# THE Wedding Checklist

Free yourself from wedding stress – and plan
your entire wedding – in less than one week

## TENILLE GREGORY

www.TheWeddingChecklist.com.au

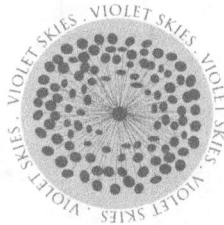

VIOLET SKIES

The Wedding Checklist

Author: Tenille Gregory

PO Box 381
Quinns Rocks WA 6030
Australia

ABN: 82 209 225 137

www.TheWeddingChecklist.com.au
Email: info@theweddingchecklist.com.au

First Published by Violet Skies 2012

Edited by Rachel Hanson
Illustrations by Pam Lostracco
Typeset by Bookhouse, Sydney
Printed and bound in Australia by Griffin Press

Special thanks to Steve, Ray, Dawn, Simone and Virginia.

Special bulk discounts are available on purchases over 12 copies.

ISBN: 978-0-646-58296-2

National Library of Australia Cataloguing-in-Publication entry

Author:    Gregory, Tenille.

Title:     The wedding checklist : free yourself from wedding stress
           and plan your entire wedding in less than one week

ISBN:      9780646582962 (pbk.)

Subjects:  Weddings--Planning.
           Wedding etiquette.

395.22

# Contents

# Introduction

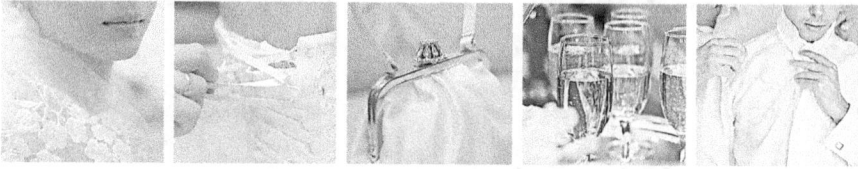

Did you know the average wedding can take over 200 hours just to plan? And that doesn't include completing all of the associated tasks, activities, errands and projects. But it doesn't have to take that much time (or energy). I can take the stress out of planning one of the most important days of your life and show you how to make every wedding decision in less than one week.

Unlike other wedding planner books, this one is designed for brides (and their grooms) who want to get down to the business of planning their wedding without having to wade through the fluff. You won't waste precious time researching every little detail – it is all written here for you. This book acts as your wedding blueprint by breaking down every task into manageable steps. It provides loads of suggestions that allow you to personalise your big day at every step and plan a completely unique wedding. It also shows you how (and when) to look to professionals for advice and suggestions in their field of expertise.

You may at first feel overwhelmed by the amount of information in this book – don't try to tackle the entire book in one sitting! Work through it in a logical sequence, one chapter at a time, and take regular breaks. This book will ensure you don't get lost in the stress and drama of planning your wedding. Above all, your wedding is a celebration of your love and planning it should be fun!

So start ticking the checkboxes and getting your ideas down on paper. It's time to get your wedding organised!

# How to use this Book

Use a pencil so you can update any changes.

Tick the main checkboxes when you complete each *task*.

☑ Decide on the type of wedding you will have
- ✗ Cultural
- ✗ Destination
- ✓ Eco-friendly
- ✓ Elegant
- ✗ Elopement
- ✗ Exotic
- ▢ Extravagant
- ▢ Fully themed
- ✓ Large party
- ✗ Modern
- ✗ Quiet drinks
- ✗ Relaxed
- ▢ Religious
- ✗ Registry office
- ✗ Small and intimate
- ✗ Surprise
- ~~Traditional~~
- ✓ Other ... *Personalised, tropical*

Make one or more *selections* in the square sub-checkboxes.

Leave checkboxes blank if you are undecided (and fill them in later).

Use the white space to jot down your own ideas, notes, sketches and reminders.

Remove items that do not apply, or that you definitely don't want, by placing a cross in the checkbox or crossing out the item entirely.

Add your own options and ideas to the lists.

# 1

# Announcing your Engagement

Congratulations, you are getting married! You're in for a wild journey, so take a deep breath and enjoy the ride. Announcing your engagement and showing off that gorgeous ring will be fun, but first be prepared for lots of questions from your adoring fans.

☐ Ask for a blessing from your family members
   - Mother and father
   - Mother and father-in-law
   - Grandmother and grandfather
   - Grandmother and grandfather-in-law
   - Children (if you feel they are old enough to understand this formality)

☐ Number the list below from 1 to 8 in the order you will announce your engagement to the special people in your lives
   - __ Children
   - __ Close family
   - __ Co-workers
   - __ Extended family
   - __ Friends
   - __ Grandparents
   - __ Parents
   - __ Siblings

*Traditionally the bride's family is told about the engagement first, then the groom's family, close friends and relatives, followed by an official announcement.*

☐ Decide how you will announce your engagement
   - At a gathering
   - Email
   - Have a family member or friend contact people for you
   - In person
   - Letters
   - Phone calls
   - Through social networks, e.g. Facebook, Twitter
   - Video call (such as Skype)

- ☐ Spread the word fast to avoid other people breaking the news for you
- ☐ Allow time for key people (such as children from previous relationships) to adjust to your engagement
- ☐ Arrange for all parents or parental figures to meet if they haven't done so already
  - Plan a special lunch or dinner
  - Spend a weekend away together
- ☐ Celebrate your engagement!

*Find ideas for your engagement party on page 39.*

- ☐ Formally announce your engagement
  - Publish in your local newspaper
  - Publish in the newspaper of your respective hometowns
  - Include a photo
  - Publish after your engagement party (if you have one)
- ☐ Arrange for premarital education, such as a marriage preparation course
- ☐ Talk with your fiancé about why you want to get married
  - Carry out a religious practice
  - Celebrate a special occasion
  - Establish a lifelong commitment
  - Maintain a family tradition
  - Make a public vow
  - Provide financial security
  - Provide security for your children
  - Provide security for future children
- ☐ Agree (or agree to disagree) on the specifics of your long-term relationship
  - Future living arrangements
  - How finances will be handled
  - How you feel about each other's family
  - How you will deal with conflict
  - If you want children and how you would like to raise them
  - Your expectations of each other
  - Your dreams for the future (as individuals and as a couple) and what you want out of life

# 2
# Planning

When creating a clear vision of your wedding day remember to be flexible, realistic, consistent and prioritise what aspects are most important to you. Not every wedding has to be a traditional ceremony followed by a grand reception. Break with tradition, dare to be different and create the personalised wedding of your dreams.

☐ Determine how much time you have to plan your entire wedding
    <3 months
    3–6 months
    6–12 months
    12–18 months
    18+ months

*The amount of planning time will be determined by a number of factors, e.g. when you can get your family members together, venue availability, time of year/season.*

## Creating your Wedding File

☐ Purchase a folder for your wedding plans and label it 'Wedding File'

☐ Fill your wedding file with plenty of blank paper to make notes, sketches and plans
    Make detailed lists of ideas and items that you would like on your wedding day and highlight those which are really important
    Record cost estimates

☐ Purchase dividers
    Label with important categories, e.g. budget, ceremony, reception, honeymoon (use the chapter headings in this book as a guide)

☐ Purchase clear sleeves to store brochures, clippings, business cards and receipts

☐ Purchase a calendar for your wedding file and mark down all important dates
    Appointments
    Attendant fittings
    Events

- Important milestones
- Special dates
- Suit fittings
- Wedding gown fittings

*Be sure to keep this calendar in a place where you will check it frequently.*

- ☐ Sort through your wedding file at the beginning of every week or month
  - Ensure everything is in its place
  - Eliminate items that you no longer need
  - Check your wedding file against your wedding calendar and update

- ☐ Purchase diaries for your wedding attendants and helpers
  - Mark important dates
  - Have your attendants mark their individual fitting schedules
  - Contact your attendants each time new appointments are made

## Wedding Research

- ☐ Research wedding trends
  - Blogs
  - Books
  - Browse through shops, e.g. stationery stores
  - Directories (both local and national)
  - Events, e.g. wedding exhibitions
  - Forums
  - Friends or family who are engaged or have recently been married
  - Newspapers (both local and national)
  - Obtain advice from those who work in the wedding industry, e.g. florists, photographers, caterers
  - Product reviews
  - Search engines
  - Social media
  - Wedding directories
  - Wedding magazines
  - Wedding websites
  - YouTube

- ☐ Collect as much information as you can and store it in your wedding file
  - Collect brochures
  - Collect pictures from magazines
  - Make note of the wedding shops and centres in your local area
  - Photocopy sections from books
  - Save or print information from internet searches
  - Take a camera everywhere you go

*Be careful not to infringe on laws and copyrights when collecting information.*

# Professional Wedding Coordinators

Using a wedding coordinator – also known as wedding planners, wedding stylists, wedding directors, bridal consultants, wedding consultants or wedding decorators – can be a fantastic way to stay organised and ease stress leading up to and on your big day.

*Advantages of Hiring Wedding Coordinators*

- Can save you money with their contacts and experience
- Can negotiate with wedding vendors on your behalf
- Offer professional guidance
- Know the latest trends
- Can help you to get things done quickly as they will have existing contacts systems
- Will have valuable local knowledge, which is important for destination weddings

☐ Hire a wedding coordinator who specialises in one or more of the following:
   Ethnic weddings
   Multicultural weddings
   Themed weddings
   Unique weddings
   Your nationality
   Your religion

☐ Decide how much your wedding coordinator will be involved
   Full planning – provides a complete service including every detail and makes major decisions on your behalf
   Partial planning – provides guidance and expert advice to help you make major decisions
   Ad hoc planning – provides assistance according to your specific needs, such as planning just the reception
   Wedding week planning – provides assistance with organising details in the week leading up to the wedding
   Wedding day assistance – provides help on the day only

☐ Complete the wedding vendor checklist for your wedding coordinator on pages 10 and 11

☐ Determine what advice and assistance you want from your wedding coordinator
   Offer expert advice and guidance
   Explain wedding etiquette
   Explain the origin of wedding traditions and rituals
   Explain the responsibilities of your attendants and helpers

- Prepare weekly or monthly schedules
- Outline aspects of bride and groom wedding attire
- Prepare a wedding budget
- Ensure you stay within your budget
- Locate wedding vendors
- Liaise between you and your vendors
- Draft vendor contracts
- Assist with invitation wording and preparation
- Organise your wedding gift registry
- Select ceremony and reception venues
- Assist with decorating at the ceremony and reception
- Assist with food selection and menu design
- Advise on music selection
- Advise on transport selection
- Create a wedding day itinerary
- Personally assist you on the day, e.g. coordinating the processional and recessional, organising gift storage, ensuring venues are decorated correctly, keeping the wedding party and guests to the time schedule, solving any problems that arise
- Provide post-wedding assistance, e.g. writing thank you notes, gown preservation

☐ Communicate openly with your wedding coordinator
- Be clear and precise with your vision and wants
- Allow your coordinator to view this book (once filled out)

☐ Speak up if things are not going in the direction you want

## DIY Projects

DIY projects allow you to utilise your creative qualities and craft unique items in your own style. They can be a lot of fun, save you money and it allows other people to get involved.

☐ Select the wedding DIY projects that you will complete

- Baking
- Beading
- Calligraphy
- Candle making
- Catering
- Cooking
- Decorating
- Drawing
- Flower arranging
- Graphic design
- Interior design
- Jewellery making
- Make-up artistry
- Menu design
- Painting
- Photography
- Picture framing
- Scrapbooking
- Sewing
- Stationery design
- Videography
- Word processing

□ Next to each of the DIY projects listed, write down the names of friends or family you know with skills, talents or interests in that area
  Ask them for their help and expertise

## Wedding Website

□ Determine how you will create your wedding website
  Create yourself from scratch
  Have a friend or family member create
  Have your wedding coordinator create
  Use an online template
  Use web design software

□ Include important information and details on your wedding website
  How you met
  Your proposal story
  Photographs of you as a couple, e.g. engagement photos
  Your wedding blog link
  Gift registry information and link
  Guestbook for guests to leave messages
  List of attendants
  Ceremony details
  Reception details
  Maps of venues
  Travel information
  Accommodation suggestions including links to hotels and resorts
  RSVP option
  Wedding photos and videos (after the wedding)
  Wedding day story (after the wedding)

□ Announce your wedding website via email or social media (Facebook, Twitter)

## Vendors

Your wedding vendors are people you have hired to provide goods or services for your wedding such as your caterer, florist and photographer.

□ Locate suitable vendors
  Blogs/forums
  Bridal guides
  Connections or referrals from family, friends and work colleagues
  Existing vendor recommendations
  Internet research
  Local and national directories
  Magazines

Wedding coordinator recommendations

Wedding expos

☐ Record all communication with your wedding vendors in your wedding file

What decisions are made

What changes are made

Each time money is exchanged

☐ Select the wedding vendors that you will hire

Baker

Bar staff

Calligrapher

Caterer

Ceremony manager

Decorator

DJ

Dressmaker/tailor

Entertainers (singers, dancers)

Florist

Graphic designer

Hairstylist

Jeweller

Legal representative

Liquor vendor

Make-up artist

MC

Musician

Officiant

Photographer

Printer

Reception manager

Stationer

Transport provider

Travel agent

Videographer

Vocalist

Waitstaff

Wedding coordinator

☐ Photocopy and complete the 'Vendor Checklist' on pages 10 and 11 for every wedding vendor that you employ

*The vendor checklist can also be printed from www.TheWeddingChecklist.com.au*

## Vendor Top Tips

- Meet personally, not over the phone or internet
- Be clear about what you want and expect from each vendor
- Explain what you *don't* want
- Don't assume anything – always ask a lot of questions
- Keep an open mind – vendors have seen it all and can give recommendations
- Show vendors your research materials, notes, photos and printouts
- Shop around, and get 2–3 quotes
- Negotiate. It's amazing the amount of discounts or extras you can receive if you just ask
- If they are the cheapest, find out why
- Check out the competition
- Be aware of how vendors will dress on the day

# Planning for the Future

- [ ] Apply for time off from work
    - Before the wedding
    - The wedding itself
    - After the wedding
    - Honeymoon
    - After the honeymoon

*Apply well in advance – especially if your employer needs to hire a replacement during your absence.*

- [ ] Book personal appointments that you require
    - Family planning
    - Financial
    - Health
    - Legal

- [ ] Determine where you will live after the wedding

- [ ] If you will be moving after the wedding, spend time well in advance researching your new home as planning a wedding can be stressful enough without the added pressure of moving and/or buying a new home

- [ ] If you are planning to get married at home or you will have wedding guests stay with you, spend time preparing your home in advance
    - Perform a thorough clean or hire a cleaning service
    - Organise clutter
    - Arrange guest bedrooms
    - Replace shabby or broken furniture
    - Paint
    - Have existing carpets cleaned or lay new carpet
    - Have a pest control spray
    - Landscape

# Vendor Checklist

### Contact Details

Company name  _____

Contact name  _____

Address  _____

_____

Phone(s)  _____

Email  _____

Website  _____

☐ Research as much as possible before hiring
- Determine how long they have been operating
- Find out if they are members of a particular professional association
- Conduct a full credentials check and background check
- Review examples of their recent wedding work
- Ask for personal recommendations and testimonials

☐ Determine how you will be charged
- By distance
- By consumption
- By the hour
- Fixed price
- Per person

☐ Enquire if you have to pay a deposit (and the size of the deposit) to secure the booking

☐ Determine other costs
- Delivery
- Set-up
- Clean-up
- Taxes
- Service charges
- Overtime fees
- Vendor travel fees
- Cancellation fees (including how much notice is required and how much money will be returned)

- ☐ Determine if they are able to stay longer on the day if required

- ☐ Enquire if they offer a back-up in case of emergency, e.g. if they cannot attend on the day

- ☐ Determine if vendors and their staff require breaks
  - The number of breaks
  - The length of each break (in minutes)

- ☐ Determine if you need to provide anything else for the vendor
  - Food
  - Drink
  - Preparation area
  - Special equipment

- ☐ Have them commit to a contract by formally agreeing to the following items:
  - Date
  - Time
  - Place
  - Cost breakdown
  - Deposit
  - Balance
  - Insurance details
  - Extras
  - Conditions
  - Breakage charges

- ☐ Determine if the contract allows for modifications

- ☐ Have two people carefully review the contract, especially the fine print

- ☐ Keep a signed copy of all contracts in your wedding file

- ☐ Have the time schedule outlined in the contract
  - Delivery time
  - Arrival time
  - Set-up time
  - Dismantling time
  - Clean-up time
  - Departure time

- ☐ Confirm that all arrangements are progressing smoothly on a regular basis, e.g. four months, two months and two weeks before the wedding

# 3
# Budget

Traditionally, the bride's family pays for almost everything but these days it's more common for the engaged couple to pay for all or a large portion of the wedding costs. You may have to compromise on various elements in order to stick to your budget. Set a realistic figure and follow it very closely – the last thing that you want to do is spend the first few years of your marriage recovering from wedding debt.

## Setting your Wedding Budget

Typically, your wedding budget consists of:
1. Existing savings
2. Money you can realistically save (up to six weeks before your wedding day)
3. Debt you are willing to commit to, e.g. credit cards, loans
4. Money from financial contributors, e.g. bride's family, groom's family, close friends
5. Minus your contingency fund (money for unforseen expenses)

☐ Calculate how much you as a couple will be contributing towards the wedding

☐ Obtain solid estimates from financial contributors
   Determine if they will be contributing a set amount or paying for one or more items
   Determine when they can make their contributions, e.g. they may need time to save
   Establish if they want to have a say in where and how their money is spent

☐ Consider the following before setting your wedding budget
   Actual expenses
   How much financial contributors are donating
   Unforseen expenses

*Use the 'Budget Breakdown' tables beginning on page 14.*

☐ Create a contingency fund for unforeseen expenses
*10–20% of your overall budget is a good rule of thumb.*

☐ Review your budget often as it is likely to change many times throughout the planning process
    Make sure you are keeping on track
    Reallocate wedding funds or locate more funds if you are over budget

☐ Apply for a wedding loan

☐ Open a savings account dedicated to your wedding finances
    Deposit a set amount of money regularly, e.g. weekly, fortnightly, monthly
    Deposit money from financial contributors into the account as soon as you receive it
    Pay wedding-related bills directly from the wedding account

☐ Assign an amount of money or a percentage of your wedding funds to each of the following categories
    Attendants' attire (if you are providing or paying a portion)
    Bomboniere
    Bride's attire
    Ceremony
    Contingency fund
    Decorations
    Flowers
    Gifts
    Groom's attire
    Honeymoon
    Jewellery
    Looking good, e.g. hair, make-up, skin, fitness
    Music and entertainment
    Photos and video
    Pre-wedding celebrations
    Reception
    Stationery
    Transport
    Wedding planning

## Budget Breakdown

☐ Review the following budget traditions
    The bride traditionally pays for personal things, such as her hair and make-up, for the day
    The groom traditionally pays for items such as his attire, the best man's attire, gifts for male attendants, the bride's ring, bouquets, buttonholes, corsages, the marriage licence, and the honeymoon

- The bride's parents traditionally pay for the announcements, stationery, wedding gown, bridesmaids' attire, young attendant outfits, officiant fees, ceremony venue, transport, flowers, photographer, videographer, musicians, decorations, reception food and the cake
- The groom's parents traditionally pay for items such as reception alcohol, music and 50% of all other reception costs
- The bride's attendants traditionally pay for their attire, the hens party, hair, make-up and nails
- The groom's attendants traditionally pay for their attire and the bucks party

*It is unlikely that you will follow the traditional format exactly; however, it gives you an idea of how a wedding budget can be portioned – weddings can be paid for in a variety of ways.*

☐ Complete the following tables with your wedding expenses
- Estimate the cost of each item
- Enter the actual cost of each item when you receive a final quote
- Leave cells blank or cross them out completely if they do not apply
- Use the blank rows at the end of each table for any additional expenses
- Enter your subtotals in the last table to calculate a total wedding cost

## Wedding/Future Planning Costs

| | Estimated | Actual |
|---|---|---|
| Wedding file | | |
| Diaries and calendars | | |
| Photocopying | | |
| Research, e.g. books, magazines, expos | | |
| Wedding website | | |
| Wedding coordinator fee | | |
| Legal fees (prenuptial agreement) | | |
| Financial planner fees | | |
| Health checks | | |
| Family planning | | |
| Premarital education/counselling | | |
| Marriage licence | | |
| Marriage certificate | | |
| Marriage certificate copies | | |
| Marriage certificate storage | | |
| Wedding insurance | | |
| Life insurance | | |
| Superannuation insurance | | |
| Professional house clean | | |
| Carpet cleaning | | |
| New carpet | | |

|  | Estimated | Actual |
|---|---|---|
| House painting | | |
| Pest control | | |
| Landscaping | | |
| New furniture | | |
| | | |
| | | |
| **Subtotal** | | |

## Stationery Costs

|  | Estimated | Actual |
|---|---|---|
| Engagement announcements | | |
| Save the date cards | | |
| Invitation paper | | |
| Invitation embellishments | | |
| Invitation envelopes | | |
| Invitation postage | | |
| Reception cards | | |
| Further information cards | | |
| Registry cards | | |
| Reply cards | | |
| Reply envelopes | | |
| Reply postage | | |
| Ceremony programs | | |
| Reserved cards | | |
| Guestbook(s) | | |
| Guestbook pen and stand | | |
| Seating chart | | |
| Table names or numbers cards | | |
| Table name or number holders | | |
| Place cards | | |
| Place card holders | | |
| Menus | | |
| Wine/beverage lists | | |
| Wedding announcement cards | | |
| Bridal shower gift thank you notes | | |
| Engagement gift thank you notes | | |
| Kitchen tea gift thank you notes | | |
| Wedding gift thank you notes | | |
| | | |
| | | |
| **Subtotal** | | |

## Pre-wedding Celebrations Costs

| | Estimated | Actual |
|---|---|---|
| Bridal shower | | |
| Engagement party | | |
| Hens party | | |
| Bucks party | | |
| Kitchen tea | | |
| Wedding eve party | | |
| Rehearsal dinner | | |
| | | |
| | | |
| **Subtotal** | | |

*For each pre-wedding celebration include the cost of invitations, venue hire, special attire, decorations, food, drink, cake, activities, entertainment, furniture hire, photography and videography.*

## Jewellery Costs

| | Estimated | Actual |
|---|---|---|
| Engagement ring | | |
| Bride's wedding ring | | |
| Groom's wedding band | | |
| Bracelet | | |
| Necklace | | |
| Chain | | |
| Choker | | |
| Cufflinks | | |
| Earrings | | |
| Headpiece | | |
| Foot jewels | | |
| Pendant | | |
| Ring pillow | | |
| Ring sizing | | |
| Engraving | | |
| Jewellery cleaning | | |
| | | |
| | | |
| **Subtotal** | | |

## Ladies' Attire Costs

| | Estimated | Actual |
|---|---|---|
| Wedding gown | | |
| Wedding gown embellishments | | |
| Gown fittings and alterations | | |
| Veil | | |
| Underskirt | | |
| Bra and inserts | | |
| Underpants | | |
| Control garments | | |
| Hosiery | | |
| Garter | | |
| Lingerie | | |
| Gloves | | |
| Bag | | |
| Shoes | | |
| Perfume | | |
| Jacket/shawl | | |
| Cultural or religious items | | |
| Reception outfit | | |
| Going-away outfit | | |
| Maid of honour attire | | |
| Maid of honour fittings | | |
| Maid of honour footwear | | |
| Maid of honour accessories | | |
| Maid of honour hair/make-up/nails | | |
| Bridesmaid attire | | |
| Bridesmaid fittings | | |
| Bridesmaid footwear | | |
| Bridesmaid accessories | | |
| Bridesmaid hair/make-up/nails | | |
| Flower girl attire | | |
| Flower girl fittings | | |
| Flower girl footwear | | |
| Flower girl accessories | | |
| Flower girl hair/make-up/nails | | |
| Junior attendant attire | | |
| Junior attendant fittings | | |
| Junior attendant footwear | | |
| Junior attendant accessories | | |
| Junior attendant hair/make-up/nails | | |
| Mother of the bride attire | | |
| Mother of the bride footwear | | |

|  | Estimated | Actual |
|---|---|---|
| Mother of the bride accessories | | |
| Mother of the bride hair/make-up/nails | | |
| Mother of the groom attire | | |
| Mother of the groom footwear | | |
| Mother of the groom accessories | | |
| Mother of the groom hair/make-up/nails | | |
| Gown cleaning | | |
| Gown preservation box | | |
| | | |
| | | |
| **Subtotal** | | |

## Gentlemen's Attire Costs

|  | Estimated | Actual |
|---|---|---|
| Suit (jacket and trousers) | | |
| Fittings and alterations | | |
| Armbands | | |
| Cummerbund | | |
| Lapel pin | | |
| Overcoat | | |
| Pocket square | | |
| Tie | | |
| Tie bar | | |
| Shirt | | |
| Waistcoat/vest | | |
| Gloves | | |
| Shoes | | |
| Belt | | |
| Underpants | | |
| Socks | | |
| Singlet | | |
| Fragrance | | |
| Cultural or religious items | | |
| Going-away outfit | | |
| Best man attire | | |
| Best man fittings | | |
| Best man footwear | | |
| Best man accessories | | |
| Groomsmen attire | | |
| Groomsmen fittings | | |
| Groomsmen footwear | | |

| | Estimated | Actual |
|---|---|---|
| Groomsmen accessories | | |
| Ring bearer attire | | |
| Ring bearer fittings | | |
| Ring bearer footwear | | |
| Ring bearer accessories | | |
| Pageboy attire | | |
| Pageboy fittings | | |
| Pageboy footwear | | |
| Pageboy accessories | | |
| Usher attire | | |
| Usher fittings | | |
| Usher footwear | | |
| Usher accessories | | |
| Father of the bride attire | | |
| Father of the bride fittings | | |
| Father of the bride footwear | | |
| Father of the bride accessories | | |
| Father of the groom attire | | |
| Father of the groom fittings | | |
| Father of the groom footwear | | |
| Father of the groom accessories | | |
| Suit cleaning | | |
| | | |
| | | |
| **Subtotal** | | |

## Looking Good – Bride Costs

| | Estimated | Actual |
|---|---|---|
| Hair treatments | | |
| Styling products | | |
| Hair trial | | |
| Haircut | | |
| Hair colour | | |
| Hairstyling for the day | | |
| Body hair removal | | |
| Make-up products | | |
| Make-up trial | | |
| Make-up artist for the day | | |
| Teeth maintenance | | |
| Teeth enhancement | | |
| Facial | | |

|  | Estimated | Actual |
|---|---|---|
| Skin care products | | |
| Beauty treatments | | |
| Manicure | | |
| Pedicure | | |
| Hand and foot products | | |
| Professional tanning | | |
| Tanning products | | |
| Invasive techniques | | |
| Fitness membership/classes | | |
| Fitness products and equipment | | |
| Professional fitness assistance/personal trainer | | |
| | | |
| | | |
| **Subtotal** | | |

## Looking Good – Groom Costs

|  | Estimated | Actual |
|---|---|---|
| Hair treatments | | |
| Styling products | | |
| Haircut | | |
| Hair colour | | |
| Professional face shave | | |
| Body hair removal | | |
| Teeth maintenance | | |
| Teeth enhancement | | |
| Facial | | |
| Skin care products | | |
| Manicure | | |
| Pedicure | | |
| Hand and foot products | | |
| Invasive techniques | | |
| Fitness membership/classes | | |
| Fitness products and equipment | | |
| Professional fitness assistance/personal trainer | | |
| | | |
| | | |
| **Subtotal** | | |

## Ceremony Costs

| | Estimated | Actual |
|---|---|---|
| Ceremony venue hire | | |
| Rehearsal venue hire | | |
| Permits, e.g. parking, liquor | | |
| Officiant fee | | |
| Donation | | |
| Marquees and tents | | |
| Set-up | | |
| Clean-up/teardown | | |
| Waste removal | | |
| Security personnel | | |
| Vocalists/musicians | | |
| Aisle runner | | |
| Ceremony decorations (excluding flowers) | | |
| Chairs (and chair decorations) | | |
| Decoration storage boxes | | |
| Items to exchange | | |
| Items for rituals and ceremonial acts | | |
| Items to release | | |
| Congratulatory items | | |
| Kneeling bench | | |
| Podium | | |
| Signature table and chair | | |
| Signature pen and pen stand | | |
| Bride's wedding morning breakfast | | |
| Groom's wedding morning breakfast | | |
| Emergency kit | | |
| Paperwork lodgement fees | | |
| Destination wedding package | | |
| Bride and groom travel costs | | |
| Bride and groom accommodation | | |
| Attendants' travel costs | | |
| Attendants' accommodation | | |
| Guests' travel costs | | |
| Guests' accommodation | | |
| | | |
| | | |
| **Subtotal** | | |

## Reception Costs

| | Estimated | Actual |
|---|---|---|
| Reception site rental | | |
| Reception room hire | | |
| Dancing lessons | | |
| Reception package | | |
| Reception manager fee | | |
| Permits, e.g. site, parking, liquor | | |
| Valet parking | | |
| Set-up | | |
| Clean-up/teardown | | |
| Waste removal | | |
| Security personnel | | |
| Amenities | | |
| Podium | | |
| Room decorations (excluding flowers) | | |
| Head table decorations (excluding flowers) | | |
| Guest table decorations (excluding flowers) | | |
| Centrepieces (excluding flowers) | | |
| Backdrops | | |
| Lighting | | |
| Cake, gift and guestbook tables | | |
| Food | | |
| Caterers | | |
| Food equipment (refer to page 182) | | |
| Generators | | |
| Wedding cake | | |
| Cake topper | | |
| Cake embellishments | | |
| Cake board, tower, platter | | |
| Cake accompaniments | | |
| Cake knife | | |
| Cake servers | | |
| Cake stand | | |
| Cake bags or boxes | | |
| Drinks | | |
| Drink equipment (refer to page 183) | | |
| Host/hostess | | |
| Furnishings (refer to page 181) | | |
| Waitstaff | | |
| Bar attendant(s) | | |
| Wedding after-party | | |

|  | Estimated | Actual |
|---|---|---|
| Tips | | |
| Wedding night accommodation | | |
| Guests' accommodation | | |
| | | |
| | | |
| **Subtotal** | | |

## Flowers Costs

|  | Estimated | Actual |
|---|---|---|
| Bridal bouquet | | |
| Throw-away posy | | |
| Attendant posies | | |
| Flower girl arrangements | | |
| Wrist corsages | | |
| Buttonholes | | |
| Sprays | | |
| Flowers for hair | | |
| Loose petals | | |
| Bouquet accessories | | |
| Ceremony flowers (refer to page 203) | | |
| Reception flowers (refer to page 205) | | |
| Vases and flower boxes | | |
| Vase fillers | | |
| Flowers for gifts | | |
| Bridal bouquet preservation | | |
| | | |
| | | |
| **Subtotal** | | |

## Photos and Video Costs

|  | Estimated | Actual |
|---|---|---|
| Pre-wedding/engagement photography | | |
| Pre-wedding photography attire | | |
| Wedding photography package | | |
| Photo booth | | |
| Photography equipment | | |
| Photography prints | | |
| Digital photos | | |
| Wedding photo albums | | |
| Photo frames | | |

|  | Estimated | Actual |
|---|---|---|
| Videography package | | |
| Videography equipment | | |
| Raw video footage | | |
| Edited footage | | |
| DVD copies | | |
| Frames for mounting photographs | | |
| Canvas prints | | |
| | | |
| | | |
| **Subtotal** | | |

## Transport Costs

|  | Estimated | Actual |
|---|---|---|
| Wedding vehicle hire | | |
| Wedding vehicle decorations | | |
| Going-away vehicle hire | | |
| Going-away vehicle decorations | | |
| Servicing | | |
| Detailing | | |
| Petrol | | |
| Drivers | | |
| Escorts | | |
| Parking attendants | | |
| Guest vans/buses | | |
| Guest van/bus drivers | | |
| | | |
| | | |
| **Subtotal** | | |

## Music and Entertainment Costs

|  | Estimated | Actual |
|---|---|---|
| Ceremony music | | |
| Ceremony musicians | | |
| Reception music | | |
| Reception musicians | | |
| Vocalists | | |
| DJ | | |
| MC | | |
| Professional entertainers | | |
| Games and activities | | |

|  | Estimated | Actual |
|---|---|---|
| Children's entertainment | | |
| Music equipment | | |
| Audio equipment | | |
| Audio visual equipment | | |
| | | |
| | | |
| **Subtotal** | | |

## Gifts Costs

|  | Estimated | Actual |
|---|---|---|
| Gifts for each other | | |
| Gifts for attendants | | |
| Gifts for close family | | |
| Gifts for helpers | | |
| Bomboniere | | |
| Thank you tags | | |
| Gift packaging and wrapping | | |
| Gift cards | | |
| | | |
| | | |
| **Subtotal** | | |

## Honeymoon Costs

|  | Estimated | Actual |
|---|---|---|
| Travel costs, e.g. flights, rail, tour packages | | |
| Guidebooks | | |
| Health check | | |
| Vaccinations | | |
| Tours and activities | | |
| Accommodation | | |
| Luggage | | |
| Passports | | |
| Travel visas | | |
| Travel insurance (including medical) | | |
| Transfers | | |
| House-sitter | | |
| Pet boarding | | |
| Mail hold | | |
| Clothing | | |
| Toiletries | | |

|  | Estimated | Actual |
|---|---|---|
| Travel accessories | | |
| Spending money | | |
| Food/alcohol | | |
| | | |
| | | |
| **Subtotal** | | |

## Grand Total Costs

|  | Estimated Subtotal | Actual Subtotal |
|---|---|---|
| Wedding/Future Planning | | |
| Stationery | | |
| Pre-wedding Celebrations | | |
| Jewellery | | |
| Ladies' Attire | | |
| Gentlemen's Attire | | |
| Looking Good – Bride | | |
| Looking Good – Groom | | |
| Ceremony | | |
| Reception | | |
| Flowers | | |
| Photos and Video | | |
| Transport | | |
| Music and Entertainment | | |
| Gifts | | |
| Honeymoon | | |
| Contingency Fund (10–20%) | | |
| | | |
| | | |
| **Total** | | |

*Visit www.TheWeddingChecklist.com.au to print copies of the budget breakdown tables.*

# 15 Simple Ways to Stretch your Budget

1. Invite fewer guests
2. Have fewer attendants or no attendants at all
3. Choose lower-priced ceremony and/or reception venues
4. Hire or borrow items rather than paying full cost, e.g. wedding gown
5. Eliminate pre-wedding celebrations, such as the engagement party
6. Get married on a day other than Saturday
7. Have the reception between meal times, e.g. brunch, afternoon tea
8. Take advantage of off-season discounts for the wedding and honeymoon
9. Avoid too many 'add-ons'
10. Negotiate, negotiate, negotiate
11. Enlist help from family and friends, e.g. take photographs, provide live music, bake the cake
12. Prioritise what is most important to you – the perfect wedding gown and a comprehensive photography package may be much more important to you than an expensive reception venue
13. Create playlists on your MP3 player instead of hiring a DJ
14. Have a friend or family member MC the event
15. Consider having a cash bar for anything other than wine, beer and soft drink

## Budget Top Tips

- Pay deposits promptly in order to secure bookings
- Establish a balance between cost and quality
- Collect receipts for anything wedding related and store them in your wedding file for reconciling your budget
- Settle all final payments 1–2 months before your wedding day
- Place cash or cheques into clearly labelled envelopes and give to a trusted family member to distribute to service providers on your wedding day
- Organise back-up money for items such as the bar tab by having a credit card or cash on standby

# 4
# Core Decisions

Put etiquette and tradition aside and spend some time talking to your fiancé about what really matters most to you both (this includes both wedding day and post-wedding day decisions). When making decisions consider how much time, money and energy you are willing to invest. Hire reputable vendors and add your own sense of style to every element. If you have a clear picture of what you want, then tell everyone involved and you can't go wrong.

## Wedding Type

- [ ] Decide how much you want tradition to play a part on your wedding day
  - Respect and follow tradition entirely
  - Mixture of traditional and nontraditional elements
  - Put your personal spin on tradition
  - Forge your own path and break with tradition completely

- [ ] Decide if, and how much, you want to involve your families in your decision making

- [ ] Select the degree of formality you would like
  - Formal
  - Semi-formal
  - Informal
  - Casual

- [ ] Spend time envisioning a wedding location and venue which has meaning for you both

- [ ] Decide on the type of wedding you will have
  - Cultural
  - Destination
  - Eco-friendly
  - Elegant
  - Elopement
  - Exotic
  - Extravagant
  - Fully themed
  - Large party
  - Modern
  - Quiet drinks
  - Relaxed

| Religious | Surprise |
| Registry office | Traditional |
| Small and intimate | Other ... |

## Wedding Date, Day and Time

☐ Select the season you would like to be married in

| Spring | Autumn |
| Summer | Winter |

☐ Consider the following points about weather and the season you have chosen

| Cloud | Snowfall |
| Glare | Sunlight |
| Heat | Sunrise and sunset times |
| Humidity | Wind |
| Rain | |

☐ Select the day of the week for your wedding

| Sunday | Thursday |
| Monday | Friday |
| Tuesday | Saturday |
| Wednesday | |

☐ Mark unsuitable dates on your wedding calendar

Birthdays of attendants, close family and friends

Commitments, e.g. work functions

Commitments of your close family and friends, e.g. planned holidays, baby due dates

Dates vendors are unavailable

Dates venues are unavailable

Family celebrations, e.g. other weddings, family reunions

Local or community events, e.g. boat shows, marathons

Public holidays

Religious holidays

☐ Select a wedding date

The date chosen will be a special one from now on so ensure you are happy with it

Inform important guests so they can reserve the date

*When setting the date remember that some vendors are very popular and may already be booked up to 12 months in advance.*

☐ Have a back-up date in place in case your original date doesn't work with venues, vendors or special guests

☐ Confirm that the proposed wedding date and time coordinates with important people and your wedding vendors

| | |
|---|---|
| Attendants | Special guests |
| Baker | Musicians |
| Caterer | Officiant |
| Ceremony venue | Photographer |
| Entertainers | Reception manager |
| Florist | Reception venue |
| Helpers | Transport |
| Honeymoon plans | Videographer |

☐ Select a time for your wedding ceremony
   Before midday
   12–2pm
   2–4pm
   4–6pm
   After 6pm

☐ Select a time for your wedding reception
   Morning tea (9–11am)
   Brunch (10–midday)
   Lunch (12–2pm)
   Afternoon tea (2–4pm)
   Cocktail (4–6pm)
   Dinner (5–7pm)

## Wedding Theme

☐ Select a wedding colour scheme, e.g. blue & green, all shades of pink, neutral tones

☐ Select a wedding theme
   African safari
   Art deco
   Beach
   Big band
   Birds
   Bohemian
   Bollywood
   Broadway
   Butterflies
   Celtic
   Country
   Destination-based, e.g. Paris, Rome, Rio
   Disco
   Enchanted forest

- Environmentally friendly
- Era, e.g. 1920s, 1940s, swinging '60s
- Fairytale
- Floral, e.g. roses
- French provincial
- Funky
- Garden
- Gothic
- Hearts
- Honeymoon destination, e.g. Hawaiian
- Indian
- Las Vegas
- Literary inspiration, e.g. The Great Gatsby
- Masked ball
- Medieval
- Mexican
- Moroccan
- Movie inspired, e.g. Alice in Wonderland
- Music inspired, e.g. jazz
- Natural
- Oriental
- Pagan
- Polka dots
- Renaissance
- Retro
- Royal
- Rustic
- Seasonal
- Shakespearean, e.g. Romeo and Juliet
- Spiritual
- Sports, e.g. football
- Tea party
- Tuscan countryside
- Underwater
- Victorian
- Vintage
- Winter wonderland
- Other ...

# 5
# Legalities

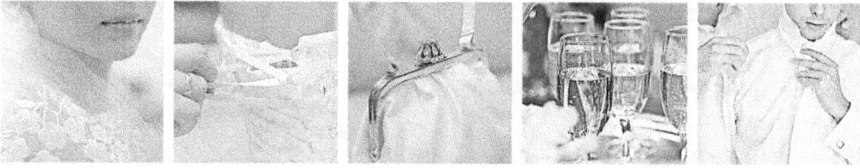

While the legal side of getting married isn't the most exciting part of a wedding, it is just as essential to make sure your day goes off without a hitch. Contact your local authorities early, arrange meetings, discuss details and then you can cross it off your list for good.

## The Legalities of getting Married

☐ Research the various legal aspects of getting married in the country and region you have selected

☐ Ensure you meet the following marriage requirements:
   - Age
   - Consent
   - Gender
   - Marital status
   - Mental capacity
   - Relationship to each other

☐ Make sure your ceremony will be legal
   - Authorised by an approved representative
   - Performed at a specific time of day
   - Performed by an approved representative
   - Performed in an approved premises
   - Performed on a specific day of the week, e.g. not on a holy day of obligation
   - Witnessed by two approved witnesses

*Only some of the above may apply depending on the country and region where you are marrying.*

☐ Consult with your local and national authorities to determine other criteria for marriage
   - Australia – www.australia.gov.au
   - Canada – www.servicecanada.gc.ca
   - NZ – www.dia.govt.nz

UK – www.direct.gov.uk
USA – answers.usa.gov

*Documents required and necessary forms may vary by state or region.*

## Marriage Certificate

☐ Apply for a marriage certificate
    Apply yourself
    Have your officiant apply on your behalf

☐ Apply for an extra copy (or several) of the marriage certificate in case the original is lost or damaged

☐ Apply for a certified copy of your marriage certificate, e.g. a commemorative certificate

☐ Arrange for the safe storage of your wedding certificate after your wedding
    Filed with your other legal documents
    Framed
    In a silver-plated gift tube
    Safe deposit box

## Legal Documentation and Order of Proceedings

☐ Provide your officiant and other representatives with legal documents
    Birth certificates
    Change of name documents
    Citizenship documents
    Death certificates of previous spouses
    Decree absolutes
    Evidence of nationality
    Passports
    Photo identification
    Previous marriage certificates
    Proof of annulment
    Statutory declarations confirming status
    Visas

*This is not an exhaustive list, you must obtain up to date advice from local/ national governing bodies.*

☐ Determine how much notice you need to give for a 'Notice of Intended Marriage' or marriage licence

☐ Contact your wedding officiant to obtain any other legal forms and documents

☐ Complete and lodge a 'Notice of Intended Marriage' form or apply for a marriage licence

☐ Update or create wills that include your fiancé
    Notify of your change in circumstances, e.g. your plans to marry

☐ If you plan to use any of the following elements in your ceremony or reception, determine if you are legally allowed to use them or if you will need copyright clearance
    Copies of sheet music for singers and musicians
    Copies of sound recordings
    Literary extracts printed in wedding programs
    Poetry printed in wedding programs
    Public performances of music
    Song lyrics printed in wedding programs
    Traditional hymns printed in wedding programs

## Prenuptial Agreement

A prenuptial agreement can also be called a financial agreement. It details assets owned before marriage and its purpose is to protect individual assets if the marriage ends. While the issue of a prenuptial agreement can be a touchy subject for some couples, it is worth discussing – especially if this is the second marriage for one or both of you, or if there are children involved.

### *Top Reasons Couples Create Prenuptial Agreements*

- To protect inheritance rights for children from previous relationships
- There is a large imbalance in income or assets
- One person holds interest in a trust fund or business
- One person has large debts

☐ Locate and contact a legal professional who specialises in prenuptial agreements

☐ Have a prenuptial agreement drawn up, focusing on items such as:
    Assets, e.g. vehicles, jewellery, artwork, valuables
    Bank accounts
    Businesses
    Items with sentimental significance
    Liabilities, e.g. existing debts and financial obligations
    Property (including appreciation, income, gains, rent, dividends)
    Retirement benefits
    Stock portfolios
    Superannuation
    Treatment of gifts and inheritances

       Treatment of income and earnings

       Trusts

☐ Include how the following items will be managed in your prenuptial agreement

       Credit card use and payments

       Expenses for children and stepchildren

       Household expenses

       Joint bank accounts

☐ Include appropriate clauses in your prenuptial agreement, e.g. a time clause where it will be invalid after a specified date

☐ Determine how financial items will be treated if you are to divorce or upon the death of one of you, e.g. spousal support, distribution of estate

☐ Ensure you consult with a reputable legal professional before making any decisions or signing anything

## Insurance

☐ Organise wedding insurance as soon as your wedding is announced

☐ Select what you would like your wedding insurance to cover

       Alcohol liability

       Cancellations

       Damages

       Flowers

       Getting married in another country

       Gifts

       Hired items

       Loss of photographs

       Loss of videos

       Personal liability

       Product liability

       Public liability

       Rescheduling costs

       Vendor contract disputes

       Vendors breaking contracts

       Wedding attire

       Wedding documents

       Wedding jewellery

       Wedding vehicles

       Other …

☐ If you expect to receive material wedding gifts, increase your house and contents insurance

- [ ] Take photos of significant items for insurance records, e.g. wedding jewellery, gifts

- [ ] Organise travel insurance for your honeymoon

- [ ] Organise life insurance or update existing policies to include your partner

- [ ] Organise superannuation life insurance or update existing policies to include your partner

## Name Changing

- [ ] Decide what your title will be after the wedding
    - Ms
    - Mrs
    - Miss

- [ ] Decide what your surnames will be after the wedding
    - Bride to take groom's surname
    - Groom to take bride's surname
    - Hyphenated with groom's surname first
    - Hyphenated with bride's surname first
    - Bride to add groom's surname without a hyphen
    - Groom to add bride's surname without a hyphen
    - Bride to take groom's surname socially and keep maiden name professionally
    - Invent a completely new name
    - No name changes

- [ ] Consider your children and future children when selecting your name changes

- [ ] Apply to the relevant authority with a certified copy of your marriage certificate to change your name(s)

## Updating Records

- [ ] If your surname, status or address is changing, present your marriage certificate to update your records
    - Banks, e.g. sole, joint and business accounts
    - Building societies
    - Car breakdown services
    - Clubs
    - Credit cards
    - Dentists
    - Doctors
    - Driver's licence
    - Electoral roll
    - Employer records

- Financial items, e.g. trusts, term deposits, stock portfolios, shares
- Insurance policies, e.g. car, house, home contents, health, life, building, boat
- Loan documentation
- Medical records
- Memberships, e.g. library and gym
- Mortgages, deeds and leases
- National health service
- Office of social security, e.g. Centrelink
- Passport office
- Payroll office
- Phones
- Post office
- Rental leases
- Schools, universities and alumni associations
- Subscriptions, e.g. books, magazines and music
- Superannuation
- Tax office
- Utilities, e.g. electricity, gas, water
- Vehicle registrations, e.g. car, boat, motorcycle, trailer
- Wills

*Often companies, such as the passport office, will let you change your name free of charge if done within a specified time frame.*

# 6
# Pre-wedding Celebrations

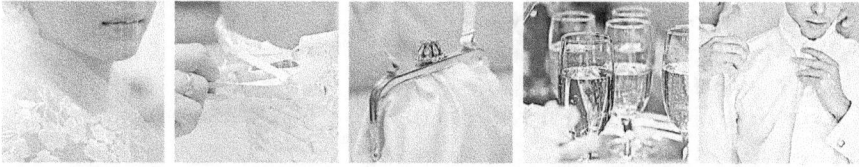

The excitement begins well before your big day. Pre-wedding celebrations are designed to pamper the couple-to-be and celebrate the special time before their official union. So let the partying begin!

## Bridal Shower

Originally, bridal showers existed to shower the bride with money or gifts for her dowry. It is now more of a shower of love and good wishes which can include both the bride and groom. It is best celebrated in a casual setting, such as your home, and only guests who are attending the wedding should be invited.

☐ Decide on the type of bridal shower
- Morning tea
- Brunch
- Lunch
- Afternoon tea
- Cocktail hour
- Dinner
- Other …

☐ Select a bridal shower host
- Bridesmaid(s)
- Close friend
- Close family member
- A group, e.g. work colleagues
- You

☐ Have your host organise the following:
- Date, e.g. 4–8 weeks before the wedding day
- Time
- Venue
- Invitations

☐ Decide who will pay for the bridal shower

☐ Select a bridal shower theme

| | |
|---|---|
| Chocolate | Kitchen |
| Coffee and dessert | Lingerie |
| Cooking | Spa and beauty |
| Craft | Tea party |
| Food, e.g. Thai, Japanese | Wine and cheese |
| Other … | |

*See a more detailed list of themes on page 30.*

☐ Put together a decorations list

☐ Purchase decorations

☐ Design your food and drinks menu
*Refer to the reception catering section on page 167.*

☐ Plan games and activities for your bridal shower
*Find a detailed list of activities on page 46.*

☐ Make or order a special cake to honour the occasion

☐ Organise for a professional, friend or family member to take photographs

☐ Organise for a professional, friend or family member to take video footage

☐ Open gifts in front of guests
   ▪ Have your maid of honour or host note each gift received and who gave it to you

☐ Send thank you notes (before your wedding day)

# Engagement Party

The engagement party gives you a chance to share your excitement with friends and family. Planning an engagement party is much like planning a miniature wedding. Although there is no set rule as to how close your engagement should be to the wedding, it's best not to have the celebrations too close to each other.

☐ Organise your engagement party
   ▪ Date
   ▪ Time

☐ Select an engagement party host
   ▪ Parents of the bride
   ▪ Parents of the groom
   ▪ Family member
   ▪ Close friend
   ▪ You (and your fiancé)

☐ Decide who will pay for the engagement party

- [ ] Decide on the degree of formality
  - Formal
  - Semi-formal
  - Informal
  - Casual

- [ ] Decide on the type of engagement party
  - Al fresco barbecue
  - Buffet
  - Casual gathering at home
  - Catered brunch
  - Other ...
  - Elegant cocktail party
  - Extravagant celebration
  - Garden party
  - Restaurant dinner

- [ ] Select and book a venue

- [ ] Select an engagement party theme
  - Disco
  - Food e.g. Thai, Mexican
  - Cultural, e.g. French, Japanese
  - Costume/masked ball
  - Music inspired, e.g. jazz
  - The same theme as the wedding
  - Wine tasting
  - Other ...

*See a more detailed list of themes on page 30.*

- [ ] Select an engagement party colour theme

- [ ] Create an engagement party guest list
  - Enlist help from both sides of your families
  - Look to the wedding guest list for support

- [ ] Prepare invitations and invite guests
  - Use matching wedding stationery
  - Post or email invitations eight weeks in advance

- [ ] Put together a decorations list

*Find a detailed list of decorations on page 165.*

- [ ] Purchase decorations

- [ ] Contact your florist and order flowers to decorate the engagement party venue

- [ ] Design your food and drinks menu
  - Give a copy to your caterer

*Refer to the reception catering section on page 167.*

- [ ] Purchase food and drinks if you are self-catering
  - Take advantage of bulk purchase discounts

☐ Contact your baker and order an engagement cake or bake your own

☐ Plan the engagement party area by designating areas to:
  - Sit
  - Mingle
  - Dance
  - Present food and drinks

☐ Hire a band, DJ or create a music playlist that you and your families and friends will enjoy

☐ Determine what equipment your chosen venue can provide, e.g. sound system, microphone

☐ Make a list of equipment that you will need to hire

| | |
|---|---|
| Dinnerware | Marquee |
| Heaters | Microphone |
| Jukebox | Sound system |
| Karaoke machine | Tables and chairs |
| Other ... | |

☐ Arrange other items that you need to hire for the party

| | |
|---|---|
| Crockery | Eskies |
| Cutlery | Tables |
| Glassware | Table linen |
| Ice | Other ... |

*Find a detailed list of furnishings, food and drink equipment on page 181.*

☐ Contact your hire company and order hired items

☐ Decide who you would like to give a toast or speech and contact them to confirm

*Typically, the bride's father announces the engagement by an official toast and the groom makes a speech.*

☐ Organise for a professional, friend or family member to take photographs
*This is a good time to trial your wedding photographer.*

☐ Organise for a professional, friend or family member to take video footage

☐ Provide your photographer and videographer with a list of items that you want documented, e.g. speeches, cake cutting, dancing

☐ Transport engagement gifts home
  - Open gifts at home
  - Make a note of each gift received and who gave it to you
  - Mark on your wedding guest list cards

☐ Write thank you notes for your engagement gifts

## Hens and Bucks Parties

This is a great excuse to let your hair down and have fun. The hens party is also known as a bachelorette party and the bucks party can be called a stag or bachelor party. Celebrate at least a few days before the wedding (or longer for weekends away) so that any after effects will have time to wear off.

☐ Organise, or have your attendants organise, your hens and bucks parties
   - Date
   - Time
   - Guest list
   - Invitations

*Guests don't have to be the same as your wedding guests.*

☐ Book, or have your attendants book, a venue
   - Club, e.g. surf club, comedy club
   - Hotel
   - Private section in bar
   - Restaurant
   - Other …

☐ Decide who will fund the hens party
   - Bride's attendants
   - Shared by all attendees, e.g. guests contribute money at the start of the party

☐ Decide who will fund the bucks party
   - Groom's attendants
   - Shared by all attendees, e.g. guests contribute money at the start of the party

☐ Decide on the type of hens and bucks parties
   Separate hens and bucks parties
   Joint hens and bucks party
   Weekend away
   Week-long holiday
   Other …

☐ Select hens and bucks party themes
   1920s flapper
   Animal inspired, e.g. cats, bunnies
   Bollywood
   Burlesque
   Cops and robbers
   Gambling
   Glam rock
   Mexican
   Movie inspired, e.g. Top Gun, Grease
   Racing
   Saints and sinners
   School uniform
   Sports
   Superhero
   Vampires
   Other …

*See a more detailed list of themes on page 30.*

☐ Design your food and drinks menu (if self-catering)
   Purchase food
   Purchase alcoholic and non-alcoholic beverages

*Refer to the reception catering section on page 167.*

☐ Organise entertainment
   Dancers                    Party games
   Jukebox                    Strippers
   Karaoke                    Other …

☐ Purchase fun attire for the bride to wear at the party
   Corset                     Garter
   Costume jewellery          Sash
   Cowgirl hat                Specialty T-shirt
   Devil horns                Tiara
   Feather boa                Veil
   Other …

- ☐ Purchase fun attire for the groom to wear at the party
  - ⬚ Beer drinking hat
  - ⬚ Bow tie
  - ⬚ Bucks party cap
  - ⬚ Other …
  - ⬚ Cowboy hat
  - ⬚ Novelty wig, e.g. a mullet
  - ⬚ Specialty T-shirt

- ☐ Have your maid of honour arrange a party bag
  - ⬚ Bride champagne flute
  - ⬚ Costume
  - ⬚ Handcuffs
  - ⬚ Lingerie
  - ⬚ Party games, e.g. dare cards, pin the hose on the fireman
  - ⬚ Sexy toys
  - ⬚ Temporary tattoos
  - ⬚ Whistle
  - ⬚ Other …

- ☐ Have your best man arrange a party bag
  - ⬚ Costume
  - ⬚ Games e.g. dare cards, drinking games
  - ⬚ Groom stubby holder
  - ⬚ Handcuffs
  - ⬚ Novelty ball and chain
  - ⬚ Sexy toys
  - ⬚ Whistle
  - ⬚ Other …

- ☐ Organise for a professional, friend or family member to take photographs at the hens and bucks parties

- ☐ Organise for a professional, friend or family member to take video footage at the hens and bucks parties

- ☐ Consider the following drinking tips if there will be alcohol involved
  - ⬚ Assign designated drivers or organise a chauffeured car service
  - ⬚ Pace yourselves
  - ⬚ Drink water between alcoholic drinks
  - ⬚ Organise for transport between pubs, clubs and home
  - ⬚ Organise accommodation close to the venue

## Kitchen Tea

Female friends of the bride traditionally organised a kitchen tea to provide her with items for her kitchen. Today, guests bring novelty or themed gifts rather than kitchen items. A kitchen tea can replace the hens party and is a great excuse to enjoy food and drinks with close family and friends.

- [ ] Select the type of kitchen tea
  - Morning tea
  - Brunch
  - Lunch
  - Afternoon tea

- [ ] Select a kitchen tea host
  - Bridesmaid(s)
  - Family member
  - Close friend
  - A group, e.g. work colleagues
  - You

- [ ] Have your host organise the following:
  - Date
  - Time
  - Guest list
  - Venue
  - Invitations

- [ ] Decide who will pay for the kitchen tea

- [ ] Plan kitchen tea games

- [ ] Coordinate your kitchen tea with your hens party, e.g. celebrate on the same day with guests not attending the hens party to depart when things heat up

## Wedding Eve Party

A wedding eve party is a gathering of your attendants and close family the night before your wedding day. It is a popular choice for couples who are not holding a rehearsal or rehearsal dinner. It may involve a casual dinner at home or a formal dinner in a restaurant. Guests share stories of the couple and discuss last-minute details of the big day.

- [ ] Organise your wedding eve party
  - Date
  - Time
  - Venue

- [ ] Decide on the type of wedding eve party
  - Morning tea
  - Brunch
  - Lunch
  - Afternoon tea
  - Dinner
  - Cocktails

☐ Prepare a guest list
  Bridesmaids
  Groomsmen
  Flower girls
  Ring bearer
  Pageboys
  Children of the bride and groom
  Parents of the bride and groom
  Grandparents of the bride and groom
  Siblings of the bride and groom
  Other …

☐ Invite guests

☐ Decide who will pay for the wedding eve party

☐ Present gifts to your attendants and special helpers
*Find a detailed list of gift ideas on page 229.*

## Pre-wedding Celebration Ideas and Activities

☐ Select from the following activities for each of your pre-wedding celebrations, e.g. bridal shower, hens party, bucks party, kitchen tea, wedding eve party

| | |
|---|---|
| Archery | Greyhound races |
| Barbecue | High tea |
| Belly dancing lesson | Home casino |
| Billiards | Horse races |
| Bonfire | Horse riding |
| Cabaret restaurant | Indoor rock climbing |
| Camping | Jazz bar/club |
| Casino | Karaoke |
| Clay shooting | Laser tag |
| Cocktail making class | Latin dancing lesson |
| Comedy club | Lawn bowling |
| Comedy show | Life painting class |
| Concert | Mini-golf |
| Cricket | Mountaineering |
| Dance studio lesson | Movies |
| Dancing | Music festival |
| Day spa | Nightclub |
| Fishing | Orienteering |
| Football | Paintball |
| Four-wheel driving | Party bus |
| Go-karts | Picnic |
| Golf | Poker night |

- Pole dancing lesson
- Pub crawl
- Quad biking
- Restaurant meal
- River cruise
- Salsa club
- Shooting
- Spa
- Speed boating
- Sports bar
- Sports car driving
- Stage show
- Strip club
- Sunset beach party
- Surf lesson
- Survival course
- Tenpin bowling
- Theatre restaurant
- Wine tasting
- Wine tour
- Whisky tasting
- Other …

# 7

# The Wedding Team

Your bridal party and helpers play a significant role in the success of your wedding. And not just on the big day! Get everyone involved by delegating wedding tasks as soon as possible. Not only will it make them feel special, it will ease a lot of your own stress to hand over some of the work to people you trust. You couldn't possibly – and aren't expected to – do everything on your own.

☐ Determine the size of your bridal party

☐ Select the types and number of wedding attendants for your ceremony
- Maid of honour
- Bridesmaids
- Best man
- Groomsmen
- Flower girl
- Ring bearer
- Pageboy
- Junior attendants
- Ushers

*Don't feel like you have to include all of the listed attendants; some couples keep it simple with only a maid of honour and best man.*

☐ Contact each attendant and ask if they would like to be part of your wedding
- Explain their role
- Explain what you expect of them

☐ Photocopy the following lists for each of your attendants and helpers
*You can also print these lists at www.TheWeddingChecklist.com.au*

## Maid of Honour

Typically, the bride's attendants include a head bridesmaid and one or more supporting bridesmaids. A maid of honour is an unmarried head bridesmaid and a matron of honour is a married head bridesmaid. The head bridesmaid is referred to as the maid of honour throughout this book.

☐ Select who will take the place of your maid of honour

| | |
|---|---|
| Sister | Daughter |
| Sister-in-law | Cousin |
| Friend (female or male) | Brother |
| Mother | Other ... |

☐ Select an alternative name for your maid of honour, such as matron of honour, best lady, best woman, chief bridesmaid, honour attendant, lead bridesmaid, male of honour (for a male maid of honour)

☐ The following is a list of tasks which are typically handled by the maid of honour. Select each task that you want completed by your maid of honour. If another person will be fulfilling the role, write their name next to it.

- Provide the wedding couple with ideas
- Offer the wedding couple emotional support
- Help with making core decisions
- Visit wedding stores and vendors with the bridal couple
- Be involved in selecting the bride's gown
- Be involved in selecting the bridesmaid dresses
- Be available for dress fittings
- Help to arrange bomboniere
- Organise the bridal shower
- Organise the hens party
- Organise the kitchen tea
- Attend pre-wedding celebrations, such as the bridal shower, engagement party, hens party, kitchen tea and the wedding eve party
- Attend the ceremony rehearsal and rehearsal dinner
- Oversee the bridesmaids
- Be available on the wedding morning for support
- Help the bride to dress on the day
- Ensure flower bouquets are ready before the ceremony
- Walk down the aisle after the bridesmaids in the processional
- Hold the bridal bouquet during ceremony
- Return the bouquet to the bride after the signing of the register
- Supervise the flower girls and junior attendants
- Be present in wedding photography
- Help to arrange the bride's train during photography
- Offer drinks to guests at the reception
- Prepare and deliver a speech at the reception
- Dance with the groom, groomsmen, father of the bride and father of the groom
- Mingle with guests at the reception
- Help the bride change into her going-away outfit
- Other ...

- [ ] Have your maid of honour complete the following immediately before the ceremony, at the top of the aisle, before any official photos, before entering the reception and throughout the reception
  - Arrange your skirt
  - Arrange your train
  - Secure your headdress
  - Fluff your veil
  - Review your hair and make-up
  - General check
  - Other …

## Bridesmaids

Traditionally, bridesmaids are sisters of the bride and groom, but now include anyone from close friends to male family members.

- [ ] Select who will take the place of your bridesmaids
  - Sister
  - Sister-in-law
  - Friend (female or male)
  - Mother
  - Daughter
  - Cousin
  - Brother
  - Other …

- [ ] If you have a specific order for your bridesmaids, write their names in your wedding file and assign a ranking number to each one

- [ ] Select an alternative name for your bridesmaids, such as bride's entourage, brideslaves, brideswenches, bridesmates (for male bridesmaids)

- [ ] The following is a list of tasks which are typically handled by the bridesmaids. Select each task that you want completed by your bridesmaids. Some bridesmaids may be suited for some tasks better than others, so feel free to assign particular tasks to individual bridesmaids and write their name next to each one. If another person will be fulfilling the role, write their name next to it.
  - Provide the wedding couple with wedding ideas
  - Offer the wedding couple emotional support
  - Be involved in selecting the bridesmaid dresses
  - Be available for dress fittings
  - Assist the maid of honour
  - Attend pre-wedding celebrations, such as the bridal shower, engagement party, hens party, kitchen tea and the wedding eve party
  - Attend the ceremony rehearsal and rehearsal dinner
  - Be available on the wedding morning for support
  - Help the bride to dress
  - Be present in wedding photography
  - Supervise young attendants
  - Offer drinks to guests at the reception

Prepare and deliver speeches at the reception

Dance with the groom, groomsmen, father of the bride and father of the groom

Gather single women for the bouquet toss

Mingle with guests at the reception

Other …

## Best Man

Typically, the groom's attendants include a head groomsman and one or more supporting groomsmen. The head groomsman is referred to as the best man throughout this book.

☐ Select who will take the place of your best man

| | |
|---|---|
| Brother | Son |
| Brother-in-law | Cousin |
| Friend (male or female) | Sister |
| Father | Other … |

☐ Select an alternative name for your best man, such as chief groomsman, lead groomsman, best woman (for a female best man)

☐ The following is a list of tasks which are typically handled by the best man. Select each task that you want completed by your best man. If another person will be fulfilling the role, write their name next to it.

Provide the wedding couple with ideas and support

Help with making core decisions

Be involved in selecting the groom's attire

Be involved in selecting the groomsmen's attire

Organise the bucks party

Attend pre-wedding celebrations, such as the engagement party, bucks party and the wedding eve party

Attend the ceremony rehearsal and rehearsal dinner

Oversee the groomsmen

Oversee the ushers

Be available on the wedding morning for support

Help the groom to dress on the day

Tie wedding ribbons to the wedding cars

Collect buttonholes

Collect the wedding programs

Carry documents to the ceremony

Carry the officiant fee to the ceremony and give to the officiant

Ensure the groom is early to the ceremony

Present wedding rings at the ceremony when prompted or give to ring bearer immediately before the ceremony

Be present in wedding photography

- Offer drinks to guests at the reception
- Prepare and deliver a speech at the reception (including collecting and relaying emails from absent guests)
- Toast the bridesmaids
- Dance with the bride, bridesmaids, mother of the bride and mother of the groom
- Mingle with guests at the reception
- Organise going-away transport for the newlyweds
- Decorate the going-away car
- Place honeymoon luggage in the going-away car
- Return hired attire
- Other …

☐ Have your best man complete the following for the groom before the ceremony, before any official photos are taken and before entering the reception
- Ensure shirt is tucked in
- Ensure tie is straight
- Ensure suit looks neat and presentable
- Check that accessories are in place
- General check
- Other …

## Groomsmen

Traditionally, groomsmen are brothers of the bride and groom, but now include anyone from close friends to female family members

☐ Select who will take the place of your groomsmen

| | |
|---|---|
| Brother | Son |
| Brother-in-law | Cousin |
| Friend (male or female) | Sister |
| Father | Other … |

☐ If you have a specific order for your groomsmen, write their names in your wedding file and assign a ranking number to each one

☐ Select an alternative name for your groomsmen, such as groom's entourage, groom's gentlemen, groomsmates, groomsmaids (for female groomsmen)

☐ The following is a list of tasks which are typically handled by the groomsmen. Select each task that you want completed by your groomsmen. Feel free to assign specific tasks to particular groomsmen. If another person will be fulfilling the role, write their name next to it.
- Provide the wedding couple with wedding ideas
- Offer the wedding couple emotional support
- Be involved in selecting the men's attire
- Be available for fittings

- Assist the best man
- Attend pre-wedding celebrations, such as the engagement party, bucks party and the wedding eve party
- Attend the ceremony rehearsal and rehearsal dinner
- Run errands on the wedding day
- Be available on the wedding morning for support
- Be present in wedding photography
- Offer drinks to guests at the reception
- Supervise young attendants
- Prepare and deliver speeches at the reception
- Dance with the bride, bridesmaids, mother of the bride and mother of the groom
- Gather single men for the garter toss
- Mingle with guests at the reception
- Return hired attire
- Other …

## Young Attendant Checklist

Young attendants include flower girls, pageboys, ring bearer, junior attendants, young bridesmaids and young groomsmen. Complete the following checklist before selecting any of your young attendants.

- ☐ Ensure each young attendant is:
  - Confident
  - Outgoing
  - Comfortable being the centre of attention

- ☐ Be aware of each young attendants' individual limits

- ☐ Be aware of each young attendants' daily routine

- ☐ Include young attendants in all wedding rehearsals

- ☐ Be very patient (especially if they are very young)

- ☐ Have a back-up plan if one or more of your young attendants change their mind about participating on the day

## Flower Girls

Typically, flower girls are aged from 4–9 years. These were traditionally daughters of immediate family members, but can be children of close friends. Some couples are even using young boys in this role.

- ☐ Select your flower girls

☐ The following is a list of tasks which are typically handled by the flower girls. Select each task that you want completed by your flower girls. If another person will be fulfilling the role, write their name next to it.

Be available for dress fittings

Practise ceremony places and duties

Attend pre-wedding celebrations, such as the bridal shower, engagement party, kitchen tea and the wedding eve party

Attend the ceremony rehearsal

Follow bridesmaids down the aisle in the processional

Scatter petals in front of the bride in the processional

Hand items for release to guests, e.g. bubbles

Be present in wedding photography

Dance with the pageboys and ring bearer at the reception

Other …

## Ring Bearer

Ring bearers are typically aged from 4–9 years; however, they can be boys or girls of any age. Your best man, pageboy or maid of honour can double as a ring bearer.

☐ Select your ring bearer

☐ The following is a list of tasks which are typically handled by the ring bearer. Select each task that you want completed by your ring bearer. If another person will be fulfilling the role, write their name next to it.

Be available for fittings

Practise ceremony places and duties

Attend pre-wedding celebrations, such as the engagement party and the wedding eve party

Attend the ceremony rehearsal

Walk in front or beside the flower girl in the processional

Carry the wedding rings at the ceremony

Present the rings to the officiant when prompted

Be present in wedding photography

Dance with the flower girls at the reception

Other …

## Pageboys

Pageboys are junior members of the bridal party, also known as pages or trainbearers. They were traditionally sons of immediate family members, but can also be male or female children of close friends.

☐ Select your pageboys

☐ The following is a list of tasks which are typically handled by the pageboys. Select each task that you want completed by your pageboys. If another person will be fulfilling the role, write their name next to it.

Be available for fittings

Practise ceremony places and duties

Attend pre-wedding celebrations, such as the engagement party and the wedding eve party

Attend the ceremony rehearsal

Carry the bride's train at the ceremony

Carry a candle, flower or bible if the bride has no train

Walk behind the bride in the processional and recessional

Help to carry the bride's train over the ceremony steps

Be present in wedding photography

Dance with the flower girls at the reception

Other …

## Junior Attendants

Typically, junior attendants are aged from 9–14 years. These are often young girls and boys from your extended families.

☐ Select your junior attendants

☐ The following is a list of tasks which are typically handled by the junior attendants. Select each task that you want completed by your junior attendants. If another person will be fulfilling the role, write their name next to it.

Be available for fittings

Practise ceremony places and duties

Attend pre-wedding celebrations, such as the bridal shower, engagement party, kitchen tea and the wedding eve party

Attend the ceremony rehearsal

Hand out flowers and programs to guests

Light candles

Hold candles

Perform a reading or poem at the ceremony

Ring bells

Be present in wedding photography

Hand out slices of wedding cake at the reception

Attend the gift table

Attend the guestbook table

Other …

# Ushers

Ushers are helpers for the groomsmen and are often needed for large weddings. Three ushers – or one for every 50 guests – is most common. They can be male and female or you can employ host/hostesses for the reception to take their place. A head usher can be nominated to oversee the other ushers and act as a messenger between the ushers and the best man.

☐ Select your ushers

☐ The following is a list of tasks which are typically handled by the ushers. Select each task that you want completed by your ushers. If another person will be fulfilling the role, write their name next to it.

   Purchase a wedding outfit with approval from the bride and groom

   Be available for fittings

   Attend pre-wedding celebrations

   Attend the ceremony rehearsal and rehearsal dinner

   Learn the ceremony seating arrangements

   Organise umbrellas for escorting guests in rain or sun

   Assist the best man and groomsmen

   Be on standby to help with last-minute problems on the wedding morning

   Arrive at the ceremony venue 45 minutes before it begins to help set up, e.g. marquees, chairs, decorations

   Assist with parking and traffic control

   Hand out wedding programs to guests

   Determine if guests are of the bride or groom and indicate where they are to sit

   Seat honoured guests, e.g. mothers and grandmothers of the wedding couple

   Even out numbers if there is a large imbalance of guests

   Inform the musicians as soon as the bride arrives

   Roll out the aisle runner

   Help to coordinate the photography

   Hand out directions to the reception

   Ensure everyone can get to the reception

   Tidy up after the ceremony

   Ensure everything is in place before the reception

   Set up welcome drinks at the reception

   Place the wedding card box on the gift table

   Circulate the guestbook at the reception

   Look after guests at the reception, e.g. introduce guests to each other

   Other …

## Mother of the Bride

☐ The following is a list of tasks which are typically handled by the mother of the bride. Select each task that you want completed by the mother of the bride. If another person will be fulfilling the role, write their name next to it.

    Support her daughter throughout the entire wedding planning process
    Be available to help with all wedding preparations
    Compile the bride's side of the guest list
    Help to select ceremony and reception venues
    Arrange engagement announcements
    Assist with or oversee catering, flowers and cake decisions
    Consult with the mother of the groom regarding wedding outfits
    Purchase a wedding outfit with approval from the bride and groom
    Meet the groom's parents before the wedding day
    Attend pre-wedding celebrations, such as the bridal shower, engagement party, hens party, kitchen tea and the wedding eve party
    Attend the ceremony rehearsal and rehearsal dinner
    Be personally available for last-minute problems on the wedding morning
    Help the bride dress on the day
    Secure the bride's veil
    Carry the emergency kit
    Travel to the ceremony with the bridesmaids
    Be the last guest to enter the ceremony
    Sit in the front row on the left of the aisle
    Be the first guest to leave the ceremony
    Greet guests at the reception
    Arrange the wedding gift display
    Sit at the parents' table at the reception
    Prepare and deliver a speech at the reception
    Introduce guests to each other at the reception
    Dance with the groom, groomsmen, father of the bride and father of the  groom
    Collect and store essential items and mementos from the day, e.g. ceremony programs, cake topper, guestbook, bouquet, horseshoes, wedding certificate
    Issue wedding announcements
    Organise photography proofs
    Distribute photography orders
    Other …

# Father of the Bride

☐ The following is a list of tasks which are typically handled by the father of the bride. Select each task that you want completed by the father of the bride. If another person will be fulfilling the role, write their name next to it.

Support his daughter throughout the entire wedding planning process

Compile the bride's side of the guest list

Prepare a reception speech

Assist the bride's mother in organising and planning the wedding

Purchase a wedding outfit with approval from the bride and groom

Meet the groom's parents before the wedding day

Attend pre-wedding celebrations, such as the engagement party, bucks party and the wedding eve party

Toast the couple at the engagement party

Attend the ceremony rehearsal and rehearsal dinner

Toast the couple at the rehearsal dinner

Chauffeur travelling guests to and from airports and the venues

Be personally available for last-minute problems on the wedding day

Travel to the ceremony with the bride

Escort the bride down the aisle

Present the bride

Sit in the front row on the left of the aisle

Be the first guest to leave the ceremony

Sit at the parents' table at the reception

Say grace (if the officiant is not in attendance) if appropriate

Toast the bride and groom

Prepare and deliver a speech at the reception

Dance with the bride, bridesmaids, mother of the bride and mother of the groom

Monitor drink supply and inform the reception manager if more is needed

Other …

# Mother of the Groom

☐ The following is a list of tasks which are typically handled by the mother of the groom. Select each task that you want completed by the mother of the groom. If another person will be fulfilling the role, write their name next to it.

Support her son throughout the entire wedding planning process

Be available to help with all wedding preparations

Compile the groom's side of the guest list

Consult with the mother of the groom regarding wedding outfits

Purchase a wedding outfit with approval from the bride and groom

Meet the bride's parents before the wedding day

Attend pre-wedding celebrations, such as the bridal shower, engagement party, hens party, kitchen tea and the wedding eve party

Attend the ceremony rehearsal and rehearsal dinner

Be personally available for last-minute problems on the wedding morning

Sit in the front row on the right of the aisle at the ceremony

Introduce guests to each other at the reception

Sit at the parents' table at the reception

Prepare and deliver a speech at the reception

Dance with the groom, groomsmen, father of the bride and father of the groom

Other …

## Father of the Groom

☐ The following is a list of tasks which are typically handled by the father of the groom. Select each task that you want completed by the father of the groom. If another person will be fulfilling the role, write their name next to it.

Support his son throughout the entire wedding planning process

Be available to help with all wedding preparations

Compile the groom's side of the guest list

Purchase a wedding outfit with approval from the bride and groom

Meet the bride's parents before the wedding day

Attend pre-wedding celebrations, such as the engagement party, bucks party and the wedding eve party

Attend the ceremony rehearsal and rehearsal dinner

Chauffeur travelling guests to and from airports and the venues

Be personally available for last-minute problems on the wedding morning

Sit in the front row on the right of the aisle

Introduce guests to each other at the reception

Sit at the parents' table at the reception

Prepare and deliver a speech at the reception

Dance with the bride, bridesmaids, mother of the bride and mother of the groom

Other …

## Behind-the-scenes Helpers

Behind-the-scenes helpers often have one or two specific tasks to complete at the ceremony and/or reception. Family members not included in the bridal party are popular choices.

☐ Select your behind-the-scenes helpers

☐ The following is a list of tasks which are typically handled by the behind-the-scenes helpers. Select each task that you want completed by your helpers. If another person will be fulfilling the role, write their name next to it.

☐ Create a DVD slideshow to show at the reception of the bride and groom's life together so far

☐ Pick up ceremony items, e.g. decorations, items to release, aisle runner

☐ Erect tents and marquees

☐ Run unexpected errands on the day, e.g. organising wet weather gear

☐ Help to set-up the ceremony, e.g. marquees, chairs, decorations

☐ Transport the going-away outfits

☐ Decorate the reception venue

☐ Arrange the reception table displays

☐ Unload liquor

☐ Park the bride and groom's going-away car at the reception and look after the keys

☐ Help load wedding gifts into the car toward the end of the reception

☐ Return hired equipment

☐ Other ...

## Wedding Team Top Tips

- Pre-wedding celebrations are a great opportunity for attendants to get to know each other
- Open communication with your attendants and helpers is crucial for a smooth wedding day
- It is likely that some members of your wedding team may not get along with each other. If necessary, create ways to keep these members on neutral ground or away from each other
- Very young babies can be included in the ceremony. For example, try seating them in a wagon or pull-along car towed by their parent or a member of the bridal party
- Children under the age of four can be unpredictable – are you prepared to handle the unexpected stress of an uncooperative child?
- Select tasks that are age appropriate for your attendants and helpers
- Pets can be part of the ceremony, e.g. as ring bearers

# 8
# Guest List

How do you envision your wedding day – a small affair or a huge bash? A lavish party or a backyard barbecue? Your guest list will be largely based on the type of reception you want and your budget. Don't let guilt (or pressure from family or friends) overcome you. If you don't want your mum's cousin twice removed at your wedding, don't invite them.

## Dividing your List

☐ Determine how many guests will be invited

| | |
|---|---|
| <50 | 150–199 |
| 50–99 | 200–300 |
| 100–149 | 300+ |

*Include yourself, your fiancé and your attendants in the guest list.*

☐ Decide how the guest list will be divided
- ½ from the bride's side and ½ from the groom's side
- ⅓ from the bride's side, ⅓ from the groom's side and ⅓ for mutual guests
- The bride and groom each invite a different amount of guests, e.g. the bride invites 50 guests and the groom invites 30 guests
- Other …

☐ Select the type of guests you will invite

| Bride | Groom |
|---|---|
| Parents | Parents |
| Siblings | Siblings |
| Grandparents | Grandparents |
| Aunts and uncles | Aunts and uncles |
| Cousins | Cousins |
| Distant relatives | Distant relatives |
| Close friends | Close friends |
| Distant friends | Distant friends |
| Friends of guests | Friends of guests |
| Work colleagues | Work colleagues |
| Neighbours | Neighbours |

- ☐ Prepare your guest list
  - Combine the guests into one big list and remove any duplications

- ☐ If your guest list is too large eliminate guests to whom you are not closely connected
  - Children of guests (young babies may have to attend)
  - Co-workers that you don't see outside of work
  - Distant cousins
  - Friends of your parents/family friends

- ☐ Redistribute guests if you still have too many
  - If space is a problem at the ceremony venue, invite some guests to the reception only
  - If space is a problem at the reception venue, invite some guests to the ceremony only
  - If money is a problem, invite everyone to the ceremony and a set number to reception only
  - If your guest list is larger than your budget and you can't eliminate any more people, consider changing elements of your wedding, e.g. change lunch to brunch

- ☐ Create a reserve guest list
  - Move all eliminated guests to the reserve list and rank in order of importance (so they can be moved to the 'invited' list as guests decline)
  - Ensure the reserve list is large enough to cover estimated declines

- ☐ Take the following steps to help avoid hurting the feelings of guests who are not invited:
  - Don't tell anyone that they are invited until your guest list is official (inform your families to do this as well)
  - If you are only inviting immediate family and close friends to the reception, explain this to guests who are only invited to the ceremony
  - If you are inviting 'companions', ensure everyone has the same rule, e.g. couples may bring a companion if they are married, engaged to be married or in a long-term serious relationship and those in short-term relationships or who are dating cannot
  - If you are inviting part of a group, e.g. work colleagues, ensure those invited are aware of who is and isn't invited so they can be sensitive to those who are not
  - Contact guests who have RSVP'd for more guests than you have invited and explain the misunderstanding

*Be clear, polite and tactful when informing guests (or their families) that they are not invited.*

- ☐ Estimate the number of guests who will decline using the following guest reply formula

*Formula:* 10% of local guests will decline and 35% of travelling guests will decline

*Example:* 100 local guests and 20 travelling guests

$$100 \times 0.10 = 10$$
$$20 \times 0.35 = 7$$
$$= 17 \text{ guests are expected to decline}$$

## Guest Information Cards

☐ Create guest cards for *each* of your invited guests

☐ Use the guest cards provided (or create your own using index cards)
- Photocopy onto card paper to make index cards
- Cut to size
- Clip them together and store in your wedding file

*You can also print these at www.TheWeddingChecklist.com.au*

☐ In addition to guests, include a guest card for each of the following
- You
- Your fiancé
- One for each of your attendants
- One for each child or infant (as they will need a place for a pram or high chair)
- One for each guest's companion, write 'Companion of...' if you don't know their name

☐ As gifts arrive, add each gift received to the card of an adult family member

☐ Use the guest cards to design your reception seating
- Lay out the cards and physically move them around until you are happy with the table settings

*Find more detailed information about reception seating plans on page 159.*

### Guest List Top Tips

- Delegate drawing up the family guest list to family members on each side
- Invite those who you know can't attend as a nice gesture
- Determine if financial contributors (or parents) expect to invite guests of their own
- Create a spreadsheet to track your replies and declines
- Inform your reception manager of your estimated guest number ASAP
- Inform your reception manager of your final guest number two weeks before your wedding
- Follow up non-replies two weeks before the wedding

Name _____ Guest Number _____

Address _____

Email _____

Phone _____

☐ Invite Sent
    ▢ Attending ceremony      ▢ Not attending ceremony
    ▢ Attending reception      ▢ Not attending reception

Meal selection _____ Table number _____

Special needs _____

Date gift received _____ Thank you card sent ☐

Gift description _____

_____

---

Name _____ Guest Number _____

Address _____

Email _____

Phone _____

☐ Invite Sent
    ▢ Attending ceremony      ▢ Not attending ceremony
    ▢ Attending reception      ▢ Not attending reception

Meal selection _____ Table number _____

Special needs _____

Date gift received _____ Thank you card sent ☐

Gift description _____

_____

# 9

# Ceremony and Reception Venues

From historical sites to modern locations to those inspired by nature, choosing your venues is one of the most important decisions you will make regarding your wedding as they will set the scene for your entire day. While your reception venue is often the most expensive component of your wedding, it is money well spent if it makes your wedding day dreams come true.

☐ Select a meaningful place for your ceremony and reception venues
- At home
- At the home or in the garden of a friend or family member
- Family tradition
- Famous landmark
- Favourite bar
- Favourite restaurant
- Romantic location
- Where the proposal took place
- Where you met
- Other ...

☐ Select a place of worship for a religious ceremony

| | |
|---|---|
| Cathedral | Mosque |
| Chapel | Synagogue |
| Church | Temple |
| Kingdom hall | Other ... |

☐ Determine the location of your ceremony and reception within the selected venues

| | |
|---|---|
| Back garden | Pool area |
| Courtyard | Property grounds |
| Front garden | Terrace |
| Indoors | Other ... |

☐ Book your ceremony and reception venues as early as possible
- Book up to 18 months in advance – the earlier the booking, the better selection you will have

# Venue Ideas

☐ Select a ceremony and reception venue

Ancestral home
Art gallery
Arts centre
Bar/tavern
Barn
Bay
Beach
Beach house
Beachfront rotunda
Boardwalk
Boat
Botanical gardens
Brewery
Café
Castle
Castle grounds
Catamaran
Cathedral
Cave
Celtic club
Chapel
Church gardens
City square
Clifftop
Community centre
Cottage
Country club
Country house
Cruise ship
Decommissioned jail
Decommissioned railway station
Estate gardens
Estate home
Events centre
Farmstead
Forest
Function centre
Gallery
Garden
Golf club
Golf course

Hall
Heritage building
Historic homestead
Historic landmark
Historic site
Homestead
Hot air balloon
Hotel
Houseboat
Inn
Lagoon
Lake
Lighthouse
Lodge
Manor
Marina
Mill
Mineral or hot spring
Mountain chalet
Mountaintop
Museum
Nature reserve
Observatory
Open field
Oriental garden
Paddle steamer
Palace
Park
Pier/jetty
Planetarium
Pontoon
Racetrack
Rainforest
Ranch
Reception centre
Registry office
Resort
Restaurant
Retreat
River
River cruise
Rose garden

| Sand dunes | Vineyard |
| Snowfields | Warehouse |
| Sports arena | Wildlife conservation centre |
| Stables | Yacht |
| Surf club | Yacht club |
| Tourist attraction | Zoo |
| Town hall | Other … |

## Narrowing down Venue Choices

☐ Ensure your ceremony and reception venues are available on special dates
  - Preferred wedding date
  - Back-up wedding dates
  - Rehearsal date

☐ Determine if there will be other celebrations at the ceremony or reception venues before, during or immediately after your wedding

☐ Ensure you are aware of details of other celebrations that will be taking place on the same day
  - The number of groups
  - If you will be sharing any facilities
  - How close the other group(s) will be

☐ Personally visit shortlisted sites
  - Obtain brochures
  - Talk to venue staff/management
  - Take notes
  - Take photos

☐ Evaluate the following points when selecting your ceremony and reception venues
  - Acoustics
  - Ages of guests (will they have trouble negotiating stairs or rocky terrain?)
  - Ammenities
  - Architectural features
  - Areas for displaying/storing gifts
  - Bar or bar space
  - Catering space and facilities
  - Ceremony space
  - Changing rooms
  - Cloakroom facilities
  - Cost
  - Council plans on the day, e.g. lawn mowing, road works
  - Council restrictions
  - Dance floor or dance floor space

Designated smoking areas
Disabled access and facilities
Dishwashing facilities
Distance from car parks
Electricity supply
Guest viewpoints
How long you will have the space (allow adequate time to decorate)
Maximum and minimum capacities (including staff)
Natural and artificial lighting
Overtime fees
Parking
Places for decorations
Room sizes
Seating potential
Site condition
Space, e.g. ensure it won't feel too cramped or too spacious on the day
Style
Venue signage, e.g. it should be easy to find
Water supply
Other …

☐ Determine if your venues have any restrictions
Alcohol
Decoration placement
Items for releasing, e.g. butterflies
Items for throwing, e.g. petals, confetti, rice
Music
Noise
Open flames, e.g. candles, lanterns
Opening and closing times
Photography and videography
Smoking
Other …

☐ Find out what your venues can provide

| | |
|---|---|
| Bar | Music (DJ, sound system) |
| Choir/vocalists/musicians | Parking |
| Cooking facilities | Storage areas |
| Decorations | Tables and chairs |
| Electricity | Toilets and washrooms |
| Heating and cooling | Water supply |

☐ Find out if there are any requirements to marry at your ceremony venue, e.g. do you have to be a member of the club or church?

☐ Contact your local council regarding public venues
- Apply for permits for venue use
- Apply for permits to take photos and video footage
- Determine the licence requirements for the ceremony location
- Obtain approval for the ceremony venue
- Reserve public areas, e.g. park gazebos

☐ Notify close neighbours of the wedding if your venue is in a residential area
- Inform them if you will be celebrating into the night at least a week in advance

☐ Determine how waste will be collected and removed
- Put something in place to collect rubbish
- Create recycling stations
- Clean up outdoor venues, leaving them in the same condition (or better) than you found them

☐ Ensure the ceremony and reception venues are child friendly by securing the following
- Electricity sources
- Fireplaces and candles
- Large drops, e.g. hills, ditches, retaining walls
- Poisons
- Stairways
- Water sources
- Other …

☐ Organise and book your wedding night accommodation
- Select the penthouse or honeymoon suite

☐ Pack an overnight bag for your wedding night and the next day so you don't have to disturb your honeymoon luggage

## Outdoor Venues

☐ Complete the following for outdoor venues
- Ensure flowers will be blooming
- Ensure sand is not eroded
- Mow grass
- Rake ground
- Repel insects, e.g. using citronella lanterns
- Set up a signature table and chair
- Set up wind breaks
- Take note of sunny and shady spots
- Other …

☐ Research the weather by a personal visit, liaising with the venue manager and by looking up the forecast for your wedding day

| | |
|---|---|
| Cloud cover | Snowfall |
| Glare | Temperature range |
| Humidity | Time of sunrise and sunset |
| Natural light | UV degree |
| Rainfall | Wind direction and speed |

☐ Discuss with your officiant and venue manager if you are able to delay the ceremony if the weather is poor on the day, e.g. until rain or heavy clouds move out

☐ Provide items to ensure your guests are comfortable in weather extremes
- Chilled bottles of water
- Electric fans
- Handheld fans/miniature battery-operated fans
- Insect repellent
- Lap blankets
- Large golf umbrellas
- Outdoor heaters
- Parasols
- Shade tents
- Sunscreen
- Windbreaks
- Other …

☐ Create a back-up plan for wet or windy weather if your venue is not weatherproof
- Have a covered area on standby, e.g. a nearby gazebo, pavilion, hut
- Erect a marquee or tent in advance
- Shelter under a nearby veranda, bridge, terrace or porch
- Reserve an alternative indoor venue, e.g. a nearby hall
- Hold your ceremony at the reception venue (if it is weatherproof)

☐ Be prepared for spectators if you have chosen a public outdoor venue
- Appoint a helper to politely 'move along' obtrusive onlookers

☐ Designate areas to accommodate all guests and equipment, e.g. arrange pot plants, flags or bamboo lanterns to create a boundary

☐ If necessary, make security arrangements
- Appoint a helper to attend the entrance and check invitations (be sure to ask guests to bring their invitations with them)
- Appoint helpers to watch the gift table and cloakroom
- Arrange for a police escort
- Erect privacy screening
- Hire security personnel

## Destination Weddings and Travelling Guests

☐ Select a destination wedding location
- Dream location
- Favourite holiday location
- Home town
- Home town of a special person, e.g. your grandmother

☐ Consult with a travel agent who is familiar with your destination

☐ Ensure guests travelling to the wedding schedule time off from work as soon as possible

☐ Reserve accommodation for close family, friends and special guests

☐ Arrange for group discounts
- Accommodation, e.g. reserve blocks of rooms
- Car rental
- Food, e.g. breakfast included in accommodation package, group dinners
- Travel fares

☐ Organise for courtesy pick-ups to and from the airport, train station and bus stops

☐ Prepare a welcome booklet/package for travelling guests and include places of interest
- Coffee shops
- Hot spots
- Local activities
- Parks
- Restaurants
- Shopping centres
- Theatres
- Other ...

☐ Entertain guests when possible

## Destination Wedding Packages

☐ Select items that you would like to be included in your wedding package
- Accommodation
- Bridal hair and make-up
- Attendant hair and make-up
- Decorations
- Discounts for multiple flight and accommodation bookings
- Flights
- Flowers
- Guest accommodation
- Honeymoon
- Musicians
- Officiant
- Photography/videography
- Reception food and drink

Venue set-up/clean-up
Wedding cake
Wedding manager
Other …

☐ Arrange for several meetings with your wedding manager
　　Ask lots of questions
　　Have them clarify anything you don't understand
　　Request a wedding day itinerary
　　Determine when you will be presented with your wedding certificate

☐ Show your wedding manager your wedding file, pictures and anything else you have prepared as soon as you arrive at the wedding destination

## Top Tips for Destination Weddings

- Be sensitive to the financial situations of invited guests
- Consider guests who won't be able to attend and what this means to you
- Don't be offended if certain guests can't attend
- Ask your travel agent for suggestions and advice
- Contact tourist boards for information, such as the climate for your selected time of year
- Arrange for the safe transport of your wedding attire – obtain advice from your dress and suit designers
- Ask guests to transport some wedding items for you
- Arrive well in advance. For example, allow more than the minimum time advised for administration documents to clear in case there are delays
- Stream your ceremony footage live on your wedding website for those who couldn't attend

## Weddings in other Countries

☐ Research wedding customs, traditions and beliefs of the destination country

☐ Contact the consulate of the country where you will be married to discuss legalities and determine the documents you will need to present

☐ Contact the relevant authorities or a lawyer to determine if your marriage will be legal when you return
　　If not, take the necessary steps to legalise your marriage before or immediately after your return

☐ Determine if you are required to register your marriage once you arrive home

☐ Ensure you, your fiancé and your guests, have valid passports

☐ Determine if you will need any documents translated; if so, organise for an interpreter

# 10
# Invitations and Stationery

Preparing your invitations will be one of the most stressful parts of your wedding plans. Just be careful not to get persuaded into purchasing needless stationery items as it is very easy to go over your budget here. Invitations can be as simple as a pre-made card from your local gift shop.

## Save the Date Cards

☐ Inform guests to hold your wedding date using themed stationery
   - Card
   - Postcard
   - Fridge magnet
   - Handwritten note
   - Email
   - Phone call
   - Text message
   - Through social networks, e.g. Facebook, Twitter

☐ Select your save the date components
   - Title, e.g. Save the Date!
   - Your names
   - Wedding date
   - Wedding venue, city or country
   - Your wedding website URL
   - A sentence or short note explaining that an invitation will follow

☐ Post your save the date information to guests six months in advance
   - Send up to 12 months in advance if you are expecting some guests to travel large distances

## Wedding Invitations

☐ Select your wedding invitation components
   - Guest name(s)
   - Host name(s)

- Bride and groom's full names
- Date
- Ceremony time
- Ceremony location
- Reception location
- Reception time
- Formality/dress requirements
- Meaningful quote, poem, song lyrics or piece of literature
- Reply by (RSVP) date

☐ Acquire the full names and titles of your guests
- Delegate this task to family members
- Don't abbreviate names on the invitation

☐ Calculate the number of invitations needed
- Create one invitation per household unless children are over 18 years
- Purchase extra invitations to cover damages, mistakes, changes and guests you decide to invite at a later date, e.g. from your reserve list

☐ Select a style for your wedding invitations

| | |
|---|---|
| Art nouveau | Modern |
| Contemporary | Traditional |
| Elegant | Vintage |
| Floral | Themed with your wedding |
| Funky | Other … |

☐ Select a type of wedding invitation

Vertical fold

Gate fold

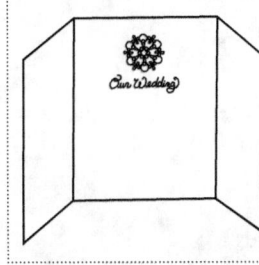

Glider

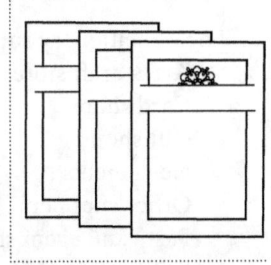

Horizontal fold

Layered

Petal fold

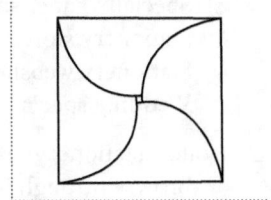

| Dual-fold | Postcard | Single panel |
|---|---|---|
|  |  | 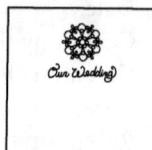 |

| Tea length | Tri-panel | Pocket fold |
|---|---|---|
|  | 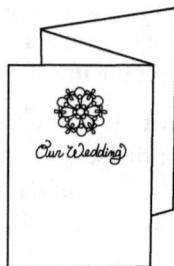 |  |

☐ Select how your invitations will be designed
    By a friend or family member
    By a professional invitation stylist
    By yourselves/DIY
    Using design software
    Use pre-designed stationery

☐ Locate stationery suppliers
    Art & craft stores
    Card shops
    Gift shops
    Newsagents
    Office suppliers
    Party and event stores
    Printers
    Scrapbooking stores
    Specialty paper shops
    Stationery stores
    Stationery websites
    Wedding specialist stores

☐ Collect stationery samples
    Browse through invitation styles
    Match paper and stationery designs with your wedding style and theme

- [ ] Create an invitation timeline using the following as a guide
  - Order and begin designing 12 weeks before the wedding day
  - Allow 3–4 weeks for printing and assembling
  - Post 6–8 weeks before the wedding day or earlier for guests travelling large distances
  - RSVP date to be 3–4 weeks before the wedding day
- [ ] Create a destination wedding invitation timeline using the following as a guide
  - Order and begin designing 12+ months before the wedding day
  - Allow 3–4 weeks for printing and assembling
  - Post 9–12 months before the wedding day
  - RSVP date to be 2 months before the wedding day

## Invitation Wording

- [ ] Draft the wording for your wedding invitations
  - Coordinate with your wedding style and theme

- [ ] Enlist the help of experts when wording your invitations
  - Printer
  - Specialty wedding books
  - Stationer
  - Wedding coordinator

- [ ] Write invitations in the third person, e.g. John and Amber invite you to …

- [ ] Spell out numbers in dates and times

- [ ] Issue your invitations in the name of one of the following
  - The bride's parent(s)
  - The bride's primary care giver at childhood
  - The groom's parent(s)
  - The hosts of the wedding
  - The bride and groom

- [ ] Include your child or children's names on the invitation, e.g. John and Amber, along with their sons Michael and Alexander, …

- [ ] Indicate guest attire
  - Beach weddings require appropriate footwear
  - Church weddings may require people to be modestly dressed
  - Lunch receptions are usually casual
  - Evening receptions generally require more formal attire, e.g. 'evening dress'
  - Request that guests bring extra clothing for cold or windy locations
  - Other …

- ☐ Specify on your invitations if children are invited
    - If children are invited, include their name on the invitation
    - If children are not invited, include a note card explaining that you are not able to invite children
    - Ensure everyone gets the same rule, e.g. all children invited or no children invited (except young babies)

- ☐ Select one or more font types for the wording components of your wedding invitation
    - Decorative – this is a dramatic font, e.g. Broadway
    - Sans serif – this is a modern font, e.g. Arial
    - Script – this font is much like handwriting, e.g. Brush script
    - Serif – this font is easy to read, e.g. Courier

## Paper, Motifs and Embellishments

- ☐ Select an invitation paper type

| | |
|---|---|
| Embossed card | Parchment |
| Handmade with natural fibres | Photo |
| Jacquard | Rice |
| Linen finish | Tinted |
| Marble | Translucent |
| Metallic | Other ... |

*Choose more than one paper type if you will be layering your invitations.*

- ☐ Match the invitation paper with your wedding theme and colours and select high-quality paper

- ☐ Purchase some test sheets and assess the print quality

- ☐ Decide how you will produce your invitations
    - Laser printed
    - Inkjet printed
    - Calligraphy
    - Handwritten by you, a family member or a friend with attractive handwriting

- ☐ Select a motif to feature on your wedding stationery

| | |
|---|---|
| Bells | Daisy |
| Celtic design | Dandelion |
| Champagne flutes | Doves |
| Cherry blossom | Fleur-de-lis |
| Cherubs | Hearts |
| Chinese love symbol | Initials |
| Claddagh | Leaves |
| Clover | Love birds |
| Combined monogram | Pear |

Photograph

Rose

Snowflake

Swan

Wedding rings

Other …

☐ Select embellishments for your wedding invitations and stationery

| | |
|---|---|
| Bows | Paper fasteners, e.g. split pins |
| Buckles | Paper lace strips |
| Charms | Pearl clusters |
| Clips | Raffia |
| Crystals | Ribbon |
| Decorative edges | Rubber stamp impression |
| Diamantes (rhinestones) | Shaped hole punches |
| Eyelets | Shaped sequins |
| Glitter | Tags |
| Metallic powder | Tassels |
| Other … | |

☐ Select decorative items to include inside the invitation envelope

Rose petals

Wedding scatters, e.g. metallic love hearts, flowers, wedding bells

Spray with perfume

## Envelopes and Postage

☐ Purchase envelopes that match your wedding invitations

☐ Line envelopes with decorative paper

☐ Acquire the full addresses of your guests

Delegate to your friends and families

Allow plenty of time to locate addresses

☐ Begin addressing envelopes while your invitations are being printed

| Guest Type | Example |
|---|---|
| Married couple with the same surname | Mr and Mrs/Ms John Jones |
| Married couple with different surnames | Ms Jane Smith and Mr John Jones |
| Unmarried couple living together | Mr John Jones and Miss/Ms Jane Smith (in alphabetical order of surname) |
| Unmarried woman | Miss/Ms Jane Smith |
| Unmarried man | Mr John Jones |
| Single guest plus a companion | *Do not include 'and guest' on the envelope* |
| Children under 18 | *Do not include on the envelope* |

☐ Select how your envelope will be sealed
  - Envelope moistener
  - Glue stick
  - Lick and stick
  - Metallic seal
  - Peel and seal
  - Personalised label
  - Wax
  - Wedding themed label

☐ Place a return address on the back of the envelope
  - Calligrapher to inscribe
  - Hand write
  - Personalised stamp
  - Printed label

☐ Decide how your invitations will reach your guests
  - Post
  - Personal delivery
  - Friend or family member to deliver
  - Email

☐ Purchase postage stamps
  - Purchase specialty wedding stamps from your post office
  - Order personalised wedding stamps, e.g. with a photo of yourselves
  - Use a standard size envelope so you only require one stamp

☐ Mail all invitations at the same time to prevent guests from becoming offended if their invitation arrives later than others

## Reception Cards

Reception cards are included with your invitations if the reception is at a different site, if the reception information does not fit on the invitation or if you are not inviting all guests to the reception.

☐ Create reception cards to include with your wedding invitations

☐ Select your reception card components
  - Title, e.g. Please Join us for Cocktails, Dinner and Dancing
  - Reception start time
  - Scheduled finish time
  - Reception address
  - The type of food that will be served
  - If drinks are not included, e.g. cash bar or BYO
  - Details about getting there and parking
  - Ideas of what to do in-between the ceremony and reception if there is a large time gap

## Gift Cards

Gift registry cards and wishing well cards allow you to inform invitees of your gift preferences in a polite and convenient way.

☐ Create a gift registry card to include with your wedding invitations

☐ Select your registry card components
    Title, e.g. Gift Registry
    Your names
    A poem or verse
    The name of the registry company/companies
    Contact details of the registry company, e.g. the website address

☐ Create a wishing well card to include with your wedding invitations
    Title, e.g. Wishing Well
    Your names
    A poem or verse
    Instructions (either a cash gift or a donation to your nominated charity)

☐ Create a note saying 'gifts not required' with the invitation if you do not want gifts

## Reply Cards

Reply cards, also known as RSVP cards, make it simple for your guests to accept or decline.

☐ Create an reply card to include with your wedding invitations

☐ Select your reply card components
    Title, e.g. Kindly Respond by
    Space for guests to write their names
    A place for guests to select if they accept or decline
    A place for indicating meal choice
    A number corresponding to the guest's name, in case they forget to write their name
    A reply envelope with your address and a postage stamp

☐ If you are having guests reply on your wedding website or responding via email, include 'how to reply' information on a separate reply card

☐ Mark all of the acceptances and declines on your index cards as they arrive and be sure to update your wedding file and/or spreadsheet

☐ Contact guests to ensure they received your invitation if you have not received a response two days before the reply-by date
    Contact by phone or in person
    Have a member of the bride's family contact guests from the bride's side
    Have a member of the groom's family contact guests from the groom's side

☐ Invite guests from your reserve list to replace those who have declined

# Further Information Cards

☐ Create information cards for travelling guests or destination weddings

☐ Select your information card components
    Nearby accommodation details including estimated rates, if bulk discounts are available and if breakfast is included
    Details of your travel agent
    Car rental companies
    Taxi phone numbers
    Details of family and friends who have offered accommodation
    Maps to the ceremony and reception venues
    Maps marked with train stations, bus routes, airports and other points of interest
    Local restaurants and attractions
    Other …

# Ceremony Programs and Reserved Cards

☐ Create a ceremony program (also known as an 'order of service' book)

☐ Select your ceremony program front cover components
    Title, e.g. The Wedding of John and Amber
    Your first names or initials
    Your wedding date
    The name of the ceremony venue
    A decorative element, e.g. your wedding motif

☐ Select components for the inside of the ceremony program
    Acknowledgements
    Attendant names
    Blessings
    Hymn or worship song
    Musicians' names
    Names of the bride's parents
    Names of the groom's parents
    Officiant's name
    Prayers
    Prelude music
    Processional music
    Readers' names
    Readings
    Recessional music
    Special messages
    Thank you messages
    Ushers' names
    Vocalists' names

- Vows
- Other …

☐ Calculate how many programs you require
- One per guest
- One per couple
- One per family

☐ Arrange for printing of the ceremony programs
- Hand write and photocopy
- Have professionally printed
- Print yourself

☐ Assemble your ceremony programs and add embellishments
- Bows
- Brooches
- Cord
- Lace
- Miniature artificial flowers
- Rhinestone accents
- Ribbon
- Themed graphics
- Themed items
- Other …

☐ Create reserved cards to let special guests know that they are seated in the reserved section (also known as pew cards)

## Guestbook

☐ Select a guestbook style
- Hard covered
- Silk covered
- Themed
- Photo guestbook – guests can insert Polaroids or prints from your photo booth and add messages

☐ Provide an alternative to a traditional wedding guestbook
- Combined monogram with surrounding signature mat
- Framed canvas with a wedding graphic and surrounding space for signatures
- Have your guests write messages on polished pebbles or shells and place them in a glass vase
- Photo puzzle pieces with space for writing messages
- Picture frame with surrounding signature mat
- Provide material squares for messages and sew into a quilt after your wedding

    Signature platter

    Signature vase

    Thumbprint tree – guests place an inked thumbprint on a pre-drawn tree and sign their name

    Video guestbook

    Wishing tree – guests write messages on tags and hang on a cherry blossom branch

    Other …

☐ Purchase a special pen or marker for your guestbook, e.g. a quill pen with stand

☐ Purchase and display two guestbooks and pens if you have over 200 guests

☐ Appoint a guestbook attendant

## Seating Chart, Table Names, Place Cards and Menus

☐ Create a reception seating chart

    List guests alphabetically by surname

    Write their table number or table name beside their name

    Provide a room plan for your guests to locate their table

☐ Prepare a poster board to display your reception seating chart

    Include a decorative element, e.g. combined monogram, a photograph, wedding motif

☐ Display your seating chart at the reception entrance or create escort cards to inform guests of their assigned reception table

☐ Create a table number and/or table name for each of the reception tables using your wedding stationery

☐ Select a theme for the table names

    Beaches

    Classic cars

    Cocktails

    Colours

    Countries you have visited together

    Hobbies you share

    Instruments

    Items relating to your wedding theme

    Music artists

    Streets you have lived in as a couple

    Other …

☐ Create a place card for each guest

- ☐ Select your place card components
  - Guest's first name
  - Guest's first name and surname

- ☐ Select items to be printed on the back of the place cards
  - Guest's name (to assist other people with name recall at the table)
  - A symbol relating to your guest's meal choice (to assist waitstaff)

- ☐ Purchase place card holders, e.g. a miniature photo frame or a themed item

- ☐ Create a menu using your wedding stationery
  - One for each table
  - One per plate

- ☐ Create a wine list using your wedding stationery
  - One for each table
  - One per plate

## Wedding Announcement Cards

Wedding announcement cards are used to announce your marriage to guests who did not attend the ceremony. They are sent after the wedding day and are often used for intimate ceremonies, destination weddings and when couples elope.

- ☐ Create wedding announcement cards

- ☐ Select your wedding announcement card components
  - Title, e.g. Amber & John
  - Your names (if not in the title)
  - A statement of marriage, e.g. We are united as one in marriage
  - Ceremony location
  - Wedding date and time
  - A photo from the day
  - An invitation to a post-wedding event
  - A link to your website that displays your wedding photos
  - Other …

- ☐ Purchase matching envelopes
  - Pre-prepare and have a helper post the day after your wedding

## Thank You Notes

- ☐ Create thank you notes for guests
  - Those who attended the ceremony/reception
  - Those who gave you a gift

- ☐ Select your thank you note components
    - Title, e.g. With Thanks on Our Wedding Day
    - Name of your guest
    - Words of thanks, e.g. thank you for sharing our day
    - A decorative element, e.g. wedding motif
    - A photo of you from the wedding day
    - A photo of you with the guest from the wedding day
    - Signed with your new married names
    - Other ...

- ☐ Personalise your thank you notes
    - Compliment a specific aspect of the gift
    - Explain how you plan to spend the money they gave
    - Explain how you plan to use the gift they sent
    - Identify something they did for you on the day and refer to it positively
    - Refer to their help, time or effort on the day
    - Write: 'It was lovely to see you' (for guests who attended)
    - Write: 'Thinking of you on our day' (for absent guests)

- ☐ Hand write or print thank you notes on your wedding stationery

- ☐ Post thank you notes
    - Send within two weeks of receiving a gift before the wedding
    - Send within eight weeks of receiving gifts on the day

- ☐ Write a card to each of your parents thanking them for everything they have done

## Stationery Top Tips

- If you are allowing guests to bring a companion write 'and Guest' on their invitation
- Use the same style of paper for all stationery
- Have two helpers check your stationery before printing
- Address envelopes before inserting the invitation
- Keep two of everything as keepsakes
- If you need to postpone or move your wedding date after your invitations have been sent creating 'Change the Date' cards is a quick and easy solution
- Place a notice in the newspaper a few days before the wedding, including the time and location of the ceremony so that well-wishers can attend your ceremony
- Generate a newspaper press release after the wedding

# 11

# Attire for the Ladies

Selecting your wedding outfits can be extremely overwhelming. There is a huge variety of wedding and attendant gowns that range from hundreds to thousands of dollars. Plus, there's coordinating the shoes, jewellery and accessories to create a consistent style. Consulting with a professional is a must. They can provide you with advice on outfits for different body shapes, personalities and tastes whilst still keeping with the wedding style.

## Finding the Perfect Wedding Gown

☐ Decide on the style of wedding gown, taking into account the type of ceremony, the venue and the wedding theme

- Casual
- City chic
- Classic
- Dramatic
- Elegant
- Funky
- Other ...
- Glamorous
- Natural
- Sexy
- Themed
- Traditional
- Vintage

☐ Decide on the type of gown

- Cocktail
- Designer
- Summer dress
- Themed
- Traditional white
- Other ...

☐ Decide how you will obtain your gown

- Buy new
- Custom designed and/or custom made
- Hire
- Borrow
- Made by you, a friend or family member
- Pre-loved/antique/vintage
- Inherited

☐ If you are considering having your gown custom made, take the following factors into consideration:

    ◻ You have plenty of time, e.g. at least eight months

    ◻ You have the budget to allow for having a unique gown

*Custom-made gowns are recommended if you are very particular or if you (or your attendants) have an unusual body shape or size.*

☐ Research dressmakers and designers

    ◻ Visit dressmakers in your local area

    ◻ Contact dressmakers in your extended area

*Fabric stores can often recommend wedding dressmakers who specialise in wedding gowns.*

☐ Appoint a dressmaker

    ◻ A dressmaker who specialises in wedding gowns

    ◻ A non-specific dressmaker

    ◻ A family member or friend

☐ Complete the wedding vendor checklist for your dressmaker on pages 10 and 11

☐ Provide your dressmaker with your thoughts and ideas including:

    ◻ Pictures (from magazines, books and the internet)

    ◻ Hand drawn diagrams and sketches

    ◻ Notes

    ◻ Precise instructions

☐ Ask your dressmaker for advice on your wedding gown

☐ Record your measurements in your wedding file, e.g. height, dress size, bust, bicep, wrist, sleeve length, waist, hip, glove, hat, shoe

☐ Find your body shape and review the following recommended styles:

| Body Shape | Recommended Styles |
| --- | --- |
| Full-figured | Vertical lines, low neckline, fitted bodice, A-line or princess line and thick structured fabric, fitted sleeves |
| Hourglass | Strapless or off-the-shoulder neckline, form fitting top, defined waist and no heavy embellishments |
| Inverted triangle | Open or V-shaped neckline, A-line skirt, smooth fabric and a simple design |
| Pear | Vertical seams, plain matte fabric with embellishments on the top half only |
| Petite | Figure hugging fabric with embellishments on the top half only |
| Rectangle | Scoop or sweetheart neckline, belted waist, layers, ruffles or details |
| Tall | Layered fabric, horizontal details, figure hugging cut and capped or short sleeves |

- ☐ Consider body size and shape changes if you are toning up, planning to lose weight or pregnant

- ☐ If you plan to purchase a new dress, decide where to shop for your gown

  | | |
  |---|---|
  | Antique stores | Evening wear stores |
  | Boutiques | Online |
  | Bridal gown stores | Retail stores |
  | Department stores | Second-hand stores |
  | Other … | |

- ☐ Allow plenty of time to shop for a gown – you may have to spend hours in each store

- ☐ Carefully select people to join you
  - People you trust
  - Those who will give an honest opinion
  - Those with similar taste and style

- ☐ Have a budget in mind before gown shopping
  - If you find a perfect wedding dress that is over your budget, decide how far you are willing to go over
  - Locate funds from other areas in your wedding budget if you feel the gown is absolutely worth the extra money

- ☐ Take items which will help you to visualise the full picture
  - Accessories
  - Shoes
  - Underwear

- ☐ Perform the following when gown shopping
  - Take notes
  - View yourself from all angles
  - Take photographs (if permitted)
  - Try on all styles – it may not look like what you want on a hanger, but it could be perfect on you

- ☐ Look for a wedding gown that makes you look and feel great
  - Accentuates your best features
  - Balances out your proportions
  - Hides any imperfections

- ☐ Allow shop assistants to assist you with gown choices and cuts

- ☐ Order your gown well in advance, e.g. six months before or 12 months before if it is being made

- ☐ Purchase your gown one size bigger than you actually are and have it tailored to fit your body shape perfectly

- ☐ Ensure your gown matches the formality of the wedding, e.g. an informal dress is perfect for a garden or registry office wedding

☐ Determine if there are any religious or cultural gown or outfit regulations, e.g. very revealing gowns may not be appropriate for a church ceremony

*You may want to wear a traditional (cultural) outfit at your ceremony and a more current outfit at your reception.*

☐ Decide how much skin coverage you would like from your wedding gown
- Neck to wrist
- Collar to bust
- Floor length
- Knee length
- Other …

☐ Consider whether to show off or cover tattoos and piercings

☐ Select an alternative to a traditional wedding gown
- Bathing suit and sarong
- Bodice and skirt
- Cocktail dress
- Corset and skirt
- Destination clothing, e.g. Polynesian attire
- Evening dress
- Fancy dress
- Jacket and skirt
- Regional/cultural/religious clothing, e.g. Indian sari
- Seasonal dress
- Summer dress
- Trouser suit
- Other …

## Gown Particulars

☐ Select from the following dress cuts and styles

Accordion pleat      A-line      Ballgown

Basque waist

Box pleat

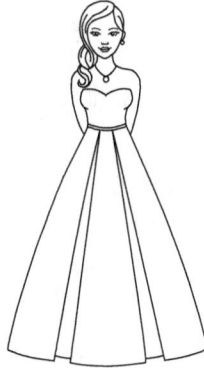

Bubble

Bustled

Column/sheath

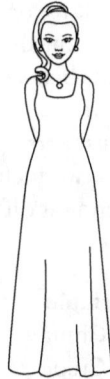

Empire waist

Mermaid/fishtail

Pickup hemline

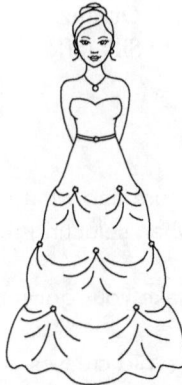

Princess line

| Shift | Slimline | Tiered |
|---|---|---|
|  | 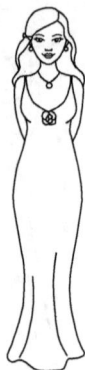 |  |

☐ Select a skirt length
- Mini – hemline ends just below the buttocks
- Knee – hemline ends at the knee or slightly above
- Street – hemline ends just below the knee
- Intermission – hemline ends between the knee and mid-calf
- Tea – hemline ends mid-calf
- Ballerina – hemline ends just above the ankles
- Floor – hemline ends up to two inches from the floor
- Asymmetrical – hemline ends at different lengths

☐ Select a gown fabric

| Light | Variable | Heavy |
|---|---|---|
| Batiste | China silk | Brocade |
| Charmeuse | Crêpe | Duchess satin |
| Chiffon | Damask | Moiré |
| Dotted Swiss | Delustred satin | Satin |
| Lace | Jersey | Velvet |
| Silk Georgette | Organza | Wool |
| Tulle | Silk taffeta | |

## Gown Fabric Top Tips

- Consider the fabric texture and what type of finish you want
- Consider the season when selecting the fabric weight, e.g. light fabrics in summer
- Changing fabric can make your gown more affordable, e.g. silk to satin
- Store appropriately to avoid creases and lines
- Press your gown according to the manufacturer's instructions

☐ Select a gown shade that matches your skin tone
- Bright white
- Champagne
- Cream
- Ivory
- Magnolia
- Natural white
- Oyster
- Stark white
- Alternative colour, e.g. icy green, pale gold, soft violet

☐ Add a splash of colour to your wedding gown using a colour panel, sash, embroidery, lace, beading and/or accessories

☐ Select a train style and length
- Watteau – begins above the shoulder and ends at the same length as the gown
- Sweep/brush – attached at the waist and ends 3–6 inches past the floor
- Court – attached at the waist and extends 3 feet past the floor
- Panel – a one foot wide panel, usually detachable, attached at the waist and ends in-between court and chapel lengths
- Chapel – attached at the waist and extends 3½–4½ feet
- Semi-cathedral – attached at the waist and ends in-between chapel and cathedral lengths
- Cathedral – attached at the waist and extends 6½–7½ feet
- Royal – attached at the waist and extends 9–10 feet
- Monarch – attached at the waist and extends 12 feet or more

☐ Select your train particulars
- Train will require a bustle
- Train to be detachable
- Wrist loop attached (for carrying your train during dancing and mingling)

☐ Organise a storage place for your detachable train after the photos

☐ Select a neckline type
*Aim for a comfortable bust that is not too tight or too roomy.*

| Asymmetric | Boat Neck | Cowl |
|---|---|---|
|  |  |  |

Elizabethan

Halter

Illusion

Jewel

Mandarin

Queen Anne

Scoop

Square

Surplice

| Sweetheart | Tank | V-shaped |
| --- | --- | --- |
|  |  |  |

☐ Select a backline type

| Backless | Crossover | High-back |
| --- | --- | --- |
| 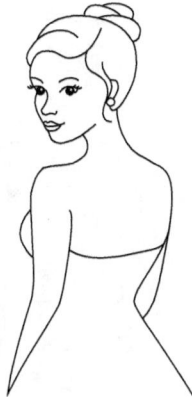 |  | 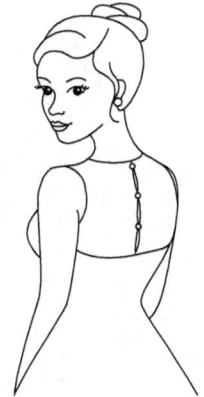 |

| Keyhole | Laced | Plunging |
| --- | --- | --- |
| 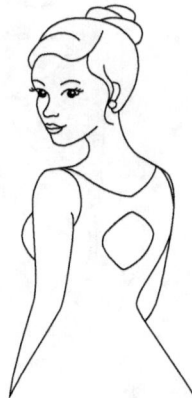 | 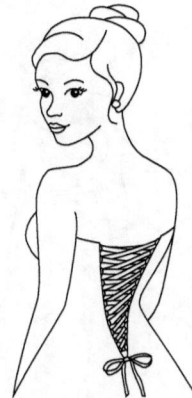 | 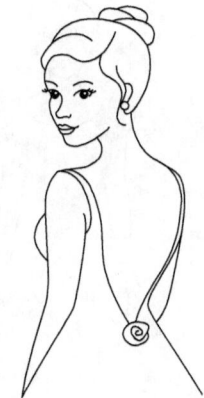 |

Scoop

V-shaped

☐ Select a sleeve type

Bell

Bishop

Fitted

Juliet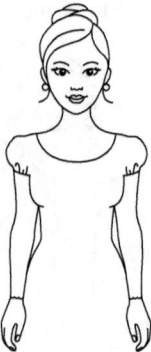

One-shoulder

Poet

Butterfly     Capped 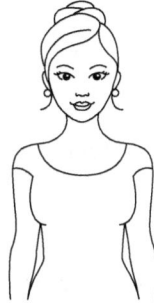    Illusion

Off-the-shoulder     Sleeveless     Spaghetti straps

☐ Select a sleeve length
- Short
- Elbow length
- Three-quarter length
- Full length

☐ Select gown embellishments

- Appliqué
- Beading
- Belt
- Bows
- Bugle beads
- Buttons
- Crystals
- Diamantes (rhinestones)
- Edging
- Embroidery
- Other …

- Fringe
- Gems
- Jewels
- Lace
- Paillettes
- Pearls
- Ribbon
- Sash
- Seed beads
- Sequins

- [ ] Practise how you will sit in your gown
  - Cross-legged
  - Legs together
  - Straight back
  - Shoulders back

- [ ] Ensure you and your attendants can perform the following comfortably in your attire:
  - Crouch
  - Dance
  - Get in and out of wedding transport
  - Go to the toilet
  - Hug
  - Kneel
  - Lift arms above your head
  - Sit
  - Twist
  - Walk
  - Walk up and down hills and/or stairs

- [ ] Consider other things you might be doing on the day when selecting a gown, e.g. getting on and off a boat

- [ ] Decide how you will pay for your wedding gown
  - In full with cash
  - In full using a credit card or funds from a loan
  - Arrange for a payment plan
  - Pay a deposit upon purchase and the remainder shortly before the wedding

- [ ] Make a list of people who you don't want to see your gown before the day, e.g. the groom

## Fittings and Alterations

- [ ] Select the types of alterations you will have made
  - Bust line lift
  - Darts inserted
  - Embellishments added
  - Entire remodelling
  - Hem lengthened
  - Hem shortened
  - Repairs, e.g. seams, zips, buttons
  - Resizing
  - Skirt made fuller
  - Skirt tapered
  - Straps or sleeves lengthened
  - Straps or sleeves shortened
  - Train bustled
  - Train shortened
  - Tucks inserted
  - Other …

*Changing or adding to the original design will make your gown one of a kind.*

- ☐ Determine the following from your dress fitter
  - How long each fitting will take
  - If alterations are added to the price and, if so, how much they will cost

- ☐ Allow plenty of time and money for alterations

- ☐ Note your fitting schedule in your wedding file
  - Allow for 3–5 fittings
  - Plan your last fitting to be less than a month before your wedding day (a must if you plan to lose weight)

## Pregnant Brides and Bridesmaids

Pregnant brides and bridesmaids are very common. Whether you decide to celebrate or disguise your pregnant shape there are a range of gowns available that will look stunning on your radiant figure.

- ☐ Select a dress cut that will flatter your pregnant figure
  - A-line
  - Empire waist
  - Medieval style
  - Princess line
  - Other …

- ☐ Ensure that your dressmaker or gown fitter knows that you are pregnant and how far along you will be on the big day
  - Let them know if you want to hide your baby bump or show it off
  - Allow for belly growth
  - Allow for an increase in bust size
  - Have your final fitting as close to the wedding day as possible

- ☐ If you decide to conceal your baby bump, try one of the following:
  - Wear a long flowing dress
  - Avoid clingy fabric
  - Have your gown focus on your arms, bust, legs or shoulders
  - Purchase a gown one size larger and have the bust taken in
  - Use a heavily patterned fabric
  - Embellish your dress with dark coloured items
  - Wear a long veil to hide shadows
  - Hold a large or cascading bouquet

- ☐ If you prefer to have *some* wedding photographs show you without your baby bump, try the following:
  - Focus on other parts of your body, e.g. bust, shoulders, face
  - Shoot directly in front or from above
  - Use low contrast lighting to minimise shadows

- Use props to block the view of your baby bump, e.g. bouquet, other people
- Use positions to block the view of your baby bump, e.g. knees up when sitting down

☐ Keep in mind that your pregnancy will make you tire easily
- Purchase a comfortable dress cut and fabric
- Purchase appropriate shoes (plus a spare pair in a larger size if you are prone to swelling)
- Plan for breaks

## Pregnant Brides Top Tips

- If you want to wear white, do it proudly!
- Consult with specialist designers and maternity formalwear stores
- Avoid corsets and tight bodices that will place pressure on your midsection
- Wear a mock wedding ring on the day if your hands are swollen

## Accessories

Don't go overboard with wedding accessories. Carefully select a few statement pieces that match the style of your wedding and your chosen attire. Aim for your accessories to complement your gown, but not overpower it.

## Veil and Headpiece

☐ Select from the following veil styles and cuts

Cage

Bandeau

Blusher

Flyaway

Pouf

Mantilla

Cascading/waterfall

Square cut

Oval cut

Drop cut

Angel cut
(back view)

Handkerchief cut
(back view)

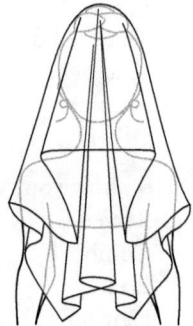

☐ Select the number of veil tiers
- Single tier
- Double tier
- Triple tier

☐ Select a veil length
  - Blusher – just enough to cover your face
  - Shoulder
  - Elbow
  - Fingertip
  - Knee
  - Ballet – falls between the knee and ankle
  - Chapel – brushes the floor
  - Church – floor length plus 20 inches
  - Cathedral – floor length plus 38 inches
  - Royal – floor length plus 82 inches

*Generally, the more formal the wedding, the longer the veil.*

☐ Select a veil fabric
  - Cage net
  - Chiffon
  - English netting
  - Illusion
  - Lace
  - Organza
  - Pleated tulle
  - Polyester
  - Shimmer tulle
  - Silk
  - Spotted tulle
  - Tulle

☐ Select veil embellishments
  - Beads
  - Bugle beads
  - Crystals
  - Diamante band
  - Embellished edging, e.g. scalloped, lace, ribbon
  - Embroidery
  - Lace appliqué
  - Pearls
  - Scattered diamantes (rhinestones)
  - Seed beads
  - Sequins
  - Other …

☐ Select how your veil will be secured
  - Barrettes
  - Comb
  - Elastic
  - Hairpins
  - Headband
  - Other …

☐ Select where your veil will be secured
  - Top of your head
  - Back of your head, e.g. above an updo or bun
  - Lower part of your head, e.g. under an updo or bun

☐ Decide how you will wear your veil for the beginning of the ceremony
　　Face covered
　　Face uncovered

*You can cover your face immediately after entering your ceremony transport or just before walking down the aisle.*

☐ Decide if you want your veil to be detachable
　　If so, organise a storage place for after the photos

## Wedding Veil Top Tips

- Consider your hair length, face shape and dress detailing before selecting a veil
- Check with your gown store or dressmaker to see if they have a matching veil
- Ensure your veil matches the style of your gown
- Hang your veil in a steamy bathroom to relax wrinkles the day before your wedding

☐ Select a headpiece type

| | |
|---|---|
| Antique brooch | Jewelled or beaded sticks |
| Bow | Juliet cap |
| Clips | Mantilla |
| Coronet | Pearls |
| Decorative comb | Picture hat |
| Fascinator | Pillbox hat |
| Feathers | Pins |
| Flowers (fresh or artificial) | Ribbons |
| Hairgrips | Snood |
| Hairpins | Tiara |
| Headband | Wreath |
| Other ... | |

☐ Select a headpiece that suits your wedding gown
　　An elaborate headpiece (for a simple gown)
　　A simple and classic headpiece (for an elaborate gown)

☐ Consider your face shape when selecting your headpiece
　　Add height with a tiara if you have a round face
　　Add width with a headband or side hairpiece if you have a narrow face
　　Provide balance with a spray of flowers or pearls to a triangular face

☐ Decide where your headpiece will be secured
　　Top of your head
　　Back of your head, e.g. above an updo or bun

Lower part of your head, e.g. under an updo or bun
Side of your head
Scattered, e.g. hairpins, pearls, jewels

## Undergarments

☐ Choose undergarments that will not show through your gown, e.g. a similar shade to your skin colour

☐ Select a wedding gown underskirt
Bridal slip                    Hoop skirt
Crinoline                      Petticoat

*Try on underskirts of varying stiffness under your gown.*

☐ Purchase a bra
Attend a professional fitting
Ensure it does not create bulges
Ensure that no material or bra straps show

*If your dress is strapless or backless don't wear a bra on the wedding morning as it may leave indents and marks on your skin.*

☐ Purchase bra inserts and accessories
Silicone/foam fillers
Push up enhancement pads
Body tape/body adhesive

☐ Purchase underpants
Make sure there are no visible lines
Make sure there are no bulges or bunches from underpants that don't fit properly

☐ Purchase control garments
Bustier – pushes up your bust and shows more cleavage
Control slip
Corset – gives you a curvy look by holding in your waist
Sculpting body wrap
Sculpting bodysuit
Sculpting underpants
Waist shaper
Other ...

☐ Purchase hosiery
Full-length pantyhose
Thigh-high stockings with garter belt
Knee-high stockings
Tights (opaque)
Footlets

*Purchase two extra pairs to store in your wedding emergency kit.*

- ☐ Purchase garters
    - One for the 'garter toss'
    - One to keep

- ☐ Embellish undergarments with diamantes, ribbons or personalised printing

- ☐ Ensure that you will be able to go to the toilet easily in your gown and undergarments
    - If you think you may have trouble, make sure your maid of honour and bridesmaids are aware that you will need their help

- ☐ Purchase lingerie for special occasions
    - Wedding night
    - Honeymoon

## Gloves

- ☐ Select a glove style
    - Fingerless
    - Gauntlet
    - Mitt
    - Ruched
    - Single finger loop

- ☐ Select a glove length
    - Wrist
    - Elbow
    - Three-quarter
    - Full

- ☐ Select a glove fabric
    - Cotton
    - Cotton spandex
    - Fur (trim)
    - Lace
    - Leather
    - Net
    - Organza
    - Satin
    - Silk
    - Velvet

- ☐ Select a glove fabric style
    - Crochet
    - Embroidered
    - Fishnet
    - Opaque
    - Sheer
    - Solid

- ☐ Decide if you will wear your gloves when exchanging rings
    - If you will be wearing your gloves for the ring exchange, split the seam of your ring finger to make it easier to get your ring on

## Shoes

- ☐ Select a shoe type
    - Boots
    - Classic pumps
    - Flats
    - Mules
    - Platforms
    - Sandals
    - Slingback pumps
    - Slippers

| Sneakers | Wedges |
| Stilettos | Barefoot (no shoes) |
| Thongs/flip flops | Other ... |

☐ Select shoes that fit correctly, e.g. allow plenty of room for your toes

☐ Select shoes that you will be able to wear comfortably for several hours
  Consider where and how much you will be walking on the day,
  e.g. stairs, gravel, sand, lawn

☐ Ensure your shoes complement your height and dress style

☐ Ensure your shoe heel is sturdy and a height that you are used to

☐ Begin 'wearing in' your shoes one month before your wedding day
  Practise walking and dancing indoors in your chosen pair

☐ Fix slippery soles
  Purchase a paint-on non-slip product
  Sandpaper the soles
  Scuff the soles on pavers

☐ Purchase items to prevent blisters

☐ Purchase cushioned insoles

## Bridal Footwear Top Tips

- Shoe colour doesn't have to be the same as your gown
- If you are getting married in summer remember that feet often swell in the heat
- Wear your shoes at all gown fittings, particularly when being hemmed
- Purchase a separate, more comfortable pair of shoes for dancing
- Place a penny in your shoe on the day for good luck

## Other Accessories

☐ Purchase a garment for extra warmth for cooler climates and evening receptions

| Bolero | Shrug |
| Cape | Stole |
| Jacket | Wrap |
| Other ... | |

☐ Select a bag type

| Clutch | Purse |
| Drawstring pouch | Shoulder bag |
| Minaudière | Wristlet |
| Other ... | |

- ☐ Purchase a bag for your wedding day envelopes and emergency kit (to be carried by someone else)

- ☐ Organise for the following:
  - Something old
  - Something new
  - Something borrowed
  - Something blue

- ☐ Purchase a horseshoe to symbolise fertility and good luck
  - Have a fabric horseshoe or horseshoe charm sewn into your wedding gown

- ☐ Select a perfume
  - Favourite brand
  - Signature scent for the day
  - Borrowed scent

- ☐ Purchase deodorant
  - Use a deodorant that dries clear on your skin
  - Apply deodorant early to let it sink in before putting on your gown

- ☐ Purchase other accessories for your wedding day
  - Charms
  - Handkerchief
  - Parasol
  - Sunglasses
  - Other …

## Special Outfits

- ☐ Purchase special outfits for your pre-wedding celebrations
  - Bridal shower
  - Engagement party
  - Hens party
  - Kitchen tea
  - Rehearsal dinner
  - Wedding eve party

- ☐ Purchase other special outfits
  - A separate outfit for your wedding reception, e.g. cultural attire
  - Going-away outfit
  - Honeymoon clothing
  - Other …

- ☐ Purchase items to complement your special outfits, e.g. shoes and accessories

# Bride's Attendants

☐ Determine who will choose the bridesmaid outfits
　　Bride
　　Maid of honour
　　Bridesmaids
　　Bride with input from attendants

☐ Decide what the bridesmaids will wear
　　Bathing suit and sarong
　　Bodice and skirt
　　Cocktail dress
　　Corset and skirt
　　Destination clothing, e.g. Polynesian attire
　　Evening dress
　　Fancy dress
　　Gown
　　Jacket and skirt
　　Regional/cultural/religious clothing, e.g. Indian sari
　　Seasonal dress
　　Summer dress
　　Trouser suit
　　Other …

☐ Decide how your bridesmaids will be unified
　　Identical attire
　　Same cut
　　Same style
　　Same fabric
　　Same length
　　Same colour
　　Varying shades of the same colour
　　Same skirt, different bodice
　　Same bodice, different skirt
　　Statement jewellery
　　Statement shoe
　　Other …

☐ Decide what your maid of honour will wear to distinguish her

☐ Record the measurements of your female attendants in your wedding file, e.g. height, dress size, bust, bicep, wrist, sleeve length, waist, hip, glove, hat, shoe

☐ Have your bridesmaids go dress shopping with you
　　Have the bridesmaids try on potential dresses
　　Take note of what your attendants like and dislike

Pay attention to which cuts, colours and styles suit each of your bridesmaids

☐ For each bridesmaid, ensure the dress complements their:
  Body shape
  Complexion
  Personal style
  Personal taste

☐ Make sure the bridesmaid dresses suit your wedding
  Ensure the bridesmaid dress colours, fabric and cut match the season
  Ensure they complement the bridal gown, e.g. elaborate bridesmaid outfits will clash with a simple bridal gown
  Coordinate bridesmaid style with male attendants

☐ If possible, choose a gown company that has a store near your bridesmaids if they live far away

☐ Select footwear for your bridesmaids
  Choose comfortable shoes
  Ensure your bridesmaids are happy to wear the chosen shoe height
  Allow bridesmaids to select their own footwear that follow certain guidelines, e.g. colour, type, heel height

☐ Select bridesmaid accessories
  Bracelets
  Earrings
  Gloves
  Hair ornaments
  Jackets or wraps
  Necklaces
  Purses or clutches
  Other …

☐ Contact your bridesmaids the day before to make sure their attire is pressed and wrinkle free

## Flower Girls

☐ Decide what your flower girls will wear
  A simplified version of the bride's gown
  A simplified version of the bridesmaid gowns
  Apron dress
  Blouse and tutu
  Party dress
  Other …

☐ Record the measurements of your flower girls in your wedding file, e.g. height, dress size, bust, bicep, wrist, sleeve length, waist, hip, glove, hat, shoe

☐ Have each flower girl and her parent go dress shopping with you
  Have your flower girls try on potential dresses

Pay attention to which cuts and styles suit your flower girls

Select a dress with room to grow

Choose something simple and comfortable that they are happy to wear

☐ Ensure the flower girl dresses suit your wedding

They complement the bridal gown

The fabric and cut match the season

They are a similar style and/or colour to the other junior attendants

☐ Select footwear for your flower girls

Ballet flats

Barefoot

Children's pumps

Sandals

Sling backs

Other ...

☐ Select complementary flower girl accessories

Baskets

Bracelets

Butterfly/fairy wings

Earrings

Gloves

Hats

Headpieces, e.g. crown of flowers

Jackets or wraps

Lace umbrellas

Necklaces

Ribbon wands

Sashes

Other ...

## Mothers of the Bride and Groom

☐ Find out what your mothers would like to wear on the day

Bathing suit and sarong

Bodice and skirt

Cocktail dress

Destination clothing, e.g. Polynesian attire

Evening dress

Fancy dress

Gown

Jacket and skirt

Regional/cultural/religious clothing, e.g. Indian sari

Seasonal dress

Skirt and top

Summer dress

Trouser suit

Other ...

☐ Shop with the mothers of the bride and groom (separately) to offer guidance and suggestions for their wedding outfits
  - Visit shops who specialise in outfits for mothers of the bride and groom
  - Select something special
  - Select something fashionable
  - Choose something that makes her feel good

☐ Ensure that each mother's outfit coordinates with the bridal party
  - Select different but complementary colours to the bridesmaids
  - Suggest outfits that will look good in the wedding photos
  - Recommend a colour other than white or cream

☐ Have the mothers consult with each other regarding their outfit styles and colour
  - Ensure the mother of the bride has the first choice

☐ Shop together for footwear
  - Ensure the mothers are comfortable as they will be on their feet for much of the day and night

☐ Shop together for accessories
  - Hat
  - Hair ornaments
  - Jewellery, e.g. pearls, heirloom earrings
  - Jacket or wrap
  - Purse, clutch or handbag
  - Other …

### Attire Top Tips for your Wedding Day

- Store your attire in the place where you will be getting dressed on the day
- Lay out your attire and accessories the night before
- Allow two hours for dressing
- Spray gowns with anti-static spray
- Dress junior attendants as late as possible
- Expect good luck and congratulatory items to be placed around your wrist by guests after the ceremony e.g. fabric horseshoes, hearts, charms, butterflies
- Avoid dark liquids, e.g. red wine and rich sauces
- Dye, shorten and/or alter the bridal or attendant dresses to wear to another special occasion, e.g. ball, cocktail event, party, wedding, races

# 12
## Attire for the Gentlemen

The groom's attire is just as important as the bride's. It must match the wedding style and theme as well as the bride's gown. If your fiancé decides to purchase a new suit, have him select a classic style that won't date so it can be worn again. The bottom line is that he should not only look good but feel good too.

### Finding the Perfect Suit

☐ Decide on the style of suit

- Classic
- Casual
- Designer
- Dramatic
- Other ...
- Natural
- Themed
- Traditional
- Vintage

*Take into account the type of ceremony, the venue and the wedding theme.*

☐ Decide on the type of suit

- Business
- Italian
- Linen
- Lounge
- Morning
- Pinstripe
- Polyester
- Seasonal
- Slim cut
- Themed
- Three piece
- Tuxedo
- Two piece
- Uniform, e.g. military
- Zoot
- Other ...

☐ Choose how the suit will be obtained

- Borrowed
- Hired
- Inherited
- Pre-loved
- Purchased new
- Tailor made

*Tailor-made suits are recommended if the groom is very particular or if he (or his attendants) has an unusual body shape or size.*

☐ Research and appoint a tailor
  ▫ Visit tailors in your local area
  ▫ Contact tailors in your extended area
  ▫ Obtain recommendations, e.g. from friends, family, fabric stores
  ▫ Select a tailor who specialises in wedding attire

☐ Complete the wedding vendor checklist for your tailor on pages 10 and 11

☐ Record the groom's measurements in your wedding file, e.g. height, shirt length, shoulder width, sleeve length, bicep, wrist, neck, chest, waist, hip, inside leg, seat, glove, hat, shoe

☐ Select your fiancé's body shape and consider the following cuts

| Body Shape | Recommended Cuts |
|---|---|
| Heavy | Dark solid colours, lightweight fabric, vertical lines, loose fit in the midsection, two button jacket with a deep V-shape |
| Inverted triangle | Athletic cut jacket with large lapels, front pleated trousers with wide legs |
| Rectangle | Long two-button jacket with double pockets on chest and shoulder pads, wide collared shirt, layered on top for bulk, semi-fitted trousers |
| Regular | Single breasted contoured jacket, lean cut trousers |
| Short | Dark solid fabric or pin stripes, jacket cut as short as possible, built jacket shoulders, low rise trousers |
| Stocky | Solid colour or vertical stripes, matching jacket and trousers, high buttoned jacket of 3–4 buttons that finishes below the chest |
| Tall and thin | Textured or heavy fabric, light colours, large cuffs, double breasted jacket, double pleat trousers |

*Consider body changes if he will be toning up, planning to build up muscle or lose weight.*

☐ Decide where to shop for the suit
  ▫ Department stores          ▫ Online
  ▫ Formalwear stores          ▫ Wedding attire stores
  ▫ Menswear stores            ▫ Other …

☐ Carefully select people to join you
  ▫ People you trust
  ▫ Those who will give an honest opinion
  ▫ Those with similar taste

☐ Have a budget in mind before suit shopping and stick to it

☐ Perform the following when suit shopping
  ▫ Take notes
  ▫ View your fiancé from all angles

- Take photographs (if permitted)
- Have him try on all styles – it may not look like what you want on the hanger, but it could be perfect once on

☐ Look for a suit that does the following:
- Accentuates his best features
- Hides imperfections
- Makes him look well proportioned

☐ Allow shop assistants to assist with suit choices and cuts

☐ Ensure the suit matches the formality of the wedding
- Have all male members dress to a similar degree of formality, e.g. attendants and immediate family

☐ Ensure you are aware of the following if hiring attire
- If cleaning is required before returning
- What happens if the item is damaged
- When it needs to be returned

☐ Select an alternative to a traditional wedding suit
- Beachwear, e.g. t-shirt and shorts
- Button down shirt with trousers
- Cultural attire, e.g. kilt
- Destination clothing, e.g. Polynesian attire
- Fancy dress
- Shirt and shorts

## Suit Particulars

☐ Select a jacket style

Cutaway

Lounge

Mandarin

Stroller    Tailcoat    Tuxedo

☐ Select a jacket type
 &#9642; Single breasted
 &#9642; Double breasted

☐ Select a trouser style
 &#9642; Boot cut     &#9642; Low rise
 &#9642; Double pleat   &#9642; Regular cut
 &#9642; Flared     &#9642; Single pleat
 &#9642; Flat front    &#9642; Slim cut
 &#9642; Full cut     &#9642; Straight leg
 &#9642; Long rise    &#9642; Wide leg

☐ Select a suit colour that complements the bridal gown
 &#9642; Beige      &#9642; Light gray
 &#9642; Charcoal gray   &#9642; Liquid black
 &#9642; Ivory      &#9642; Navy blue
 &#9642; Jet black    &#9642; Other …

☐ Select a suit fabric type

| Light | Variable | Heavy |
|---|---|---|
| &#9642; Cotton | &#9642; Cashmere | &#9642; Flannel |
| &#9642; Linen | &#9642; Polyester | &#9642; Herringbone |
| &#9642; Poplin | | &#9642; Tweed |
| &#9642; Seersucker | | &#9642; Wool |
| &#9642; Silk | | |

☐ Select a shirt collar type

Button down

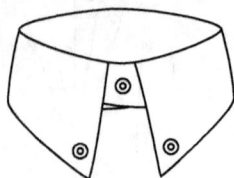

Classic point

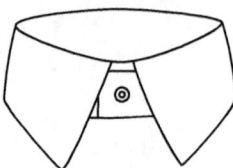

Hidden button

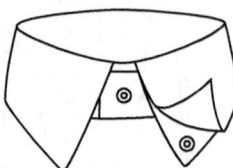

Band

Cutaway

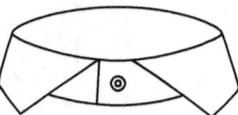

Pinned

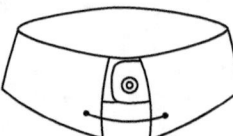

Round

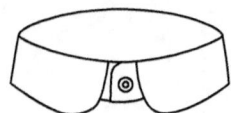

Spread

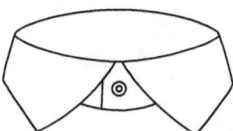

Wing

Tab

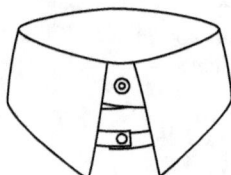

☐ Select a shirt cuff type
   Button – single cuff with 1, 2 or 3 buttons
   French – double cuff folded back and secured with cufflinks

☐ Ensure your fiancé (and his attendants) can perform the following
comfortably in their attire:
   Crouch
   Dance
   Get in and out of wedding transport
   Hug
   Kneel
   Lift arms above head
   Sit
   Twist
   Walk up and down hills and stairs

- ☐ Decide how the suit will be paid for
  - In full with cash
  - In full using a credit card or funds from a loan
  - Payment plan
  - Pay a deposit upon purchase and the remainder shortly before the wedding

## Fittings and Alterations

- ☐ Select the types of alterations to be completed
  - Alter shoulders
  - Embellishments added
  - Entire remodelling
  - Lengthen jacket hem and sleeves
  - Lengthen trousers
  - Repairs, e.g. seams, zips, buttons
  - Resizing
  - Shorten jacket hem and sleeves
  - Shorten trousers
  - Other …

*Make the suit a one of a kind by changing or adding to the original design.*

- ☐ Determine the following from the fitter or tailor
  - How long each alteration will take
  - How much it will cost, if not included in the suit price

- ☐ Allow plenty of time and money for suit alterations

- ☐ Have your fiancé take items that will aid the suit fitter, e.g. shirt and shoes

- ☐ Note the fitting schedule in your wedding file
  - Allow for 3–5 fittings
  - Plan the last fitting to be less than a month before your wedding day (a must if you plan to lose weight)
  - Collect suits from the tailor with plenty of time to spare

## Accessories

- ☐ Choose additional items for the groom's attire
  - Armbands
  - Cummerbund
  - Lapel bar, pin or clip
  - Overcoat
  - Other …
  - Pocket square
  - Tie
  - Tie bar
  - Waistcoat/vest

☐ Select a type of tie

Ascot

Bolo
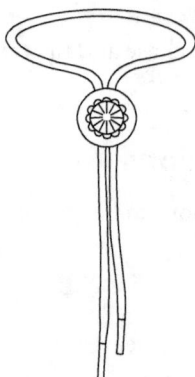

Classic necktie
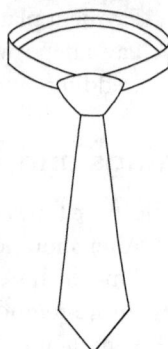

Colonel
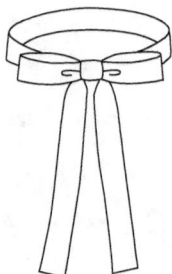

Fat boy

Scarf
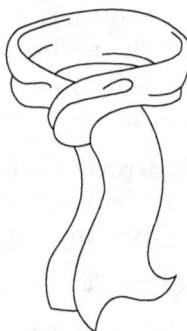

Bow tie
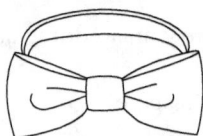

Crossover
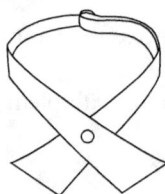

☐ Determine the tie colour
   Traditional, e.g. black bow tie
   The colour of the wedding gown
   The colour of the bridesmaid gowns
   Other ...

## Gloves

☐ Select a glove type
   Fingerless
   Full
   Gauntlet

☐ Select a glove fabric
   Cotton
   Leather
   Nylon
   Polyester/cotton
   Wool

☐ Decide if your fiancé will wear gloves when exchanging rings
   If he will be wearing gloves for the ring exchange, split the seam of the ring finger to make it easier to get the ring on

## Shoes

☐ Select a shoe type
   Boots
   Derbys/Bluchers
   Leather thongs/flip flops
   Monks/loafers
   Oxfords/Balmorals
   Sandals
   Wing tips
   Barefoot (no shoes)
   Other …

☐ Ensure the shoes complement the groom's suit style

☐ Consider where and how much he will be walking on the day, e.g. stairs, gravel, sand, lawn

☐ Ensure you purchase shoes that he will be able to wear comfortably for several hours

☐ Have him begin 'wearing in' his shoes one month before the wedding day
   Have him practise walking and dancing indoors

☐ Fix slippery soles
   Purchase a paint-on non-slip product
   Sandpaper the soles
   Scuff the soles on pavers

☐ Purchase items to prevent blisters

☐ Purchase cushioned insoles

# Undergarments

☐ Purchase new underwear
  - Briefs
  - Boxers
  - Boxer briefs
  - Personalised underwear

☐ Ensure underwear can't be seen under the groom's trousers

☐ Purchase a sleeveless tank or singlet to be worn under the shirt
  - Ensure that it cannot be seen under the shirt

☐ Purchase socks
  - Ensure the socks match the attire as there will be times when they are exposed

# Other Accessories

☐ Purchase a belt
  - Match with the shoe colour
  - Ensure the belt is darker than the suit fabric
  - Use quality full grain leather

☐ Purchase a belt buckle

☐ Purchase deodorant
  - Ensure he applies deodorant in advance to let it settle before putting on his suit

☐ Select a scent
  - Aftershave
  - Cologne
  - His favourite brand
  - Signature scent for the day

☐ Have him apply fragrance behind his ears, on his neck and upper chest

☐ Purchase other accessories for the wedding day
  - Braces
  - Cane
  - Handkerchief
  - Hat
  - Studs and cufflink set
  - Sunglasses
  - Tie pin
  - Top hat
  - Watch
  - Other …

# Special Outfits

☐ Purchase outfits for the pre-wedding celebrations
  - Engagement party
  - Bucks party
  - Rehearsal dinner
  - Wedding eve party
  - Other …

- ☐ Purchase other special outfits
  - A separate outfit for the wedding reception, e.g. cultural attire
  - Going-away outfit
  - Honeymoon clothing
  - Other ...

- ☐ Purchase items to complement the special outfits, e.g. shoes and accessories

## Groom's Attendants

- ☐ Select the type of suit the groomsmen will wear

| | |
|---|---|
| Business | Slim cut |
| Italian | Themed |
| Linen | Three piece |
| Lounge | Tuxedo |
| Morning | Two piece |
| Pinstripe | Uniform, e.g. military |
| Polyester | Zoot |
| Seasonal | Other ... |

- ☐ Decide what the best man will wear to distinguish him

- ☐ Record the measurements of the male attendants in your wedding file, e.g. height, shirt length, shoulder width, sleeve length, bicep, wrist, neck, chest, waist, hip, inside leg, seat, glove, hat, shoe

- ☐ Have the groomsmen go suit shopping with you
  - Have the groomsmen try on potential suits
  - Pay attention to which cuts and styles suit them
  - Take note of what they like and dislike

- ☐ Make sure the groomsmen's suits complement your wedding
  - Ensure the suit colours, fabric and cut match the season
  - Ensure they complement the groom's attire
  - Coordinate groomsmen's attire with the bridesmaid dresses

- ☐ If possible, choose a suit company that has a store near the groomsmen if they live far away

- ☐ Select footwear for the groomsmen
  - Choose comfortable shoes
  - Allow groomsmen to select their own footwear that follow certain guidelines, e.g. colour and type

- ☐ Select complementary accessories for the groomsmen

| | |
|---|---|
| Armbands | Cummerbunds |
| Belts | Gloves |
| Braces | Handkerchiefs |

| | |
|---|---|
| Lapel bars, pins or clips | Ties |
| Overcoats | Tie bars |
| Pocket squares | Top hats |
| Socks | Waistcoats/vests |
| Studs and cufflinks | Watches |
| Sunglasses | Other ... |

☐ Contact attendants the day before to make sure their attire is clean and wrinkle free

# Ring Bearer and Pageboys

☐ Decide what the ring bearer and pageboys will wear
    A simplified version of the groom's outfit
    A simplified version of the groomsmen's outfits
    Miniature tuxedo
    Morning suit
    Sailor suit
    Trousers and waistcoat
    Other ...

☐ Record the measurements of the ring bearer and pageboys in your wedding file, e.g. height, shirt length, shoulder width, sleeve length, bicep, wrist, neck, chest, waist, hip, inside leg, seat, glove, hat, shoe

☐ Have each pageboy and his parent go shopping with you
    Have them try on potential outfits
    Pay attention to which cuts and styles suit them
    Select an outfit with room to grow
    Choose something simple and comfortable that they are happy to wear

☐ Ensure the chosen outfits suit your wedding
    The fabric and cut match the season
    They complement the groom's attire
    They are a similar style and/or colour to the other junior attendants

☐ Select footwear for the ring bearer and pageboys

| | |
|---|---|
| Barefoot | Loafers |
| Boots | Sandals |
| Dress shoes | Other ... |

☐ Choose complementary ring bearer and pageboy accessories

| | |
|---|---|
| Clip on ties | Socks |
| Gloves | Waistcoats/vests |
| Jackets | Other ... |

☐ Purchase or create a ring carrying device for the ring bearer
  ☐ Cushion with ties, e.g. a small velvet or satin pillow
  ☐ Hollow book, e.g. bible, poetry book
  ☐ Plate or dish
  ☐ Plush toy with ties, e.g. a teddy bear
  ☐ Silver tray
  ☐ Single flower stem with ties
  ☐ Small decorated box
  ☐ Other ...

## Fathers of the Bride and Groom

☐ Find out what your fathers would like to wear on the day

| | |
|---|---|
| ☐ Casual attire | ☐ Themed attire |
| ☐ Seasonal attire | ☐ Tuxedo |
| ☐ Shirt and trousers | ☐ Uniform |
| ☐ Suit | ☐ Other ... |

☐ Take the father of the bride and groom shopping to help select a wedding outfit

☐ Record the measurements of the fathers of the bride and groom in your wedding file, e.g. height, shirt length, shoulder width, sleeve length, bicep, wrist, neck, chest, waist, hip, inside leg, seat, glove, hat, shoe

☐ Ensure that each father's outfit coordinates with the bridal party
  ☐ Suggest outfits that will look good in the wedding photos
  ☐ Select complementary colours

☐ Shop together for footwear
  ☐ Ensure shoes are comfortable as they will be on their feet for much of the day and night

☐ Shop together for accessories

| | |
|---|---|
| ☐ Armbands | ☐ Socks |
| ☐ Belts | ☐ Studs and cufflinks |
| ☐ Braces | ☐ Sunglasses |
| ☐ Cummerbunds | ☐ Ties |
| ☐ Gloves | ☐ Tie bars |
| ☐ Handkerchiefs | ☐ Top hats |
| ☐ Lapel bars, pins or clips | ☐ Waistcoats/vests |
| ☐ Overcoats | ☐ Watches |
| ☐ Pocket squares | ☐ Other ... |

☐ Contact each of your fathers the day before to make sure their attire is clean and wrinkle free and their shoes are freshly polished

## Men's Attire Top Tips

- If the groom has pale skin, select a navy or grey coloured suit rather than black
- Avoid too many layers if the weather will be hot
- Ensure the jacket is comfortable across the groom's back
- Ensure the lines are clean and smooth
- Make sure trousers are not too tight or loose around his waist
- Have the trouser cuffs just touch the top of his shoes
- Coordinate the sock colour with the male attendants
- Polish shoes the day before as boot polish can stain

☐ Decide where the following people will dress on your wedding day

| | |
|---|---|
| Bride | Pageboys |
| Maid of honour | Junior attendants |
| Bridesmaids | Ushers |
| Flower girls | Mother of the bride |
| Groom | Father of the bride |
| Best man | Mother of the groom |
| Groomsmen | Father of the groom |
| Ring bearer | Special helpers |

# 13
# Jewellery

Select a wedding ring that you really like and fits your style – you will be wearing it for the rest of your life! Don't be put off if you don't find one straight away. Try on all types and styles, those you don't like the look of in the cabinet may take your breath away once on your finger. You might decide to go slightly over budget with your rings as you will be looking at them every day, but do your best to choose affordable pieces; remember you have a wedding on the horizon.

## Wedding and Engagement Rings

☐ Determine who will choose the engagement ring
  ▢ Groom
  ▢ Bride
  ▢ Bride and groom together

☐ Select a type of engagement ring
  ▢ New                                    ▢ Family heirloom
  ▢ Self-designed                          ▢ Antique
  ▢ Altered design of existing ring        ▢ Vintage

☐ Consider the following when selecting your (and your fiancé's) wedding and engagement rings
  ▢ Lifestyle, e.g. sport, hobbies         ▢ Personal taste
  ▢ Occupation                             ▢ Personality

☐ Select an engagement ring setting

  ▢ Bar                    ▢ Bezel                    ▢ Channel

Claw

Flush/gypsy

Pavé

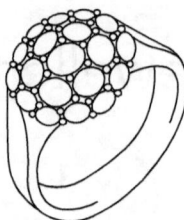

Tension

☐ Decide on the precious stones or gems for your rings (and other wedding jewellery)

| | |
|---|---|
| Alexandrite | Garnet |
| Amber | Opal |
| Amethyst | Pearl |
| Aquamarine | Peridot |
| Birthstone | Quartz |
| Citrine | Ruby |
| Diamond | Sapphire |
| Emerald | Topaz |
| Family gemstone | Other … |

☐ Select a diamond shape/cut

Asscher

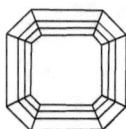

Baguette

Cushion

Emerald

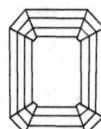

Heart

Marquise

Oval

Pear

| Princess | Radiant | Round | Trilliant |
|:---:|:---:|:---:|:---:|

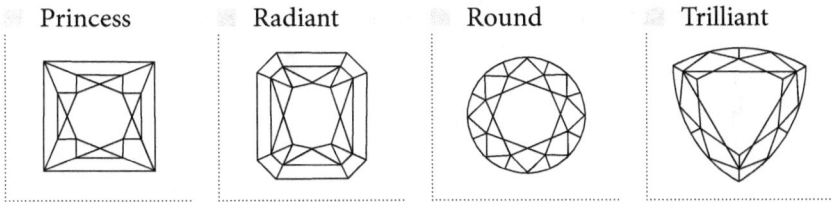

☐ Establish your (and your fiancé's) ring size
  - Have your ring finger professionally sized
  - Allow for finger swelling and shrinkage in hot and cool weather
  - Note your ring sizes in your wedding file

☐ Give your jeweller your engagement ring when they are sizing your wedding band to ensure a perfect fit

☐ Select a style and type of wedding band
  - New
  - Self-designed
  - Altered design of an existing ring
  - Family heirloom
  - Antique
  - Vintage
  - Solid band
  - Band with design
  - Band with precious stones
  - Interweaving rings that lock together
  - Matching his-and-her wedding bands

☐ Select a style and type of wedding band for the groom
  - New
  - Self-designed
  - Altered design of an existing ring
  - Family heirloom
  - Antique
  - Vintage
  - Solid band
  - Band with design
  - Band with precious stones
  - Matching his-and-her wedding bands

☐ Decide on a type of metal for you (and your fiancé's) rings
  - Palladium
  - Platinum
  - Rhodium
  - Rose gold
  - Silver
  - Titanium
  - White gold
  - Yellow gold

☐ Select the carat that you want (if you are choosing gold rings)
- 9
- 14
- 18
- 22
- 24

☐ Choose the same metal and carat for your wedding and engagement rings as it will reduce metal erosion

☐ Have your (and your fiancé's) wedding band engraved
- Names
- Initials
- Wedding date
- Nicknames
- A romantic, humorous, spiritual or religious saying
- A romantic, humorous, spiritual or religious quote
- Song name
- Song lyrics
- Words, e.g. together forever

*Enquire with your engraver as to how many characters you can have and the cost for engraving.*

☐ Have your engagement ring cleaned at least two days before the wedding

☐ Appoint a helper to carry the rings on the wedding morning
- Best man
- Groom
- Maid of honour
- Ring bearer
- Other …

*If your ring bearer is young, entrust the wedding rings with the groom or best man and have him give them to the ring bearer just before the ceremony.*

☐ Have stones and rings professionally cleaned yearly
- Enquire if cleaning is included with the ring purchase

☐ Obtain advice from your jeweller on how to clean your particular ring selection so you can do it throughout the year

☐ Select an alternative item to exchange rather than traditional wedding rings
- Amulet
- Bracelet
- Love token, e.g. a handcrafted gift, painting, poem
- Necklace with his-and-her lockets or pendants
- Tattoo, e.g. on your ring finger or somewhere else
- Other …

# Wedding Jewellery

☐ Select a wedding jewellery style or theme

| | |
|---|---|
| Antique | Diamonds |
| Birthstone | Pearls |
| Bohemian | Period, e.g. Renaissance |
| Chic | Retro |
| Classic | Vintage |
| Other ... | |

☐ Consider your wedding attire when selecting your jewellery pieces, e.g. gown neckline, shape, fabric, embellishments

☐ Browse various places for your wedding rings and wedding jewellery
- Antique shops
- Gown stores
- Jewellery stores
- Markets
- Online
- Pawn brokers
- Vintage jewellers
- Wholesale jewellers, e.g. purchase the stones and have them set into a band

☐ Purchase from respected and reputable jewellers

☐ Complete the wedding vendor checklist for your jeweller on pages 10 and 11

☐ Carefully select wedding jewellery to complement your wedding style and theme

| Jewellery Type | Example |
|---|---|
| Ankle and foot jewels | beaded barefoot sandals, chain, charm |
| Bracelet | crystal, diamond line, pearl, solid bangle |
| Brooch/pin | fabric corsage, floral, vintage, wreath |
| Chain | box, cable, rope, rolo |
| Choker | double or triple row, pendant, Victorian, vintage rose |
| Cufflinks | novelty, gem encrusted, personalised, themed |
| Earrings | chandelier, drop, hoop, pendant, solitaire, stud, tassel |
| Headpiece | hair brooch, headband, jewelled clips, sticks, tiara |
| Necklace | backdrop, draping fringe, statement, Y necklace |
| Pendant | diamond solitaire, locket, pearl solitaire |

*Select timeless jewellery pieces.*

- ☐ Purchase jewels to be used with other wedding items
  - ☐ Attire, e.g. crystal beads or pearls sewn onto your wedding gown
  - ☐ Bomboniere
  - ☐ Cake
  - ☐ Decorations
  - ☐ Flowers
  - ☐ Hair
  - ☐ Invitations
  - ☐ Stationery

## Jewellery Cost

- ☐ Determine how much will be spent on the bride's engagement ring
  - ☐ Equivalent to one month of the groom's salary
  - ☐ Equivalent to two months of the groom's salary
  - ☐ A set budget
  - ☐ An unlimited budget

- ☐ Decide how your rings and wedding jewellery will be paid for
  - ☐ Outright – cash, credit, EFTPOS or cheque
  - ☐ Finance – in-store payment plan or bank loan
  - ☐ Lay-by plan – pay a deposit upfront and the remainder at a selected time

- ☐ Request a ring guarantee

- ☐ Obtain written documentation of rings
  - ☐ Ensure the documents identify the carat and description of gems

- ☐ Ensure all jewellery and diamonds come with legitimate valuation certificates

- ☐ Keep receipts for the rings and other jewellery for insurance purposes and have them insured immediately after purchasing

- ☐ Have pre-loved rings valued independently

# 14
# The Look

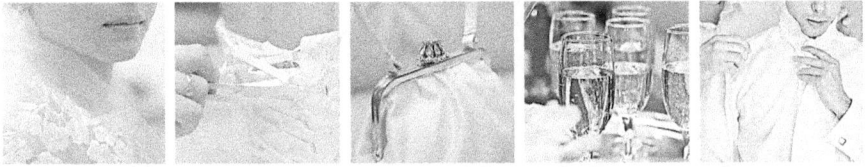

Break out the face cream, hairspray and lip gloss, it's time to plan your primping and preening regime. When it comes to the total image, you want to create a cohesive look with your dress, veil, hair and make-up. Don't go overboard with the fake tan and make-up – the key is to create the most beautiful version of yourself.

## Bride's Hair

- ☐ Focus on hair care several months in advance to ensure it is healthy for the big day
    - Apply weekly deep conditioning treatments
    - Control dandruff
    - Match your hair products to your hair type
    - Minimise heat from dryers and straightening irons (to protect hair from drying out)
    - Regularly sterilise combs and brushes
    - Remove split ends with regular trimming
    - Thicken with scalp massages

- ☐ If you want longer hair for your wedding, allow plenty of time to grow it out
    - Have regular trims for faster growth, e.g. every 6–8 weeks

*Hair grows approximately 15cm (6 inches) per year.*

- ☐ Decide who will style your hair on the day
    - Professional hairstylist
    - Bridal hair specialist
    - Family member
    - Friend
    - You

- ☐ Complete the wedding vendor checklist for your hairstylist on pages 10 and 11

- ☐ Book your hairstylist at least four months in advance

☐ Determine where you will have your hair done on the day
  ⬚ Hair salon
  ⬚ The location where you will be dressing
  ⬚ Family member or friend's house
  ⬚ Your home

☐ Decide what time you will have your hair styled on the day
  ⬚ Wedding morning
  ⬚ Midday
  ⬚ Afternoon

*Hair can take up to 2 ½ hours to style, so be sure to schedule in enough time.*

☐ Research a hairstyle that will look great on you
  ⬚ Consider your facial structure
  ⬚ Look through magazines, online and talk to your attendants about hairstyles
  ⬚ Shortlist hairstyles that complement both your gown and your face shape
  ⬚ Collect photos and diagrams to show your hairdresser

☐ Select a wedding hairstyle
  ⬚ Beehive
  ⬚ Bob
  ⬚ Braids
  ⬚ Bun
  ⬚ Down
  ⬚ Finger wave
  ⬚ French twist
  ⬚ Half updo
  ⬚ Long and flowing
  ⬚ Other ...
  ⬚ Loose curls
  ⬚ Low do
  ⬚ Ponytail
  ⬚ Side curls
  ⬚ Side do
  ⬚ Straight
  ⬚ Twist
  ⬚ Updo
  ⬚ Weave

☐ Inform your hairdresser if your ceremony or reception is outdoors and explain the elements you are likely to encounter, e.g. strong winds

☐ Experiment with hair colours several months in advance and talk to your hairdresser about the best colours for your skin tone

☐ Select an appropriate hair colour
  ⬚ Full permanent recolour
  ⬚ Full semi-permanent recolour
  ⬚ Full colour rinse
  ⬚ Root touch-up
  ⬚ Highlights
  ⬚ Foils

*Have your hair colouring completed 1–2 weeks before your wedding day to let it settle.*

☐ Arrange for your hair to be cut well before the wedding day

☐ Organise for hair extensions

☐ Select hairstyles for your bridesmaids, flower girls and junior attendants

☐ Consult with your hairstylist to ensure they understand the hairstyle that you have selected
- Determine if your hairstyle will hold for the entire day – including activities such as dancing
- Find out what you will need to help the hairstyle last the day, e.g. a comb and hairspray

☐ Obtain advice from your hairdresser about a suitable veil and/or headpiece
*See the detailed list of headpieces and hair ornaments on page 100.*

☐ Organise and attend a bridal hair trial
- Invite your bridesmaids, junior attendants and flower girls to attend
- Take hair ornaments, headpieces and your veil
- Take photos at your hair trial to make sure it looks good on camera
- Make adjustments to the hairstyles as necessary

☐ Wash your hair the day before your wedding day so that it will be easier to style
- Dry your hair immediately after washing

☐ Wear a button up shirt or robe when having your hair styled so you won't risk damaging it
- Inform your bridesmaids, junior attendants and flower girls to do this as well

## Groom's Hair

☐ Have your fiancé focus on hair care several months in advance to ensure it is healthy for the big day
- Apply weekly deep conditioning treatments
- Control dandruff
- Match hair products with his hair type
- Regularly sterilise combs and brushes
- Remove split ends with regular trimming
- Thicken with scalp massages

☐ Decide on a wedding hairstyle
- Clipped or shaved
- Fauxhawk (a mini mohawk without shaving the sides of your head)
- Messy and textured
- Pompadour
- Short back and sides
- Slicked back

- Spiked
- Other …

☐ Select a hair colour
- Camouflage colour
- Full permanent recolour
- Full semi-permanent recolour
- Full colour rinse
- Root touch-up

*Have hair colouring completed 1–2 weeks before your wedding day to let it settle.*

☐ Consider hair building techniques (if necessary)
- Hair replacement surgery
- Purchase a toupee – recent advances have made them look more realistic

☐ If he is thin on top arrange for the following:
- Have his hair cut as short as he is comfortable with
- Have him grow facial hair to help detract from hair loss
- Arrange for a scalp conditioning

☐ Arrange for his hair to be cut 1–2 weeks before the wedding day

☐ Purchase hair products for the wedding day
- Cream
- Gel
- Mousse
- Oil
- Pomade
- Shiner
- Spray
- Volumiser
- Wax

☐ Select hairstyles for the groomsmen, pageboys, ring bearer and junior attendants

☐ Help him select the type of facial hair to grow or keep for the day
- Chin curtain
- Extended side burns
- Full beard (long or short)
- Goatee
- Moustache
- Mutton chops
- Soul patch
- Stubble
- Van Dyke
- None (clean shaven)

☐ Purchase tools for facial hair maintenance
- Combs
- Disposable razors
- Electric razor
- Scissors
- Straight cut razor
- Trimmer

☐ Organise a professional straight blade shave

☐ Arrange a skin cleanse, face massage and a hot steam facial wrap for the wedding morning

## Face Shaving Top Tips for the Groom

- Moisturise before shaving
- Use a fresh razor that is from a trusted brand
- Shave wet skin with a gel, foam or oil
- Double check for stray hairs and clumps
- Use a high-quality aftershave balm
- Apply a moisturiser with SPF 30+ sunscreen after shaving

## Body Hair Removal

☐ Explore the different types of hair removal
- Electrolysis
- Hair removal cream
- Intense pulsed light (IPL) treatment
- Laser removal
- Plucking
- Shaving
- Threading
- Tweezing
- Waxing

☐ Select the areas you will be removing hair

| Bride | Groom |
|---|---|
| Bikini (American, French, Brazilian) | Arms |
| Chin | Back |
| Eyebrows | Chest |
| Legs | Ears |
| Underarms | Eyebrows |
| Upper lip | Full body |
| | Legs |
| | Neck |
| | Nose |
| | Shoulders |
| | Speedo |
| | Stomach |

☐ Gently exfoliate before hair removal to reduce the risk of ingrown hairs

☐ Complete all hair removal at least 48 hours in advance

☐ Moisturise daily

# Make-up

- ☐ Research a make-up style that will look great on you
  - Consider your facial structure and skin colour
  - Look through magazines, online and talk to your attendants
  - Collect photos and diagrams to show your make-up artist

- ☐ Select a make-up artist
  - Book as soon as possible
  - Enquire if they can also style your hair as they may offer a bundled discount

- ☐ Complete the wedding vendor checklist for your make-up artist on pages 10 and 11

- ☐ Have your eyelashes tinted

- ☐ Have your eyebrows tinted or lightened
  - Consider a semi-permanent option, e.g. cosmetic tattooing

- ☐ Organise and attend for a make-up trial
  - Invite your bridesmaids, junior attendants and flower girls to attend
  - Talk to your make-up artist about your preferred style, e.g. natural, glam, retro
  - Indicate shades and colours that you *don't* want
  - Take photos at your make-up trial to make sure it looks good on camera
  - Make adjustments to the make-up as necessary

- ☐ If you are doing your own make-up, seek out advice from make-up professionals or your local department store
  - Aim for a natural look
  - Select a foundation according to the season, e.g. consider the humidity of summer and use an oil-free product
  - Use a foundation for your individual skin tone and complexion (consider the difference if you will be fake tanning)
  - Use cream eye shadows as they last longer and don't crease
  - Select a waterproof mascara in case of tears
  - Curl eyelashes before you apply mascara
  - Apply only two coats of mascara and allow time to dry in-between
  - Apply less mascara on your lower lashes
  - Hold eyebrows in place with a tiny amount of Vaseline
  - Test lipstick colours on your fingertips as it is the closest colour to your lips
  - Select a volume boosting lip gloss for fuller lips

- ☐ Pack foundation, lipstick and eye make-up in your wedding emergency kit for reapplying throughout the day and night

## Teeth

☐ Ensure your teeth and gums are kept healthy starting several months in advance
  - Brush, floss and use mouthwash twice a day
  - Rinse with water after meals
  - Avoid food and drink with strong colouring, e.g. red wine, coffee
  - Have a regular dental clean, e.g. twice yearly
  - Have a professional gum treatment

☐ Use a quality toothbrush that is not too hard; most dentists recommend soft-to-medium bristles

☐ Teeth take time but if you have a long engagement consider the following:

| | |
|---|---|
| Bridges | Orthodontics |
| Crowns | Reshaping |
| Dentures | Tooth jewels |
| Implants | Tooth whitening treatment(s) |
| Laser light bleaching | Veneers |

## Hands

☐ Protect your hands with moisturising creams, gloves and sunscreen

☐ Ensure your fingernails are kept healthy starting months in advance
  - Trim and tidy fingernails regularly
  - Treat infections around your nails and cuticles
  - Use a fortified nail polish
  - Use a high-quality polish remover
  - Give your nails a few days break between nail polish applications

☐ Begin to strengthen and condition your fingernails 12 weeks in advance
- Massage your hands daily with a cuticle cream
- Massage your nails to stimulate growth
- Apply nail hardener twice a week

☐ Visit your manicurist for nail enhancements

| | |
|---|---|
| Acrylic nails | Natural tips |
| French polish | Overlays |
| French tips | Refills |
| Gel nails | Shape and polish |
| Manicure | Temporary tips |

☐ Arrange nail enhancements for your bridesmaids and junior attendants

☐ Select a fingernail colour for your wedding day
- Clear
- Light pink or nude
- French manicure
- Matched with the bridesmaid dresses
- Matched with the wedding colours
- Other …

☐ Select a fingernail colour for your bridesmaids and junior attendants

☐ Have henna designs applied to your hands

☐ Select fingernail embellishments and jewellery
- Diamantes (rhinestones)
- Gems
- Glitter
- Nail art
- Nail dangles
- Nail stickers
- Patterns, e.g. houndstooth
- Shaped gems, e.g. butterflies, hearts, flowers

## DIY Nail Colour

- File and shape before removing existing polish as the nail is stronger
- Apply a base coat
- Apply two coats of nail polish colour
- Allow to dry between coats
- Apply a clear top coat

## Feet

☐ Ensure your feet are kept healthy starting months in advance
- Trim and tidy your toenails regularly
- Scrub and clean feet with soap in the shower daily
- Exfoliate
- Remove calluses with a pumice stone
- Treat athletes foot, warts and toenail fungus
- Keep hydrated with a high-quality foot cream
- Have regular foot massages to increase circulation and relieve stress

☐ Wear breathable footwear and spend time daily without shoes and socks to allow your feet to breathe

☐ Keep your feet dry as much as possible
- Dry thoroughly between toes
- Use powder and change socks often if your feet sweat excessively

☐ Visit your pedicurist and have one or more of the following
- Callus peel
- Cuticle tidy
- Dead skin removal
- Foot spa
- Pedicure
- Scrub
- Soak
- Toenail clip and file

☐ Arrange a pedicure for your bridesmaids and junior attendants

☐ Select a toenail colour for your wedding day
- Clear
- Light pink or nude
- French manicure
- Matched with the bridesmaid dresses
- Matched with the wedding colours
- Other …

☐ Select a toenail colour for your bridesmaids and junior attendants

☐ Select toenail embellishments and jewellery
- Diamantes (rhinestones)
- Gems
- Glitter
- Nail art
- Nail dangles
- Nail stickers
- Patterns, e.g. houndstooth
- Shaped gems, e.g. butterflies, hearts, flowers

☐ Have henna designs applied to your feet

## Skin and Face

☐ Visit a skin specialist
      Have a complete skin health check
      Treat the appearance of burns, moles, scars or sun spots

☐ Obtain skin health advice from a skin care professional or pharmacist

☐ Minimise skin blemishes by learning what triggers your breakouts
      Treat existing blemishes with high-quality spot removers

☐ Limit UV exposure and apply SPF 30+ sunscreen often

☐ Avoid cigarettes and smoky areas

☐ Use the correct skin care products for your skin type
*Dry skin has uneven tone, visible capillaries and flakiness whereas oily skin has visible pores and areas of pigmentation which are prone to breakouts.*

☐ Begin a skin care regime 12 weeks in advance
      Cleanse 1–2 times daily (don't over cleanse)
      Tone
      Moisturise with day and night cream
      Moisturise according to the season
      Soothe tires eyes with cucumber
      Gently exfoliate daily in the shower
      Give yourself a daily full body oil massage

☐ Select products for your skin care regime
      Masks
      Peels
      Scrubs
      Moisturiser with added sunscreen
      Alcohol free toner
      Products made with plant-based ingredients
      Products containing antioxidants
*Take note of skin products use-by dates.*

☐ Visit your beautician and have one or more of the following
      Antioxidant facial
      Chemical peel
      Facial massage (to tone and tighten face muscles)
      Oil and dead skin removal
      Stress relief facial
      Ultrasonic peel
*It's best to do these well in advance of your wedding day (at least one week before).*

- [ ] Select a tanning option
  - Bronzing powder
  - Cream
  - Gel
  - Mousse
  - Professional spray tan
  - Spray
  - Tinted moisturiser

- [ ] Test tanning products on your skin at least four weeks in advance
  - Apply a small amount first; it is simple to apply another coat but difficult to remove tan

- [ ] Apply fake tan 1–2 days before your wedding

## Tanning Top Tips

- Wax or shave the day before applying your tan
- Shower on the day, exfoliate thoroughly and remove all traces of make-up and deodorant
- Lightly moisturise dry or creased areas such as your elbows, knees and heals to prevent them soaking up more tan
- Enlist a helper for hard to reach areas
- Cover your hands with tight-fitting disposable gloves
- For an even, streak-free finish apply with gentle circular motions (do not rub in)
- Take your time – focus on an even application
- Avoid showering, bathing, swimming or exercising for at least eight hours
- Gently wash your skin on your wedding day (don't scrub!)
- Moisturise your entire body daily so your tan will stay for your honeymoon!

## Invasive Options

- [ ] Consider invasive techniques
  - Anti-sweating injections
  - Cellulite treatments
  - Fillers and relaxers
  - Implants
  - Laser treatments
  - Lifts
  - Liposuction
  - Plastic surgery
  - Skin removal and tightening
  - Surgical facelift, e.g. brows, around eyes, lower face, neck
  - Tucks

# 15
# Keeping Well

Exercise, following a healthy diet and getting enough sleep will go a long way towards improving your mental and physical health, as well as reducing your stress levels! Start setting goals at the same time you start planning for the big day – you'll notice the results (and the benefits) in no time at all. Here's to a better you!

## Healthy Living

- [ ] Set general health and exercise goals
  - Increase fitness
  - Increase flexibility
  - Increase muscle mass
  - Lose a large amount of weight (10kg+)
  - Lose a small amount of weight (less than 10kg)
  - Tone your body, e.g. arms, legs, abdomen, entire body

- [ ] Break down your goals into smaller, more manageable mini-goals
  - Write down your mini-goals and keep them in a visible area, e.g. on the fridge

- [ ] Monitor your progress and log it in your wedding file
  - Reward yourself for achieving your goals with a movie, massage or manicure/pedicure session

- [ ] Select the parts of your body that you want to focus on
  - Abdominals
  - Back
  - Biceps
  - Calves
  - Chest
  - Core
  - Legs
  - Shoulders
  - Triceps

☐ Calculate your body measurements and note your goals

|  | Bride | Bride's goal | Groom | Groom's goal |
| --- | --- | --- | --- | --- |
| Weight | | | | |
| Bust/chest | | | | |
| Waist | | | | |
| Hips | | | | |
| Upper right arm | | | | |
| Upper left arm | | | | |
| Right thigh | | | | |
| Left thigh | | | | |
| Seat | | | | |
| Clothing size (upper) | | | | |
| Clothing size (lower) | | | | |

☐ Organise for weekly wellness coaching by a professional (dietician, nutritionist, and/or personal trainer)

☐ Have a diet plan constructed by a nutritionist or dietician
- Low-sodium diet
- Low-fat diet
- Muscle building diet
- Natural foods diet
- Raw foods diet
- Sugar-busting diet
- Weight loss diet

## Fitness

☐ Construct a fitness timeline from now until your wedding day

☐ Create an exercise regime which includes both aerobic and weight bearing/ weight resistance exercises

☐ Select from the following activities for increasing your fitness
- Aerobics
- Cycling
- Dancing
- Exercise ball routines
- Jogging
- Jumping rope
- Kickboxing
- Rock climbing
- Pilates
- Other ...
- Rowing
- Running
- Spin classes
- Squash
- Swimming
- Treadmill
- Walking
- Weight/resistance training
- Yoga

- ☐ Select exercises that you enjoy
  - ☐ Do something physical every day

- ☐ Organise for personal training sessions

- ☐ Purchase fitness items to make exercising more enjoyable and to make it easier to fit into your schedule
  - ☐ Exercise apps
  - ☐ Exercise ball
  - ☐ Fitness DVDs
  - ☐ Free weights
  - ☐ Jump rope
  - ☐ Music, audio book or instructional downloads
  - ☐ Pedometer
  - ☐ Resistance bands
  - ☐ Stepper
  - ☐ Treadmill
  - ☐ Workout outfits/clothes

- ☐ Encourage others to exercise with you, e.g. your fiancé, attendants, friends, parents, siblings

## De-stressing

Remaining calm under pressure is key to surviving wedding planning. You can find stress relief in a variety of ways—from crossing off completed tasks in this book to engaging in meditation or having massages. Find out what works for you and incorporate it into your schedule.

- ☐ Commit tasks to paper to free your brain from having to remember them
  - ☐ Write down every wedding detail, date and reminder in your wedding file
  - ☐ File paperwork so it is easy to locate documents when needed

- ☐ Don't let small details consume you
  - ☐ Make a decision, tick it off your list and move on

- ☐ Set goals
  - ☐ Set achievable daily, weekly and monthly goals
  - ☐ Establish ways to stick to your goals
  - ☐ Share your goals so you can support each other through stressful times

- ☐ Practise one or more of the following stress busters
  - ☐ Deep breathing
  - ☐ Exercising
  - ☐ Goal-oriented visualisation
  - ☐ Listening to your favourite music
  - ☐ Meditation
  - ☐ Relaxation massage
  - ☐ Stretching
  - ☐ Yoga
  - ☐ Other …

☐ Try to separate yourself from electronic devices on a daily basis, e.g. no computers or phones once you have gone to bed

☐ Allow yourself to feel good

☐ Take frequent breaks from wedding planning
   Schedule regular time blocks that *don't* involve wedding planning or wedding talk
   Make time for yourself
   Make time for your relationship without the wedding interfering

☐ Practise restful sleep (especially the night before your wedding)
   Air the room so you have clean fresh oxygen to breathe
   Clear your mind by thinking about something else
   Enjoy aromatherapy, e.g. chamomile, lavender
   Ensure you are comfortable, e.g. temperature, clothing
   Have a soothing bubble bath with calming oils before bed
   Listen to soothing music
   Remove yourself from electrical appliances, technology and digital devices
   Use ear plugs

☐ Complete wedding planning tasks that you enjoy and delegate the rest to friends, family and professionals

*This is part of the joy of being the bride!*

## Healthy Living Tips

- Exercise regularly doing activities you enjoy
- Drink pure water
- Reshape bad eating habits
- Follow a fresh and balanced diet
- Eat a wide variety of foods (fruits, vegetables and wholegrains)
- Eat oily fish or other foods containing essential fatty acids 2–3 times per week
- Consult with a nutritionist or dietician about vitamin supplements
- Learn to recognise and manage stress triggers
- Sleep 7–9 hours a night
- Have no more than two standard drinks a day, e.g. 2 x 100ml glasses of wine
- Keep an up-to-date diary and schedule everything wedding related

# 16
# Ceremony: Planning

Many brides and grooms are moving away from a traditional wedding to a more unique and tailored ceremony (be it civil, religious, spiritual or cultural). Remember that this is *your* day so don't be afraid to add humour, edginess and originality into your ceremony. Most of all, make it meaningful for the two of you. Inject your personalities and style into the readings, vows and general atmosphere.

☐ Discuss, with your fiancé, the type of ceremony that you would both like
- Civil
- Religious
- Interfaith
- Elopement
- Registry office
- Commitment
- Other, e.g. double, themed, tea ceremony, gothic, medieval

## Civil Ceremony

A civil ceremony is performed by an authorised wedding officiant and joins a couple by law. Civil ceremonies often contain little or no religious elements or connotations.

☐ Contact your local authority and obtain information on the laws of marriage
- For destination weddings, you must also contact the authority in the place of marriage

☐ Decide if you will add spiritual elements to your civil ceremony, e.g. psalms, scripture, religious music

☐ Lodge necessary paperwork within specified times, e.g. in Australia, you need to submit a Notice of Intended Marriage form at least 32 days before your wedding day
- Provide essential paperwork, e.g. current identification, divorce papers

☐ Select two people over the age of 18 to witness your wedding

# Religious Ceremony

A religious ceremony is where a couple is united in marriage under their practicing faith. It contains religious traditions, rituals and is performed by a religious leader in a house of worship.

- ☐ Select a religious ceremony type

| | |
|---|---|
| Anglican | Pagan |
| Baha'i | Parsi |
| Buddhist | Protestant |
| Cao Dai | Quaker |
| Catholic | Rasta |
| Church of England | Roman Catholic |
| Church of Ireland | Scientologist |
| Hindu | Shinto |
| Jain | Sikh |
| Jehovah's Witness | Spiritualist |
| Jewish | Taoist |
| Mormon | Tenrikyo |
| Muslim | Unitarian |
| Orthodox | United Church |
| Other … | |

- ☐ Contact your religious representative or a leader in your nominated place of worship
    - Obtain information on the laws of marriage under your chosen faith
    - If necessary, enquire if there are objections to second marriages

- ☐ Some faiths require an invitation into the faith if you are not a current member. If this is the case, find out what steps are involved
    - Attend classes to help understand the teaching of a faith you are not practicing

- ☐ Attend religious services
    - Arrange for publication of banns, an official public announcement of your intended marriage

- ☐ Lodge necessary paperwork within specified times, e.g. in Australia, you need to submit a Notice of Intended Marriage form at least 32 days before your wedding day
    - Provide essential paperwork, e.g. current identification, divorce papers

- ☐ Select two people over the age of 18 to witness your wedding ceremony

# Interfaith Ceremony

Interfaith ceremonies unite couples of different faiths. Rituals, traditions and symbols from both religions can be chosen for the wedding ceremony. There are religious leaders who specialise in interfaith ceremonies.

☐ Respect each other's religious beliefs and consider both religions when planning the ceremony

☐ Meet with a religious advisor from each faith
    Obtain information on the laws of marriage for each religion
    If necessary, enquire if there are objections to second marriages

☐ Decide how you will incorporate both faiths
    Have the ceremony performed by an officiant from each faith, e.g. divide your officiants between vows, readings and blessings
    Find one officiant who is capable of performing all religious elements
    Arrange for two ceremonies, one for each faith (decide which will be legally recognised)

☐ Hold the ceremony in a neutral place, e.g. a garden

☐ Attend classes to help understand the teaching of a faith you are not practicing

☐ Attend religious services
    Arrange for publication of banns, an official public announcement of your intended marriage

☐ Lodge necessary paperwork within specified times, e.g. in Australia, you need to submit a Notice of Intended Marriage form at least 32 days before your wedding day
    Provide essential paperwork, e.g. current identification, divorce papers

☐ Select two people over the age of 18 to witness your wedding

# Elopement Ceremony

Eloping is when a couple gets married in secret. Couples choose this type of ceremony for a variety of reasons, such as urgent military service. You may choose to marry in private and then have a reception at a later date. Getting married in another country is popular for eloping couples and you can still have professional photos taken to honour the day.

☐ Contact the local authority and obtain information on the laws of marriage
    For destination weddings, you must also contact the authority in the place of marriage

□ Lodge necessary paperwork within specified times, e.g. in Australia, you need to submit a Notice of Intended Marriage form at least 32 days before your wedding day
  Provide essential paperwork, e.g. current identification, divorce papers

□ Select two people over the age of 18 to witness your wedding

## Registry Office Ceremony

Registry office ceremonies are an intimate and economical way to get married. They can take place in a city registry office or courthouse and typically take 10–20 minutes to complete.

□ Decide how many guests will be invited
  No guests
  A few selected guests, e.g. your parents and immediate family
  Up to 30 guests (for large registry offices only)

□ Contact the registry office and obtain information on the laws of marriage
  For destination weddings, you must also contact the authority in the place of marriage

□ Lodge necessary paperwork within specified times, e.g. in Australia, you need to submit a Notice of Intended Marriage form at least 32 days before your wedding day
  Provide essential paperwork, e.g. current identification, divorce papers

□ Select two people over the age of 18 to witness your wedding

*Top reasons to elope, have an intimate ceremony or be married in a registry office:*

- Inexpensive
- Easy to organise
- Low-key
- Less planning and stress involved
- It may avoid family conflict

□ Organise the following after eloping, a registry office ceremony and/or a destination ceremony:
  Create and distribute a wedding announcement
  Send a copy of your wedding photos and DVD to those who couldn't attend
  Host a post-wedding party or reception where you wear your wedding attire, deliver toasts and speeches, display wedding photos, show a DVD and share memories of the day

## Commitment Ceremony

A commitment ceremony is a union between two people without legal standing. Couples are free to design the ceremony to their liking or incorporate all the aspects of a civil or religious wedding ceremony. It provides an option for same-sex partners or couples who can't legally get married (as yet!) but still want to make public vows and celebrate their union.

☐ Organise a registry office ceremony to legalise your marriage
   Before the commitment ceremony
   After the commitment ceremony

☐ Organise a blessing ceremony in a house of worship to legalise your marriage
   Before the commitment ceremony
   After the commitment ceremony

## Your Officiant and Ceremony Manager

☐ Select the type of officiant for your wedding ceremony
   Chaplain
   Civil celebrant
   Honoured guest (for commitment ceremonies)
   Imam
   Judge
   Justice of the Peace
   Magistrate
   Minister
   Notary public
   Ordained friend or family member
   Pastor
   Priest
   Rabbi
   Recognised leader
   Registrar

☐ Locate officiants who operate in the vicinity of the ceremony venue
   Attorney general's department
   Local directories
   Newspapers
   Officiant associations
   Online
   Personal recommendations
   Religious venues/houses of worship
   Wedding directories

- ☐ Shortlist officiants by ensuring they are:
    - Available for pre-wedding meetings, rehearsals and on the day
    - Legally allowed to marry you
    - A specialist in your type of ceremony
    - Able to marry people of different faiths
    - Willing to perform the ceremony away from a house of worship
    - Able to provide you with resources and suggestions
    - Willing to listen and tailor the ceremony to your wants
    - Able to address a group of people with confidence and energy
    - Someone you would both like to be part of your wedding
    - Someone who has a friendly personality, a natural flair and a sense of humour

- ☐ Complete the wedding vendor checklist for your officiant on pages 10 and 11

- ☐ Meet and discuss the following ceremony details with your officiant
    - Date and time of your wedding
    - Fees
    - Music choices
    - Order of service
    - Special rituals to be included
    - Venue restrictions, e.g. photography, attire
    - Wedding location
    - Wedding style and theme
    - Other, e.g. items you do not want included

- ☐ Look to your officiant for advice in all areas of your wedding ceremony

- ☐ Ensure your officiant organises their side of the legal arrangements
    - Inform your officiant if you have been married before

- ☐ Arrange for premarital education, e.g. a marriage preparation course

- ☐ Arrange for premarital counselling

## Ceremony Ambience

- ☐ Select the type of atmosphere you would like at your ceremony
    - Cosy
    - Dramatic
    - Elegant
    - Fun
    - Funky
    - Intimate
    - Luxurious
    - Other …
    - Magical
    - Natural
    - Romantic
    - Rustic
    - Stylish
    - Themed
    - Warm

- ☐ Obtain a floor plan of the ceremony venue
    - Mark detailed measurements on the floor plan, e.g. the room size

- ☐ Plot the following on your ceremony floor plan
    - Aisle
    - Altar
    - Areas for equipment, e.g. music, sound system
    - Chancel
    - Electrical points
    - Entrance
    - Foyer
    - Guest seating
    - Kneeling bench
    - Lectern
    - Lights
    - Musicians and singers places
    - Podium
    - Signature table and chair
    - Stage or platforms
    - Stairways
    - Vestry
    - Walkways
    - Window locations
    - Other …

- ☐ Have your officiant or ceremony manager view and make suggestions to your floor plan

- ☐ Appoint a ceremony decorating team, e.g. florist, ceremony manager, ushers, friends, family

- ☐ Create a point of focus for the ceremony, e.g. a flower arrangement, existing architecture

- ☐ Select decorations for your ceremony
    - Aisle runner, e.g. red carpet
    - Archway, e.g. flowers, balloons
    - Backdrop
    - Balinese flags
    - Balloons with loosely curled ribbon
    - Banners
    - Beaded curtains
    - Candles
    - Chair covers
    - Chair sashes
    - Decorative fabric, e.g. tulle, lace
    - Decorative lighting, e.g. hurricane lamps, chandeliers, fairy lights wrapped around columns or trees

- Flags
- Flower displays
- Flower petals
- Garden umbrellas
- Glass ornaments
- Incense
- Leaves
- Luminaria, e.g. a small candle set in sand inside a paper bag
- Palm fronds
- Pebbles
- Potted plants
- Ribbon
- Seashells
- Sculptures
- Smoke machine
- Themed props
- Other ...

## Top Tips for Aisle Runners

- Create your own aisle runner using any thick sturdy fabric, fabric tiles, dance floor panels or paving stones
- Attach a non-stick backing so it doesn't slide around easily
- Ensure it doesn't stick to your shoes
- Ensure it doesn't make noise when walked on
- Line aisles with flower petals, large paper confetti or themed items

☐ Locate places for your ceremony decorations
- Archways
- Attached to doors
- Backs of chairs
- Behind the altar
- Ceiling
- Columns
- Entrance
- Free-standing displays
- Pew-ends
- Podium
- Trees
- Walkways
- Windowsills
- Other ...

☐ Store decorations in clearly labelled crates or boxes

☐ Use existing venue features or nature as your decorations
- Amphitheatres
- Attractive buildings
- Beautiful views
- Blooming gardens
- Bridges

- Carved ceilings
- Fountains
- Gazebos, rotundas, pavilions or huts
- Historical items
- Murals
- Potted trees
- Stained glass windows
- Trees
- Water features
- Other …

☐ Liaise with your officiant or ceremony manager regarding your decorations
- Show them your plans
- Obtain advice and guidance
- Enquire if the venue can provide any decorations

☐ Select the type of ceremony chairs for your guests

| | |
|---|---|
| Bench seats | Hay bales |
| Cube seats | Padded chairs |
| Cushions | Pews |
| Daybeds | Picnic rugs |
| Driftwood logs | Pillows |
| Folding chairs | Wicker chairs |
| Garden chairs | Wooden chairs |
| Other … | |

☐ Decorate your ceremony chairs with various items

| | |
|---|---|
| Bows | Organza |
| Burlap | Ribbon |
| Feathers | Sashes |
| Flowers | Shells |
| Garlands | Slipcovers |
| Herbs | Other … |

☐ Purchase items for ceremony rituals, e.g. candles, glasses, religions artefacts

☐ Incorporate items from each of your family's heritages and cultures when decorating the ceremony

☐ Purchase a kneeling bench or cushion for the ceremony

☐ Purchase or hire a signature table and chair for the ceremony

☐ Purchase a special pen, pen stand and tablecloth for the signature table

☐ Decide when the decorating team or venue staff will begin decorating the ceremony venue
- Inform each member of their schedule and tasks

# Second, Third and Fourth Marriages

☐ Consider how a subsequent wedding may differ from a first wedding, e.g. your parents may not feel obliged to contribute financially

☐ Inform your children of the engagement early on and include them in decision making

☐ Announce your engagement to loved ones (in the following order)
   Children
   Parents
   Ex-partner (only if you share children together)
   Close relatives and friends

☐ Treat your wedding as though it is your first if:
   You had a small first wedding
   You didn't enjoy your first wedding
   You didn't have much choice over your first wedding
   This is a first wedding for one of you

☐ Include your children in the ceremony as a way of bringing your families together
   Appoint as attendants, junior attendants or ushers
   Have a blessing for the new family
   Have them deliver a reading
   Have them escort the bride
   Have them participate in a ritual, e.g. candle lighting
   Have them play an instrument
   Have them sing
   Include them in your vows
   Make a separate vow to your children and present them with a small gift
   Other …

☐ Include your children in the reception festivities, e.g. as guestbook attendants or to participate in a special dance

☐ Obtain consent from the other parent if you wish for your children to be involved

☐ Contact your local (and destination) authority to obtain legal details of subsequent marriages
   Obtain a certificate of divorce
   Obtain proof of annulment

☐ Determine if there are any restrictions for subsequent marriages if you wish to marry at a place of worship

# 17
# Reception: Planning

Your reception layout will largely be influenced by your personal wants, your religion, family traditions and the location. This is the time to celebrate and have fun. Make sure that your reception reflects your style as a couple.

☐ Book your reception venue as early as possible
  - Book up to 12 months in advance – the earlier the booking the better venue choice you will have

☐ Decide on the type of reception that you would like
  - Ballroom dinner
  - Drinks in the garden
  - Elaborate soiree
  - Grand reception
  - Intimate luncheon
  - Lively party
  - Picnic on the lawn
  - Quiet celebration
  - Small casual gathering
  - Other …

☐ Decide on the type of reception meal that you would like
  - Breakfast
  - Brunch
  - Luncheon
  - Afternoon tea, e.g. high tea
  - Dessert, e.g. champagne and cake
  - Cocktail
  - Dinner
  - Supper

☐ Obtain one or more of the following legal items
  - Council permit
  - Entertainment licence
  - Function licence
  - Liquor licence
  - Music licence

*Refer to the legalities section for other legal matters on page 32.*

## Reception Manager

- ☐ Select what you would like your reception package to include
  - Accommodation, e.g. bridal suite, guest suites
  - Bar staff
  - Catering
  - Centrepieces
  - Chairs
  - Changing room
  - Clean-up/dismantling
  - Cloakroom
  - Crockery
  - Dance floor
  - Decorations, e.g. backdrops, table skirting, chair covers
  - DJ
  - Drinks
  - Glassware
  - Host or hostess
  - Linen, e.g. underlays, overlays, runners, napkins
  - Marquee
  - MC (Master of Ceremonies)
  - Onsite amenities
  - Reception room
  - Set number of hours, e.g. five hours
  - Set-up
  - Silverware
  - Tables, e.g. bridal, guest, cake, gift, guestbook
  - Waitstaff
  - Wedding cake
  - Other ...
- ☐ Complete the wedding vendor checklist for your reception manager on pages 10 and 11
- ☐ Have your reception contract specify times, including set-up and clean-up
- ☐ Determine if your reception manager will attend the reception
  - Beginning only
  - Entire reception
- ☐ Ensure that there will be someone to help with emergencies, e.g. a hotel manager to oversee the event
- ☐ Ask your reception manager for vendor recommendations, e.g. musicians, DJs, caterers, bakers
- ☐ Take place cards, seating chart and the final guest head count to the reception manager a few days before the wedding

# Room Layout

- [ ] Select the type of atmosphere you would like for your reception room
  - Cosy
  - Dramatic
  - Elegant
  - Fun
  - Funky
  - Intimate
  - Luxurious
  - Other …
  - Magical
  - Natural
  - Romantic
  - Rustic
  - Stylish
  - Themed
  - Warm

- [ ] Obtain a floor plan of the reception venue
  - Mark detailed measurements on the floor plan, e.g. the room size, entrances

- [ ] Determine how many people can be comfortably accommodated
  - Allow one square metre per guest for a sit down meal (plus tables)

- [ ] Plot the following on your floor plan
  - Areas for equipment, e.g. music, sound system
  - Bar
  - Bathroom facilities
  - Cake table
  - Cloak room
  - Coffee and refreshments station
  - Dance floor
  - DJ
  - Electrical points
  - Entrance(s)
  - Foyer
  - Gift table
  - Guestbook table
  - Guest tables
  - Head table
  - Kitchen facilities
  - Large decorations
  - Lights
  - Musicians and singers places
  - Podium
  - Servery
  - Stage
  - Stairways
  - Structural features
  - Walkways
  - Window locations
  - Other …

☐ Select the different types of tables you will need at the reception
    Buffet
    Cake
    Gift
    Guest
    Guestbook
    Head
    Photo
    Utility, e.g. refreshments station
    Other ...

## Seating Plan

☐ Select the type of seating for your guests
    Assigned chairs – guests are assigned a specific table and chair
    Assigned tables – guests select their own chair at an assigned table
    Open seating – guests select their own table and chair

☐ Select a seating style
    Ambassador – all guests sit around one large oval table
    Banquet – a bridal table and many round or hexagonal guest tables
    Cabaret – round guest tables facing live music or a performance
    Canteen – a horizontal bridal table with vertical rows of long
    rectangular guest tables
    Chevron – rectangular guest tables set-up diagonally toward the
    bridal table
    Dinner dance – round or hexagonal tables arranged around the
    dance floor
    Lounge seating – lounges, armchairs and ottomans arranged for a
    stand-up reception
    Royal table – all guests sit around one large rectangular table
    Scattered bistro tables and stools (for a cocktail reception)
    S-shaped – a long communal table shaped into an S, a striking set-up
    for outdoor receptions
    T-shaped – a horizontal bridal table and vertical guest table
    U-shaped – tables set in a U-shape around the dance floor

☐ Select the shape of your guest tables
    Hexagonal
    Long feasting tables
    Oval
    Rectangular
    Round
    Square
    Sweetheart (half circle)

☐ Calculate the number of guest tables you will have and how many guests will sit at each table

☐ Select the type of bridal table
   Head table with your attendants
   Head table with your attendants and their partners
   Head table with your parents
   Sweetheart table for just the two of you

☐ Decide where your bridal table will be positioned in the reception room
   Front and centre
   Front and to the left side
   Front and to the right side
   In the middle of the room
*Ideally, the bridal table is placed where all guests can see the newlyweds.*

☐ Elevate your bridal table approximately 15–20cm higher than the guest tables using a stage or wooden platform

☐ Draft a seating plan
   Use the guest index cards provided on page 64
   Move guest cards around until you are happy with the mix

☐ Decide how you will assign guest tables
   Seat couples together
   Seat relatives together
   Seat close friends together
   Mix families and friends
   Mix single guests with couples
   Combine guests who share similar interests
   Combine guests of similar ages
   Combine guests who already know each other

☐ Determine how you will seat children
   All children to sit with their parents
   All children to sit with their parents in the children and parents section
   Children under 5 to sit with their parents
   Children over 5 to sit at a children's table
*Older siblings make great supervisors for the children's table.*

☐ Consider problem areas when arranging your guest seating
   Divorced couples or divorced parents
   Feuding guests
   People who don't get along
*Place these guests on different and non-neighbouring tables.*

- ☐ Decide how you will seat couples
  - Side by side (recommended for round tables)
  - Across from each other (recommended for long rectangular tables)
- ☐ Seat close family and friends nearest to the bridal table
  - Parents of the bride to sit to the right of the bridal table
  - Parents of the groom to sit to the left of the bridal table
  - Partners of attendants to sit at a table near to the bridal table
- ☐ Seat specific guests at the front tables
  - Hard of hearing
  - Poor eyesight
- ☐ Seat specific guests close to amenities
  - Disabled
  - Guests with young children
  - Pregnant
  - Very elderly
- ☐ Seat specific guests away from loud music and speakers
  - Elderly
  - Parents with young babies
- ☐ Provide a place for your wedding vendors to eat
  - In the main reception room, e.g. at the back of the room
  - Away from your guests, e.g. in the foyer
- ☐ Create spaces for high chairs, prams and strollers
- ☐ Designate an usher or helper to monitor children at the reception
- ☐ Have your reception manager view and make suggestions on your floor and seating plans
- ☐ Inform your caterer and reception manager of the final seating arrangements

## Seating Plan Top Tips

- Always seat couples at the same table with the exception of attendant spouses
- Sit honoured guests at the parent tables
- Ensure that every guest knows at least one other person seated at their table
- Provide a mixture of loud and quiet guests at each table
- Alternate women and men as much as possible
- Provide an ice-breaker on each guest table, e.g. a quiz about the couple

# Table Setting and Decorations

☐ Select a bridal table backdrop
  Balloon display
  Curtain
  Embroidery hanging
  Hanging lights
  Hanging ribbon display
  Large vases
  Natural backdrop (for outdoor weddings or reception rooms with a view)
  Projector displaying photographs, muted video or a themed scene
  Sweeping fabric with lighting and crystal accents
  Tall columns
  Themed art display, e.g. oriental fans
  Other ...

☐ Select a bridal table centrepiece
  3D letters displaying 'Mr & Mrs' or 'Love'
  Goblets, e.g. pewter, crystal
  Low floral arrangement
  Personalised 'Mr and Mrs...' sign
  Pillar candle display
  Wedding candelabra

*See the more detailed list of centrepieces provided on page 164.*

☐ Select items to make the bridal table unique
  Ceremony bouquets
  Engraved toasting flutes
  Lighting, e.g. fairy lights, lighting underneath the table
  Linen colour different or opposite to the guest tables
  Personalised napkins, e.g. bride, groom, bridesmaid
  Personalised table banner with your names and wedding date

☐ Select the items to be included in your table settings

| | |
|---|---|
| Bread plate and knife | Menu |
| Candles | Napkin |
| Cocktail fork or spoon | Place card and holder |
| Coffee cup | Salad plate and fork |
| Dessert fork or spoon | Soup bowl and spoon |
| Dinner plate, knife and fork | Table number |
| Glassware (champagne, red wine, white wine, water) | Teaspoon |
| | Wine list |

☐ Have a separate setting for each course
  Crockery is set top down, e.g. first course on top

- ☐ If you are setting your own tables, set cutlery from the outside in, e.g. the first course is on the outside and you work inwards
  - Knives on the right (with blades facing inwards)
  - Forks on the left
  - Spoons on the right
  - Dessert cutlery placed above

- ☐ Have reception tables set as early as possible
  - The day before
  - The wedding morning
  - After the ceremony

*Have perishable items, such as fresh flower centrepieces, placed on the table just before the reception begins.*

- ☐ Decide which table linens you will use
  - Coasters
  - Napkins
  - Placemats
  - Tablecloths
  - Table runners
  - Table skirting
  - Table underlays

- ☐ Select your preferred table linen fabric
  - Cotton
  - Hemp
  - Linen
  - Paper
  - Polyester
  - Satin
  - Silk

- ☐ Select a linen style
  - Crochet
  - Damask
  - Embroidered silk
  - Hemstitched
  - Jacquard
  - Lace
  - Monogrammed
  - Printed
  - Vintage

- ☐ Select a colour for each piece of your table linen
  - Coordinated with your wedding colours
  - Coordinated with your wedding theme
  - Neutral tones

- ☐ Fold your napkins creatively with one of the following designs
  - Blossom
  - Bouquet
  - Bow tie
  - Clamshell
  - Crown
  - Fan
  - Fleur-de-lis
  - Heart
  - Orchid
  - Rosebud
  - Swan
  - Tulip
  - Tuxedo

- [ ] Select a napkin ring type
  - Antique
  - Bamboo
  - Beaded
  - Ceramic
  - Crystal
  - Glass
  - Pewter
  - Ribbon
  - Silver
  - Themed
  - Vintage
  - Wooden

- [ ] Select guest table centrepieces
  - Balloon displays, e.g. helium, miniature balloons
  - Bonsai
  - Candelabras
  - Candles
  - Chocolate bouquets
  - Decorative vases
  - Fish in fish bowls
  - Floating candles and flower petals
  - Flower arrangements
  - Fruit arrangements, e.g. pomegranates or limes in clear vases
  - Glass columns
  - Glassware filled with sugared almonds
  - Herb bouquets
  - Hurricane lamps
  - Lanterns
  - Lolly jars filled with sweets
  - Miniature potted topiaries (shaped trees)
  - Organic arrangements, e.g. cut branches in a vase
  - Pillar candles clustered at varying heights
  - Potted plants, flowers or herbs
  - Tabletop chandeliers
  - Other …

- [ ] Give away your centrepieces at the end of the night
  - Attendants
  - Close family
  - Close friends
  - Helpers
  - Special guests

- [ ] Purchase other table decorations
  - Drip-free candles
  - Feathers
  - Flower petals
  - Flowers
  - Lanterns
  - Scatters, e.g. metallic shapes, acrylic gems, glitter, confetti, sugared almonds
  - Tea light candles

Themed ornaments
  Vases
  Other …

☐ Decorate your reception chairs with themed items

| | |
|---|---|
| Bows | Organza |
| Burlap | Ribbon |
| Feathers | Sashes |
| Flowers | Shells |
| Garlands | Slipcovers |
| Other … | |

## *Table Setting Top Tips*

- Ensure table linens are wrinkle free
- Ensure silver is freshly polished
- Avoid cluttering the table with too many pieces
- Make sure guests can see each other across the table
- Folded napkins can double as place card holders

## Reception Room Decorations

☐ Select reception room decorations
  Backdrops
  Bali flags
  Balloons with loosely curled ribbon
  Banners
  Beaded curtains
  Candles
  Chair covers
  Chair sashes
  Decorative fabric, e.g. tulle, lace
  Decorative lighting, e.g. hurricane lamps, chandeliers
  Fabric canopies, e.g. fabric fastened in the centre of the ceiling and draped outwards
  Fairy lights hanging from the ceiling, wrapped around columns or trees
  Flower displays
  Flower petals
  Fountains
  Garden umbrellas
  Glass ornaments
  Glow-in-the-dark products
  Ice sculptures
  Lanterns

- Leaves
- Luminaria
- Mirror balls
- Pebbles
- Petals
- Photo board displays
- Potted plants
- Ribbon
- Sculptures
- Shells
- Smoke machine
- Streamers
- Themed props
- Tulle draped around windows
- Wall hangings
- Other …

☐ Use existing venue features or nature as your decorations
- Attractive buildings
- Beautiful views
- Carved ceilings
- Colourful blooming gardens
- Fountains
- Gazebos rotundas or pavilions
- Historical features
- Murals
- Other …

☐ Incorporate items from each of your family's heritages and cultures when decorating the reception

☐ Visit the venue at the time of day your reception will take place and take notice of the existing lighting

☐ Use lights and lighting as a decoration
- Bamboo torches
- Chandeliers
- Disco lights/disco ball
- Fairy lights
- Floating candles
- Lanterns
- Other …
- Laser lights
- Luminarias
- Neon lights
- Pillar candles
- Spotlights
- Tea light candles

☐ Store decorations in clearly labelled crates or boxes, e.g. one for each table

- [ ] Use audio visual effects as a decoration
  - Projector
  - Television screens
  - Laptop

- [ ] Create a muted childhood video or photo slideshow and play it on repeat during the meal

- [ ] Liaise with your reception manager regarding your decorations
  - Show them your plans
  - Obtain advice and guidance
  - Enquire if the venue can provide decorations and if they will set them up for you

- [ ] Appoint a reception decorating team

- [ ] Decide when your decorating team will begin decorating the reception room
  - Inform each member of their schedule and tasks

## Food and Caterer

- [ ] Decide on the type of reception meal that you will provide
  - Banquet
  - Barbecue
  - Cocktail – hors d'oeuvres (mains served in small bowls)
  - Desserts – sweet delicacies, tasting plates, cake and champagne
  - Finger buffet – canapés, sandwiches, pastries and dips
  - Fork buffet – bite-sized portions that can be served and eaten with a fork
  - Formal sit down meal – a full service dinner
  - Hot or cold buffet
  - Light refreshments – canapés and snacks
  - Picnic
  - Tapas
  - Other ...

- [ ] Appoint a caterer
  - Check to see if your reception venue can provide catering (or requires you to use their catering)
  - If not, select a company who specialises in weddings
  - Ensure you are allowed to provide your own catering at the reception venue

- [ ] Complete the wedding vendor checklist for your caterer on pages 10 and 11

- [ ] Design your wedding menu
  - Contact your caterer and discuss menu plans

    View sample menus
    Take part in tastings
    Shortlist into options that work with your budget
    Consider the colour and presentation of your food
    Incorporate family traditions and culture in the menu
    Consider the time of day and season when selecting the type of meal

☐ Ensure your menu reflects your desired level of formality

☐ Consider the balance of the overall meal
    Taste
    Texture
    Spice
    Hot vs. cold
    Light vs. rich or creamy
    Protein vs. carbohydrate

☐ Consider the needs and tastes of your guests by providing appropriate food

| | |
|---|---|
| Allergy-friendly | Kosher |
| Child-friendly | Low-calorie/low-fat |
| Diabetes-friendly | Organic |
| Dairy-free | Vegan |
| Gluten-free | Vegetarian |

☐ Decide how the food will be served

| | |
|---|---|
| Buffet style | Serving trays |
| Food stations | Silver platters |
| Individual plates | |

☐ Serve finger foods, canapés and appetisers on:
    Bamboo skewers
    Cocktail toothpicks
    Miniature noodle boxes
    Napkin-lined baskets
    Silver platters
    Spoons/forks
    Themed items, e.g. mini bamboo steamers for Asian style food

☐ Provide different food stations for guests to serve themselves

| | |
|---|---|
| Chocolate fountain | Meat carving station |
| Crêpe station | Omelette station |
| Dessert buffet | Sandwich buffet |
| Fondue | Soup bar |
| Fresh fruit bar | Waffle and ice-cream station |
| Gelato bar | |

☐ Contact your caterer and advise of the preliminary guest numbers
    Inform of final guest numbers a week before your wedding day

## Breakfast Receptions

☐ Select the types of food you will serve at your breakfast reception

| | |
|---|---|
| Bacon | Ham |
| Bagels | Hash browns |
| Cereals | Muesli |
| Crêpes | Muffins |
| Croissants | Mushrooms |
| Doughnuts | Omelettes |
| Eggs Benedict | Pancakes |
| Eggs Florentine | Pastries |
| Eggs to order | Sausages |
| Fish | Scrambled eggs |
| French toast | Toast and jam |
| Fresh fruit | Waffles |
| Fruit bread | Yoghurt |
| Grapefruit | Other ... |

*Serve with juice, tea, coffee, mimosas and Bloody Marys.*

## Brunch and Luncheon Receptions

☐ Select the types of food you will serve at your brunch or lunch reception

| | |
|---|---|
| Bagels | Grilled vegetables |
| Baguettes | Pasta dishes |
| Banana bread | Pastries |
| Chicken | Pickled vegetables |
| Cold meats, e.g. sliced turkey, ham, salami, roast beef | Potato dishes |
| Cold salads | Quiches |
| Cocktail croissants | Rice dishes |
| Crab cakes | Savoury muffins |
| Fish, e.g. smoked salmon | Scones |
| Frittatas | Soup |
| Fruit salad | Stuffed mushrooms |
| Gourmet sandwiches | Wraps |
| | Other ... |

*Serve with smoothies, light drinks, lemonade, Bellinis and Bloody Marys.*

☐ Select from the following platter ideas
- Antipasto
- Breads and spreads
- Chocolate dipping trays
- Deli
- Caramel or chocolate fondue
- Cheese fondue
- Fresh fruit

- Fruit and yoghurt
- Gourmet cheese board with crackers
- Mediterranean, e.g. marinated olives, sun-dried tomatoes, feta
- Middle Eastern, e.g. hummus, baba ganoush, tabouli
- Mixed nuts
- Nuts and dried fruit
- Oysters
- Sandwiches or wraps
- Sushi
- Vegetable sticks and dip
- Vegetarian
- Other ...

*Serve with sparkling wine, lemonade and gin & tonics.*

☐ Select from the following picnic hamper ideas

| | |
|---|---|
| Baguettes | Potato salad |
| Banana bread | Quiches |
| Cold meats | Rice salad |
| Focaccia | Smoked salmon |
| Fruit salad | Sweet buns |
| Gourmet cheeses | Vegetables and dip |
| Gourmet sandwiches | Wraps |
| Pasta salad | Other ... |

*Serve with ginger beer, iced tea, sparkling wine, picnic rugs and chequered linen.*

## Afternoon Tea Receptions

☐ Select the types of food you will serve at your afternoon tea reception
- Cupcakes
- Finger sandwiches, e.g. smoked salmon, cucumber, roast beef
- Homemade biscuits
- Macaroons
- Meringues
- Mini quiches
- Profiteroles
- Scones with jam and cream
- Shortbreads
- Sponge rolls
- Tartlets
- Other ...

*Serve with a variety of flavoured loose leaf teas in teapots, champagne and punch.*

## Dessert Receptions

☐ Select from the following dessert ideas

Assorted candy
Biscotti
Brownies
Cake balls
Caramels
Chocolate dipped fruit
Chocolate fountain
Cream puffs
Crème brûlée
Crêpes
Cupcakes
Éclairs
Fresh fruit
Fruit pies
Fudge
Gourmet cheese with crackers
Ice-cream sundaes
Macaroons
Other ...

Meringues
Mini cheesecakes
Mini jam doughnuts
Mousse cups
Parfaits
Pavlova
Petits fours
Pralines
Profiteroles
Rich desserts
Rum balls
Stuffed dates
Tartlets
Tiramisu
Toasted nuts
Tortes
Trifle
Truffles

*Serve with champagne, tea and flavoured coffee.*

## Cocktail Receptions

☐ Select from the following cocktail food ideas

Asparagus spears
Baby potatoes
Barbecue prawns
Beef tenderloin
Beef Wellington
Bruschetta
Calamari rings
Canapés
Chicken drumettes, tenders and/or wings
Crab cakes
Croquettes
Crostini
Devilled eggs
Empanadas
Filo triangles
Finger sandwiches
Focaccia bites

Fondue
Frittata bites
Gourmet pizzas
Lamb cutlets
Meatballs
Mini burgers
Mini quiches
Mini tacos
Mixed seafood samples
Olives
Oyster shots
Oysters in shells
Pappadums
Pastries
Pinwheels
Potato cakes
Potato skins
Prawns

Riblets
Rice paper rolls
Samosas
Sashimi
Savoury tarts
Sea scallops
Sliced vegetables
Sliced wraps

Spring rolls
Steamed dim sims
Stuffed dates
Stuffed mushrooms
Sushi
Vegetable balls
Wontons
Other ...

*Find a list of cocktail desserts on page 171.*

☐ Select from the following food that can be served in small bowls for
cocktail and stand-up receptions

Asian noodles
Asian vegetables
Chilli con carne
Chowder, e.g. cauliflower, crab
Curries
Fried rice
Gnocchi
Grilled vegetables
Meat dishes with mashed
potato
Other ...

Meat dishes with rice
Nachos
Paella
Pastas
Prawn cocktails
Ragout
Ravioli
Risotto
Soup, e.g. creamy potato,
lobster bisque

## Cocktail Reception Top Tips

- Provide 5 pieces per person for the first hour
- Provide 3–4 pieces per person per hour for each hour after
- If served at meal time you can include something more substantial,
  e.g. gourmet pizzas
- Serve cold foods first, then hot foods
- Change from savoury to sweet two-thirds of the way through the
  reception
- Offer plenty of napkins
- Offer plenty of bowls for discarded toothpicks and spoons

## Buffet Receptions

☐ Select the types of food you will serve at your buffet reception

Cold meats
Dessert
Pasta
Potato dishes

Roast meats
Salads
Seafood
Sides

| Soup | Vegetarian/vegan dishes |
| Vegetables | Other ... |

☐ Select side dishes
- Bread, e.g. rolls, sticks, garlic, Turkish, Naan
- Corn on the cob
- Couscous
- Glazed carrots
- Green beans
- Peas
- Potato, e.g. mashed, baked, stuffed, skins
- Rice
- Steamed vegetables
- Other ...

## Buffet Reception Top Tips

- Provide enough crockery for multiple buffet visits
- Send guests in groups to avoid long waits
- Have guests line up in two or more lines
- Appoint a helper to keep the lines moving
- Provide an alternative to lining up, e.g. place large serving dishes on each table and change after each course (family style)

## Sit-down Receptions

☐ Decide on the number of food courses that you will offer

☐ Select the types of courses

| Appetizer | Poultry |
| Soup | Red meat |
| Salad | Dessert |
| Palate cleanser | Wedding cake |
| Fish | Cheese |

☐ Review the following 50 main meal dishes for sit-down receptions
- Baked garlic parmesan chicken
- Barbecued spiced lamb cutlets
- Beef Wellington
- Butternut squash ravioli
- Caramel vinegar glazed pork belly
- Chicken breast stuffed with spinach and feta
- Chicken marsala
- Chicken piccata

- Citrus-marinated chicken thigh
- Confit duck
- Couscous and feta stuffed vegetables
- Creamy wild mushroom risotto
- Eye fillet with red wine sauce
- Filet minion with balsamic vinegar sauce
- Ginger-soy marinated tuna
- Grilled rack of lamb with chilli-mint sauce
- Herb crusted prime rib
- Herb crusted salmon fillet
- Honey rosemary braised veal shanks
- Hoisin marinated duck
- Lamb korma
- Mediterranean chicken
- Moroccan lamb tagine
- Moroccan vegetable stew
- Mushroom stroganoff
- Oven roasted chicken with mango glaze
- Pan roasted sea bass with ginger and chilli
- Pan seared T-bone with caramelised onion
- Penne aioli
- Pepper crusted porterhouse steak
- Polenta with char grilled vegetables
- Pork and rosemary fillet
- Portuguese whole roasted spatchcock
- Prawns al Cartoccio
- Roast pork with garlic and thyme
- Roast turkey with cranberry sauce
- Roasted pork loin with cranberry apple stuffing
- Rosemary and garlic roast lamb
- Sage and feta stuffed veal roulade
- Salmon and herb filo parcel
- Salmon stuffed crab cakes
- Salt and pepper calamari
- Scotch fillet with garlic and chilli butter
- Seared barramundi fillet with lemon and basil
- Spinach, ricotta and pine nut ravioli
- Veal loin stuffed with capsicum and goats cheese
- Veal scaloppine with creamy mushroom sauce
- Vegetable and goat cheese towers
- Vegetable stuffed cannelloni
- Whole snapper with lime and chilli

☐ Select from the following condiments

| | |
|---|---|
| Barbecue sauce | Mustard |
| Butter | Olive oil |
| Cheese sauce | Pepper |
| Chilli sauce | Pickles |
| Chutney | Relish |
| French dressing | Salt |
| Garlic sauce | Sour cream |
| Gravy | Soy sauce |
| Honey | Syrup |
| Horseradish | Tartar sauce |
| Italian dressing | Thousand island dressing |
| Jam | Tabasco sauce |
| Margarine | Tomato sauce |
| Mayonnaise | Vinaigrette |
| Other … | |

## Wedding Food Top Tips

- If you are on a budget, have your caterer prepare the main meal only and provide entrées and dessert yourself
- Selecting a few types of hors d'oeuvres is more cost effective than offering a large range of selections
- Provide plenty of high-quality bread and butter
- Provide vegetarian options that non-vegetarian guests will also enjoy
- Offer a cheese plate or fruit platter with ice-cream as a dessert option
- Have children's food come out early or provide them with pre-dinner snacks
- Ensure your food servers inform you (and your attendants) when your meal is placed at your table if you aren't there

## Self-catering

☐ Inform your reception manager if you intend to self-cater
    Enquire if they have any restrictions or extra charges

☐ Ensure there is enough preparation and storage space
    Bench tops
    Electrical outlets
    Freezers
    Refrigerators
    Tables
    Water sources

- [ ] Enlist help with self-catering
  - Ask reliable people who are not in the bridal party
  - Ask people who have a flair for the task that you require, e.g. baking, cake decorating
  - Give lots of people small jobs
  - Write a list of who is doing what, including short job descriptions and diagrams and distribute to your helpers

- [ ] Follow strict food safety and cleanliness practices
  - Wash hands with soap before and after contact with each different food
  - Sanitise work spaces regularly
  - Observe proper refrigerating, freezing and thawing procedures
  - Don't put hot and cold foods side by side

*Ensure all helpers are aware of these practices.*

- [ ] Make detailed lists for shopping items

- [ ] Purchase non-perishable items early

- [ ] Prepare as much food as you can ahead of time

## Drinks

- [ ] Arrange for pre-dinner drinks to be served while you are having photos taken
  - Hire waitstaff or enlist a helper to serve drinks
  - Provide a cocktail bar

- [ ] Offer a welcome drink to guests upon arrival
  - Champagne
  - Cocktail
  - Mocktail
  - Punch
  - Sherry
  - Signature drink
  - Wine

- [ ] Design a signature drink
  - Create a drink (or ask your bartender to do so) in line with your wedding theme
  - Name the drink

- [ ] Select which drinks you will provide for your guests at the reception
  - Soft drink
  - Beer, wine and soft drink
  - Beer, wine, signature drink and soft drink
  - Beer, wine, spirits and soft drink
  - All drinks

☐ Select the types of drinks you will be serving

| | |
|---|---|
| ☐ Beer (full, mid and light strengths) | ☐ Liqueurs |
| ☐ Champagne | ☐ Mocktails |
| ☐ Cider (alcoholic and non-alcoholic) | ☐ Port |
| ☐ Cocktails | ☐ Punch |
| ☐ Coffee | ☐ Sherry |
| ☐ Cognac | ☐ Soft drink |
| ☐ Frozen drinks | ☐ Spirits |
| ☐ Fruit juice | ☐ Tea |
| ☐ Other … | ☐ Tonic water |
| | ☐ Water (still and sparkling) |

☐ Select the types of wine you will be serving

| | |
|---|---|
| ☐ Dessert | ☐ Rosé |
| ☐ Fortifieds | ☐ Sparkling red |
| ☐ Port | ☐ Sparkling white |
| ☐ Red | ☐ White |

☐ Select spirits for making cocktails. Next to each, write which brands you will serve, or write 'house'

| | |
|---|---|
| ☐ Bourbon | ☐ Tequila |
| ☐ Gin | ☐ Vodka |
| ☐ Rum | ☐ Whisky |
| ☐ Scotch | ☐ Other … |

☐ Select the types of 'exotic' drinks you will be serving
- ☐ Flavoured coffee
- ☐ Frozen drinks, e.g. daiquiris, margaritas
- ☐ Sparkling juices
- ☐ Tropical iced teas

☐ Select the drink garnishes you will need
- ☐ Cherries
- ☐ Coarse salt
- ☐ Coconut
- ☐ Ice, e.g. whole, cracked, shaved
- ☐ Lemon, lime or orange slices or wedges
- ☐ Mint
- ☐ Olives
- ☐ Sugar
- ☐ Other …

☐ Taste test reception drinks

☐ Estimate the number of drinks your guests will consume using the following drink formula

    *Formula*:      Each guest will drink two drinks in the first hour and one drink per hour after

    *Example*:      120 guests, four-hour reception

                    $120 \times 2 = 240$

                    $+$

                    $120 \times 3 = 360$

                            $= 600$ drinks

☐ Adjust the estimated number of drinks if you expect some of your guests to be drinking lighter or heavier than average, e.g. allow for 25% more

☐ Review the following drinks guide when planning the quantity you will need

    A standard glass of beer is 285ml

    750ml wine bottle holds 5 x 150ml glasses

    750ml champagne bottle holds 6 x 125ml flutes

    750ml bottle of spirits holds 25 x 30ml shots

    2L bottle of soft drink holds 8 x 250ml glasses

    10kg of ice serves 20 adults

*It is best to overestimate even when using this guide.*

☐ Consult with your reception manager regarding reception drinks

    Enquire if the venue charges on a consumption basis or as a package deal

    Ask what they can provide, e.g. ice, lemons, limes, stirrers, other bar items

    Ask what brands of drinks they stock

☐ Inform your reception manager of how you want drinks to be served, e.g. alcohol to only be obtained from the bar

☐ Enquire about liquor laws at your reception venue

    Determine if you are legally allowed to serve alcohol at the venue

    Determine if you require a licence to serve alcohol

    Determine if there are time restrictions, e.g. no alcohol to be served after midnight

☐ Decide how you will fund the drinks .

    Open bar – you pay for unlimited drinks

    Set price bar – you place a set amount of money on the bar and once used guests pay

    Time limit – you pay for drinks until a certain time and guests pay after

    Cash only bar – guests pay for their own drinks

    BYO – guests bring their own drinks

☐ Supply your own reception drinks
  - Ask for advice from a liquor store
  - Find a company who will accept returned alcohol
  - Consider price as well as quality
  - Purchase specials in advance
  - Find an appropriate storage facility
  - Enquire if your venue charges a corkage fee

### Reception Drinks Top Tips

- Supply more glassware than guests attending
- Sparkling wine is more budget-friendly than champagne for toasting
- Provide a non-alcoholic toasting option
- Place carafes of chilled water on each guest table
- Serve dry white wines with white meat or fish
- Serve red wines with red meat or hearty meals
- Serve port with cheese platters
- Serve a dessert wine with coffee

## Waitstaff and Helpers

☐ Appoint a host or hostess
  - Professional
  - Provided by your catering company
  - Provided by your reception manager
  - Friend or family member

☐ Decide how many serving staff you require
  - Calculate a staff-to-guest ratio, e.g. one server per 15 guests

☐ Appoint food waitstaff
  - Professionals
  - Provided by your catering company
  - Provided by your reception manager
  - Friends or family members

☐ Appoint bar attendants
  - Professionals
  - Provided by your catering company
  - Provided by your reception manager
  - Friends or family members

*Determine if bar attendants require a licence to serve alcohol,
e.g. a Responsible Service of Alcohol (RSA) licence.*

- ☐ Complete the wedding vendor checklist for your waitstaff and bar staff on pages 10 and 11

- ☐ Appoint coat check staff

- ☐ Appoint a guestbook attendant
    - Have your guestbook attendant ask guests to sign the guestbook or take a photo of each guest as they arrive and attach it to the guestbook

- ☐ Ensure your waitstaff and reception helpers will be wearing appropriate attire

- ☐ Determine what your waitstaff and helpers will require on the day
    - Preparation equipment
    - Food
    - Drinks
    - Breaks

- ☐ Determine when your waitstaff, bar staff and helpers are available to start and finish on the day

- ☐ Determine if your waitstaff, bar staff and helpers will charge overtime fees and the rate of overtime fees

## Reception Equipment and Furniture

- ☐ Explore the following ways to obtain reception equipment and furniture
    - Borrow from friends or family members
    - Borrow or hire from your catering company
    - Borrow or hire from your reception manager
    - Borrow or hire from your reception venue
    - Purchase new
    - Rent from a specialty hire companies
    - Use your own

- ☐ Purchase, hire or borrow marquees and tents
    - Have your hire company visit, or provide them with photos, to assess the sites before selecting marquees or tents

- ☐ Consider the following when constructing marquees
    - Access to electricity, water and kitchen facilities
    - Access to amenities
    - The surface which you are placing it on, e.g. you may need to set up carpet or wood flooring

- ☐ Select from the following list of reception items, enter the quantity needed, who you will obtain them from and the cost

| Furnishings | Qty | Obtained from | Cost |
|---|---|---|---|
| Ashtrays | _____ | _____ | _____ |
| Banquet tables | _____ | _____ | _____ |
| Booster seats for children | _____ | _____ | _____ |
| Candelabras | _____ | _____ | _____ |
| Bridal table and platform | _____ | _____ | _____ |
| Candles | _____ | _____ | _____ |
| Card box | _____ | _____ | _____ |
| Chair covers, sashes and bows | _____ | _____ | _____ |
| Chairs | _____ | _____ | _____ |
| Children's tables and chairs | _____ | _____ | _____ |
| Coffee tables | _____ | _____ | _____ |
| Cushions | _____ | _____ | _____ |
| Dance floor | _____ | _____ | _____ |
| Guest tables | _____ | _____ | _____ |
| Fans | _____ | _____ | _____ |
| Flooring | _____ | _____ | _____ |
| Heaters (indoor or outdoor) | _____ | _____ | _____ |
| High chairs | _____ | _____ | _____ |
| Leather benches and cubes | _____ | _____ | _____ |
| Marquees or tents | _____ | _____ | _____ |
| Marquee awnings | _____ | _____ | _____ |
| Placemats | _____ | _____ | _____ |
| Plant stands | _____ | _____ | _____ |
| Portable bar | _____ | _____ | _____ |
| Portable toilets | _____ | _____ | _____ |
| Stage | _____ | _____ | _____ |
| Stools | _____ | _____ | _____ |
| Table skirting | _____ | _____ | _____ |
| Tablecloths and runners | _____ | _____ | _____ |
| Utility tables | _____ | _____ | _____ |
| Vases | _____ | _____ | _____ |
| Water fountain | _____ | _____ | _____ |
| Wishing well or birdcage | _____ | _____ | _____ |
| | | **Total** | _____ |

| Food Equipment | Qty | Obtained From | Cost |
|---|---|---|---|
| Bain-maries | ___ | _____ | _____ |
| Barbecues | ___ | _____ | _____ |
| Bread knives | ___ | _____ | _____ |
| Bread plates | ___ | _____ | _____ |
| Butter or margarine dishes | ___ | _____ | _____ |
| Cake stands | ___ | _____ | _____ |
| Cake table | ___ | _____ | _____ |
| Cocktail forks | ___ | _____ | _____ |
| Dessert forks | ___ | _____ | _____ |
| Dessert spoons | ___ | _____ | _____ |
| Dinner forks | ___ | _____ | _____ |
| Dinner knives | ___ | _____ | _____ |
| Dinner plates | ___ | _____ | _____ |
| Disposable cutlery | ___ | _____ | _____ |
| Disposable plates | ___ | _____ | _____ |
| Food warmers | ___ | _____ | _____ |
| Freezers | ___ | _____ | _____ |
| Gravy boats | ___ | _____ | _____ |
| Microwaves | ___ | _____ | _____ |
| Napkins | ___ | _____ | _____ |
| Ovens | ___ | _____ | _____ |
| Refrigerators | ___ | _____ | _____ |
| Roasters | ___ | _____ | _____ |
| Roasting spit | ___ | _____ | _____ |
| Rotisserie | ___ | _____ | _____ |
| Salad forks | ___ | _____ | _____ |
| Salad plates | ___ | _____ | _____ |
| Servery | ___ | _____ | _____ |
| Serving bowls | ___ | _____ | _____ |
| Serving platters | ___ | _____ | _____ |
| Serving spoons | ___ | _____ | _____ |
| Soup bowls | ___ | _____ | _____ |
| Soup spoons | ___ | _____ | _____ |

| Food Equipment | Qty | Obtained From | Cost |
|---|---|---|---|
| Steak knives | ___ | _____ | _____ |
| Steamers | ___ | _____ | _____ |
| Storage boxes | ___ | _____ | _____ |
| Teaspoons | ___ | _____ | _____ |
| Toothpicks | ___ | _____ | _____ |
| | | Total | _____ |

| Drink Equipment | Qty | Obtained From | Cost |
|---|---|---|---|
| Beer glasses | ___ | _____ | _____ |
| Blenders | ___ | _____ | _____ |
| Bottle openers | ___ | _____ | _____ |
| Carafes | ___ | _____ | _____ |
| Champagne flutes | ___ | _____ | _____ |
| Chopping boards | ___ | _____ | _____ |
| Cocktail glasses | ___ | _____ | _____ |
| Cocktail napkins | ___ | _____ | _____ |
| Cocktail picks | ___ | _____ | _____ |
| Cocktail shakers | ___ | _____ | _____ |
| Coffee mugs | ___ | _____ | _____ |
| Coffee machines | ___ | _____ | _____ |
| Collins glasses | ___ | _____ | _____ |
| Corkscrews | ___ | _____ | _____ |
| Frozen drink machine | ___ | _____ | _____ |
| Highball glasses | ___ | _____ | _____ |
| Ice | ___ | _____ | _____ |
| Ice buckets or tubs | ___ | _____ | _____ |
| Ice tongs | ___ | _____ | _____ |
| Knives | ___ | _____ | _____ |
| Measuring pourers | ___ | _____ | _____ |
| Measuring spoons | ___ | _____ | _____ |
| Milk jugs | ___ | _____ | _____ |
| Mixing jugs | ___ | _____ | _____ |
| Mixing spoons | ___ | _____ | _____ |
| Punch bowl and ladle | ___ | _____ | _____ |

| Drink Equipment | Qty | Obtained From | Cost |
|---|---|---|---|
| Punch cups | | | |
| Serving trays | | | |
| Shot glasses | | | |
| Signs for caffeinated, decaffeinated, alcoholic and non-alcoholic | | | |
| Spirit measures | | | |
| Strainers | | | |
| Straws | | | |
| Sugar bowls | | | |
| Swizzle sticks | | | |
| Teacups and saucers | | | |
| Tea dispensers | | | |
| Teaspoons | | | |
| Specialty toasting glasses for the bridal party | | | |
| Urns | | | |
| Water jugs | | | |
| Water glasses | | | |
| Wine glasses (red and white) | | | |
| | | **Total** | |

*Visit www.TheWeddingChecklist.com.au to print copies of the furnishings, food and drink equipment tables.*

## Renting Top Tips

- Place deposits on hired equipment as early as possible
- Have the rental company explain how to use each item safely and correctly
- Be aware of any extra charges for set-up, delivery, dismantling and collection
- Determine how your rental company will deal with breakdowns, damages, or breakages due to misuse or negligent use
- Obtain a signed 'proof of return' receipt for each rental item

# 18
# Capturing Memories

Photographs and video footage from your wedding day will provide lasting memories for years to come. Selecting wedding photography specialists to capture the emotions and essence of the day and tell a story is much more precious than simply posing for shots. Ensure your photography team knows exactly what you want – whether it is an elegant, modern, humorous or exotic look.

## Photography Before the Wedding

☐ Have pre-wedding photos taken
- Engagement portraits
- Engagement shoot with your attendants
- Engagement shoot with your parents
- Bridal portrait – a professional photograph of you in your wedding dress for the wedding announcements or to display at the reception
- Professional photographer to attend pre-wedding parties, e.g. the engagement party, hens party, bucks party

☐ Theme your pre-wedding photos, e.g. romantic, boudoir, fantasy

☐ Decide where you will have your pre-wedding photos, e.g. at the beach, city, botanical gardens

☐ Purchase attire for your pre-wedding photography

☐ Use your engagement portraits for one or more of the following:
- Wedding website
- Engagement announcements
- Save the date cards
- Wedding invitations
- Reception entrance photo
- Guestbook cover
- Wedding announcements

*An engagement session is highly recommended if:*

- You want professional photos taken in your local area (for destination weddings)
- You want the photographs to include friends, family, pets etc
- You want to get to know your photographer better
- You want to feel more relaxed in front of a camera
- You want to test ideas for your wedding day photography

## Your Photographer

☐ Decide how many photographers you require for the wedding day
- One
- One plus an assistant
- A team of photographers

☐ Research professional photographers who service your local area or your wedding venue
- Ask friends, family and acquaintances for referrals

☐ Contact and meet with potential photographers
- Consider their personality
- Ensure you are relaxed in their presence
- View examples of their recent work
- View examples from an entire wedding

☐ Select a photographer
- Book as early as possible, up to 12 months before your wedding day

☐ Complete the wedding vendor checklist for your photographer on pages 10 and 11

☐ Advise your photographer on the style of photographs that you would like

| | |
|---|---|
| Candid | Intimate |
| Casual | Photojournalistic |
| Elegant | Posed |
| Formal | Quirky |
| Fun | Romantic |
| Glamorous | Other … |

☐ Discuss the following with your photographer
- The type of couple you are, e.g. outdoorsy, casual, glam, focused on details
- What you *don't* want, e.g. flash photography, cliché images
- Who will own the rights to the images
- What they will wear on the day

If you need to provide their food and drink

How quickly they can produce the images

☐ Obtain your officiant's or ceremony manager's approval to take photographs at the ceremony venue and grounds

☐ Obtain your reception manager's approval to take photographs at the reception venue and grounds

☐ Have your photographer visit the ceremony and reception venues if they aren't familiar with them already

Visit at the same time of day as your ceremony and reception

Look for photograph locations

Discuss good angles and camera positioning

Discuss lighting

☐ Select what you would like your photography package to include

Pre-wedding meeting

Engagement portrait session

Bridal portrait session

Specific number of photographers

Specific number of hours, e.g. eight hours

Bride's preparation on the day

Groom's preparation on the day

Ceremony venue photography

Guests arriving at the ceremony

Groom arriving at the ceremony

Bride arriving at the ceremony

Full ceremony photography

Ceremony specifics only, e.g. bride's entrance, ring exchange, signing of the register

Group shots

Posed photographs of the newlyweds and their attendants

Candid shots of family and friends

Reception venue photography

Full reception photography

Reception specifics only, e.g. grand entrance, cutting the cake

Printed photos

Wedding album

Digital images

DVD slideshow

Photo retouching and special effects

Other items, e.g. photo book, framed portraits, canvas prints

*Find a comprehensive list of ceremony and reception photo suggestions at www.TheWeddingChecklist.com.au*

- ☐ Inform your photographer of when you will require their services on the day
  - With the bride before the ceremony
  - With the groom before the ceremony
  - Entire ceremony
  - Post ceremony
  - In-between the ceremony and reception
  - Part of the reception, e.g. leave after the speeches
  - Entire reception
  - After-party

- ☐ Allow approximately 1½ hours between the ceremony and reception for photography

- ☐ Enquire if your photography company can also provide videography

## Amateur Photography

- ☐ Select an amateur photographer
  - Family member
  - Friend
  - Work colleague
  - Photography enthusiast

- ☐ Select an assistant (or two) for your amateur photographer
  - Ask your photographer if they have someone in mind already

- ☐ Ensure your amateur photographer is 100% confident with their camera and equipment

- ☐ Schedule a meeting with your amateur photographer
  - If necessary, discuss how you will pay for their services, e.g. with cash, camera equipment

- ☐ Discuss camera views and ideas
  - Use natural light as much as possible
  - Study shadows and highlights
  - When to expose

- ☐ Inform your amateur photographer of the variety of shots you want on the day
  - Full-length
  - Three-quarter
  - Head and shoulder portraits
  - Group shots
  - Sequence shots
  - Creative angles
  - Other …

☐ Ensure your photographer has studied and tested various specifics with the selected camera and equipment

| | |
|---|---|
| Continuous shooting mode | Shutter speed control |
| Flash brightness and control | Using diffused light |
| Handling backlight problems | When to use a tripod |
| Iris control | Zoom control |

*It is also a good idea to turn off the camera function and shutter sounds so they don't cause distraction.*

☐ Discuss photography equipment that will be needed
- Accessories bag
- Batteries
- Battery belt
- Cables
- Camera
- Film
- Filters
- Flashes, e.g. speedlights, diffusing dome
- Lens cleaning materials
- Lenses, e.g. zoom, prime, wide angle
- Light meter
- Memory cards
- Reflective discs
- Reflectors
- Small step ladder
- Tabletop tripod
- Tripod

☐ Have extra equipment on standby, e.g. back-up camera, spare batteries, memory cards

☐ Survey the ceremony and reception venues with your photographer
- Identify suitable camera positions
- Utilise natural backgrounds
- Be aware of night time shooting, low light and indoor colours

☐ Have a photography trial with the camera your amateur photographer will be using
- Body placement and angle
- Face placement and angle
- Camera angles, e.g. looking up or down
- Practise relaxed and happy expressions
- Practise poses and looks that are flattering

☐ Reimburse your photographer for any costs they will outlay, e.g. batteries, memory cards

# Photo Suggestions

☐ Utilise your ceremony and reception venue for photograph backdrops

| Category | Examples |
|---|---|
| Architecture | balcony, columns, fireplace, fountain, staircase, terrace |
| Grounds | courtyard, gardens, golf course, lawns, walkways |
| Landscape | buildings, forest, hills, mountains |
| Nature | animals, birds, fields, flowering gardens, grass, plants, trees |
| Romantic | kissing behind a tree, lying on the sand or lawn, rose garden |
| Water-inspired | lake, ocean, pond, river, reflecting pools, waterfall |

☐ Arrange for photographs of wedding items

- Bridal gown on hanger
- Bride's bouquet
- Bride's shoes
- Cake
- Candles
- Ceremony program
- Cufflinks
- Decorated going-away car
- Flower arrangements
- Other …
- Garter
- Gift table
- Guestbook
- Menu
- Perfume
- Rings
- Seating board
- Toasting flutes
- Wedding invitation

☐ Compile a wedding photo list using the hundreds of suggestions found at www.TheWeddingChecklist.com.au

☐ Inform your photographer, before the wedding day, of any other specific photographs that you require

# Photography Enhancements, Printing and Distribution

Much of the following will not apply if a professional photographer will be enhancing the photographs for you. However, you may wish to request some of the listed items to be performed by your photographer.

☐ Create several back-up copies of your wedding photographs
- Store at different locations

☐ Never work on an original image

☐ Organise editing equipment
- Computer
- Specialised software, e.g. Adobe Photoshop
- Scanner
- CD or DVD burner

- ☐ Enhance your wedding photos
  - Air-brush effect
  - Automatic contrast
  - Colour adjustments, e.g. brightening your wedding gown
  - Crop
  - Red eye reduction
  - Remove flaws
  - Shadow reduction
  - Sharpen
  - Soften
  - Other ...

- ☐ Add effects to your wedding photos
  - Blur background
  - Diffuse glow
  - Filters, e.g. stained glass, sketch, oil painting
  - Frames
  - Lighting effects
  - Vintage look
  - Other ...

- ☐ Consider different photograph colours for some shots
  - Black and white
  - Full colour
  - Sepia
  - Spot colour
  - Vintage tone

- ☐ Have your photographer print out a thumbnail catalogue of your photos
  - Look through the catalogue with help from your attendants, members of both families and close friends
  - Mark the shots you want
  - Mark the shots your families and friends want

*300 photo proofs is usually enough; any more and it will be difficult to select your favourites.*

- ☐ Distribute the ordered photographs

- ☐ Enlarge your favourite photos

- ☐ Arrange your wedding photos
  - Display in a beautiful wedding album
  - Enlarge and display around your home in elegant frames
  - Print onto canvas
  - Have a wedding photo book printed
  - Include prints in your wedding scrapbook
  - Other ...

# Your Videographer

☐ Decide how many videographers you require
    ▢ One
    ▢ One plus an assistant
    ▢ A team of videographers

☐ Research professional videographers who service your local area
    ▢ Ask friends, family and acquaintances for referrals

☐ Contact and meet with potential videographers
    ▢ Consider their personality
    ▢ Ensure you are both relaxed in their presence
    ▢ View examples of their recent work
    ▢ View a DVD from an entire wedding

☐ Select a videographer
    ▢ Book as early as possible, up to 12 months before

☐ Complete the wedding vendor checklist for your videographer on pages 10 and 11

☐ Advise your videographer on the style of recording that you would like

| | |
|---|---|
| ▢ Candid | ▢ Glamorous |
| ▢ Casual | ▢ Intimate |
| ▢ Elegant | ▢ Quirky |
| ▢ Formal | ▢ Romantic |
| ▢ Fun | ▢ Other ... |

☐ Discuss the following with your videographer
    ▢ The type of people you are
    ▢ What you *don't* want, e.g. extreme close ups
    ▢ Who will own the rights to the footage
    ▢ What they will wear on the day
    ▢ If you need to provide their food and drink
    ▢ If you can choose your own background music and DVD menu layout
    ▢ How quickly they can edit and produce the footage

☐ Obtain your officiant's or ceremony manager's approval to record video at the ceremony venue and grounds

☐ Obtain your reception manager's approval to record video at the reception venue and grounds

☐ Have your videographer visit the ceremony and reception venues if they are not already familiar with them
    ▢ Visit at the same time of day as the ceremony and reception
    ▢ Look for filming locations
    ▢ Discuss good angles and video camera positioning
    ▢ Discuss lighting and sound

- [ ] Select what you would like your videography package to include
  - Pre-wedding meeting
  - Specific number of videographers
  - Specific number of hours, e.g. eight hours
  - Bride's preparation on the day
  - Groom's preparation on the day
  - Ceremony venue footage
  - Guests arriving at the ceremony
  - Groom arriving at the ceremony
  - Bride arriving at the ceremony
  - Full ceremony footage
  - Ceremony specifics only, e.g. bride's entrance, ring exchange, signing of the register
  - Footage of arranging group photography
  - Candid footage of family and friends
  - Reception venue footage
  - Full reception footage
  - Reception specifics only, e.g. entrance, cutting the cake, special dances
  - Video messages/guestbook
  - Raw footage DVD
  - Special effects
  - Short film edit with menu and chapters, e.g. 20–25 minutes
  - Other …

- [ ] Inform your videographer when you will need their services on the day
  - With the bride before the ceremony
  - With the groom before the ceremony
  - Entire ceremony
  - Post ceremony
  - In-between ceremony and reception
  - Part of the reception e.g. leave after the speeches
  - Entire reception
  - After-party

## Amateur Filming

- [ ] Select an amateur videographer
  - Family member
  - Friend
  - Work colleague
  - Acquaintance

- [ ] Select an assistant (or two) for your amateur videographer
  - Ask your videographer if they have someone in mind already

- [ ] Ensure your amateur videographer is 100% confident with their video camera and equipment

- ☐ Schedule a meeting with your amateur videographer
  - If necessary, discuss how you will pay for their services, e.g. with cash, camera equipment

- ☐ Discuss video camera views and ideas
  - Use natural light as much as possible
  - Study shadows and highlights

- ☐ Ensure your videographer has studied and tested various specifics with the selected video camera and equipment
  - Focus control
  - Handling backlight problems
  - Iris control
  - Setting audio levels
  - When to use a dolly
  - When to use a tripod
  - Zoom control

*It is also a good idea to turn off the video camera function sounds so they don't cause distraction.*

- ☐ Discuss filming equipment that will be needed
  - Accessories bag
  - Adapters
  - Batteries
  - Cables
  - Diffuser panels
  - Dolly (for smooth moving)
  - DVDs
  - Extension power cables
  - Lens cleaning materials
  - Lights to attach to the top of the video camera
  - Microphones
  - Reflectors
  - Small step ladder
  - Tabletop tripod
  - Tapes
  - Tripod (for smooth panning side to side and up and down)
  - Video camera

- ☐ Have extra equipment on standby, e.g. back-up video camera, spare batteries, DVDs, tapes

- ☐ Ensure they select the correct microphones as sound is extremely important
  - Handheld
  - In camera
  - Lavalier (lapel mic)
  - Wired
  - Wireless

- ☐ Remind your amateur videographer to limit talking as their voice will be the loudest on the camera microphone

- ☐ Survey the ceremony and reception venues with your videographer
  - Identify suitable camera positions
  - Locate microphone, tripod and dolly positions
  - Utilise natural backgrounds
  - Be aware of night time shooting, low light and indoor colours

- ☐ Have your videographer set up and test the equipment an hour before the ceremony or earlier if they are recording footage of the bride and groom getting ready

- ☐ Reimburse your videographer for any costs they will outlay, e.g. batteries, DVDs, memory cards

## Video Suggestions

- ☐ Select the pre-ceremony footage that you would like
  - Bride and bridesmaids getting ready, e.g. applying make-up, fastening the bridal gown
  - Groom and groomsmen getting ready, e.g. tying shoes, adjusting ties
  - Bride and groom messages to each other before the ceremony
  - Ceremony location inside and out before guests arrive including flower arrangements, decorations and architecture

- ☐ Select ceremony videography
  - Guest arrivals
  - Groom's arrival
  - Groom greeting guests
  - Bride's arrival
  - Bride's entrance
  - Full wedding ceremony
  - Guest congratulations
  - Ceremony departure
  - Message from officiant

- ☐ Select pre-reception videography
  - Reception location inside and out before guests arrive including decorations, table settings, unique aspects and the cake

- ☐ Select reception videography
  - Grand entrance
  - Important guests
  - Cake cutting
  - Speeches
  - First dance
  - Bouquet toss
  - Garter toss
  - Video messages, toward the end of the reception
  - Send-off
  - After-party
  - Other …

- [ ] Have video messages from
    - Bride and groom
    - Attendants
    - Parents and close family friends
    - All guests

- [ ] Inform your videographer, before the wedding day, of any other specific footage that you require

## Video Editing and Special Effects

Much of the following will not apply if a professional videographer will be editing the footage for you. However, you may wish to request some of the listed items to be performed by your videographer.

- [ ] Create back-up copies of your wedding video
    - Create at least two copies of the raw footage
    - Store at different locations

- [ ] Never work on the original footage

- [ ] Organise video editing equipment
    - Computer
    - Software, e.g. Cyberlink Power Director
    - DVD burner

- [ ] Enhance your wedding footage
    - Blur
    - Brighten
    - Colour balance
    - Contrast
    - Soft-focus filter
    - Zoom in
    - Zoom out
    - Other …

- [ ] Select photographs to include in your wedding DVD
    - Incorporate photos in slideshow format in-between video snippets
    - Use the pan and zoom feature for still photographs

- [ ] Edit your video
    - Design a DVD menu
    - Create an opening montage, e.g. the bride and groom's names, wedding date, bride and groom getting ready, ceremony venue, guests arriving
    - Tell your wedding day story through selected snippets of footage
    - Select background music
    - Create a short film edit 15–25 minutes (perfect for distributing to family)
    - Design and print a cover for DVD case
    - Design and print onto the DVD

- [ ] Add special effects to your wedding video with specialised software
    - Audio, e.g. cross-fading audio
    - Bubbles

- Filters, e.g. old movie
- Fireworks
- Lighting effects, e.g. moonlight, spotlight
- Slow motion
- Text

☐ Consider changing the colour for different scenes
- Black and white
- Full colour
- Sepia
- Spot colour
- Vintage tone

☐ Make DVD copies and distribute to:
- Attendants
- Bride's family
- Groom's family
- Close friends
- Those who couldn't attend

## Photography and Videography Top Tips

- While everyone is focusing on the bride as she enters the ceremony, have someone take a few snaps of the groom's reaction to her entrance
- Organise for a group photo immediately after the ceremony before anyone vacates
- Stream live footage on your wedding website for those who can't attend
- Request copies of wedding photos taken by guests on their private cameras
- Upload photos to your wedding website
- Upload video footage to your wedding website

# 19
# Flowers

Flowers can provide a burst of bold colour, set the tone and enhance the atmosphere of your entire wedding. Don't feel like you have to crowd your venue with flowers – smaller arrangements can often make powerful statements.

## Selecting a Florist

☐ Select a flower designer
   Professional florist
   Family member
   Friend
   You

☐ Visit florists in your local area
   View examples from a recent wedding
   Evaluate photos of their work
   Request samples

☐ Complete the wedding vendor checklist for your florist on pages 10 and 11

☐ Provide your floral designer with the following
   Your personal flower preferences
   Arrangement samples that you like from magazines and online
   How you would like to personalise your arrangements
   Your wedding colours
   Bride and bridesmaid dress fabric samples
   The type and style of wedding
   The type of ceremony venue
   The type of reception venue
   The proposed wedding date

☐ Give your florist plenty of notice – Saturday is typically their busiest trading day

- ☐ Decide how your flowers will arrive on the day
  - Floral designer to deliver
  - A helper to pick up

- ☐ Pick up or have flowers delivered as close to the ceremony as possible
  - Wedding morning, for pre-lunch ceremonies
  - Midday, for afternoon ceremonies
  - Afternoon, for late afternoon or evening ceremonies

- ☐ Enquire if your florist can provide other items, e.g. vases, flower boxes, ribbon for pews and chairs

## Flower Theme

- ☐ Match flowers to your wedding style and theme
  - Have a common flower theme, e.g. a particular variety or colour
  - Coordinate flowers with the location, e.g. frangipanis for a tropical location

- ☐ Select a flower theme
  - Exotic
  - Native
  - Seasonal, e.g. spring
  - Other ...
  - Succulents
  - Tropical
  - Wild flowers

- ☐ Select the types of flowers for your bouquets and displays
  - Artificial
  - Dried
  - Fresh
  - Mixture of fresh and artificial

- ☐ If using artificial flowers, select a type
  - Carved wood
  - Cloth
  - Crystal
  - Dried silk
  - Felt
  - Glass
  - Latex
  - Leather
  - Paper
  - Silk
  - Suede
  - Other ...

- ☐ Decide on a floral colour theme, e.g. shades of one colour, two (or more) colours, rainbow effect

- ☐ Select bouquets of contrasting colours for your bridesmaids to carry so the colour won't blend into their dresses
  - Have the bridesmaid bouquets made one-third smaller than the bridal bouquet

- ☐ Keep a consistent colour intensity, e.g. pastels with pastels, bold colours with bold

☐ Consider flower availability according to the season
    ▦ Use seasonal flowers as they will offer the best value
    ▦ Import flowers that are not in season

*Find over 100 flower types and their season of availability at
www.TheWeddingChecklist.com.au*

☐ Consider the fragrance of your chosen flowers
    ▦ Strong scented flowers can activate allergies
    ▦ The fragrance of your table centrepiece flowers may be too strong
    when eating

## Bouquets and Buttonholes

☐ Choose a bridal bouquet type
    ▦ Flower basket
    ▦ Freeze-dried posy
    ▦ Mixed blooms
    ▦ Single stem
    ▦ Other …

☐ Choose a bridal bouquet style

    ▦ Arm sheaf         ▦ Wrist

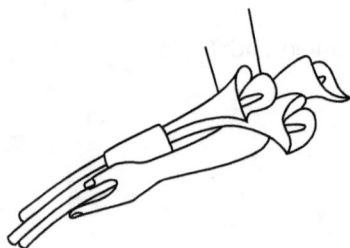 

    ▦ Ballerina     ▦ Cascading     ▦ Cone

Crescent

Fan

Nosegay

Pomander

Posy

Round

Sceptre

Single stem

Wreath

☐ Choose a feature flower

▫ Daffodil
▫ Frangipani
▫ Freesia

▫ Gardenia
▫ Gerbera
▫ Hyacinths

Hydrangea
Iris
Lily
Orchid
Peony

Ranunculus
Rose
Stephanotis
Tulip
Other …

*Find over 100 flower types, their colour(s) and their season of availability at www.TheWeddingChecklist.com.au*

☐ Select a bouquet filler

Asters
Baby's breath
Berry stems
Branches, e.g. cherry blossom
Fern
Greenery
Israeli ruscus
Other …

Ivy
Leather leaf
Pom-pom
Queen Anne's lace
Solidago
Statice
Wax flowers

☐ Select accessories for your flower bouquets and displays

Bead strings
Beads
Bows
Buckles
Charms
Crystal branches
Crystals
Diamantes (rhinestones)
Feathers
Glass diamonds
Other …

Glitter
Lace
Pearls
Raffia
Ribbon
Sea shells
Small sentimental items
Themed items
Trailing ribbon
Twine

☐ Select an alternative to a floral bouquet

Bible
Candle
Cotton ball bouquet
Fan
Feather bouquet
Felt and button bouquet
Fern
Fur muff
Gem or crystal bouquet

Herbs
Horseshoe
Ivy
Lantern
Leaves
Parasol
Prayer book
Purse
Other …

*Pageboys (who don't have a train to bear) and male bridesmaids may also appreciate having something to hold in the processional and recessional.*

☐ Select flowers for buttonholes
- White carnations
- Double red carnations
- Other ...
- Roses
- Your wedding feature flower

☐ Position buttonholes on the left side

## Ceremony Flowers

☐ Select flowers for the bride

| | Qty | Type |
|---|---|---|
| Bridal bouquet | _____ | _____ |
| Wrist corsage | _____ | _____ |
| Flowers for hair | _____ | _____ |
| Throw-away posy | _____ | _____ |
| Going-away corsage | _____ | _____ |

☐ Select flowers for the groom

| | Qty | Type |
|---|---|---|
| Buttonhole | _____ | _____ |

☐ Select flowers for the bride's attendants

| | Qty | Type |
|---|---|---|
| Maid of honour posy | _____ | _____ |
| Bridesmaid posy | _____ | _____ |
| Wrist corsage | _____ | _____ |
| Flowers for hair | _____ | _____ |

☐ Select flowers for the groom's attendants

| | Qty | Type |
|---|---|---|
| Best man buttonhole | _____ | _____ |
| Groomsman buttonhole | _____ | _____ |

☐ Select flowers for the flower girls

| | Qty | Type |
|---|---|---|
| Flower girl posy | _____ | _____ |
| Pomander | _____ | _____ |
| Flower hoop | _____ | _____ |
| Wrist corsage | _____ | _____ |
| Loose petals | _____ | _____ |
| Flowers for hair | _____ | _____ |

☐ Select flowers for the ushers, pageboys and ring bearer

|  | Qty | Type |
|---|---|---|
| Buttonhole | _____ | _____ |
| Wrist corsage | _____ | _____ |

☐ Select flowers for the mother and grandmother of the bride and groom

|  | Qty | Type |
|---|---|---|
| Wrist corsage | _____ | _____ |
| Spray | _____ | _____ |

☐ Select flowers for the father and grandfather of the bride and groom

|  | Qty | Type |
|---|---|---|
| Buttonhole | _____ | _____ |

☐ Select flowers for other special guests that you wish to honour

☐ Select the types and places for flower arrangements at the ceremony venue

|  | Qty | Type |
|---|---|---|
| Altar | _____ | _____ |
| Archways | _____ | _____ |
| Attached to doors | _____ | _____ |
| Backs of chairs | _____ | _____ |
| Boxed arrangements | _____ | _____ |
| Chancel steps | _____ | _____ |
| Columns | _____ | _____ |
| Entrance arrangement | _____ | _____ |
| Free-standing displays | _____ | _____ |
| Garlands | _____ | _____ |
| Hanging displays | _____ | _____ |
| Lectern | _____ | _____ |
| Marquee | _____ | _____ |
| Petals for scattering | _____ | _____ |
| Pew-ends | _____ | _____ |
| Pillars | _____ | _____ |
| Potted trees or plants | _____ | _____ |
| Signature table | _____ | _____ |
| Transport | _____ | _____ |

|  | Qty | Type |
|---|---|---|
| Vase displays | _____ | _____ |
| Wedding cars | _____ | _____ |
| Windowsills | _____ | _____ |

☐ Consider the size of the ceremony venue when selecting the number of flower arrangements

☐ Discuss the placement of your selected flower arrangements with your officiant

☐ Organise where your flower arrangements will go after the ceremony
- Take ceremony flowers to reuse at the reception
- Use bouquets to decorate bridal and guest tables
- Donate your ceremony flowers to the ceremony venue or local hospital after the ceremony

## Reception Flowers

☐ Select the types and places for flower arrangements at the reception venue

|  | Qty | Type |
|---|---|---|
| Archways | _____ | _____ |
| Attached to doors | _____ | _____ |
| Backs of chairs | _____ | _____ |
| Bar | _____ | _____ |
| Boxed arrangements | _____ | _____ |
| Bridal table arrangements | _____ | _____ |
| Buffet tables | _____ | _____ |
| Centrepieces | _____ | _____ |
| Cake | _____ | _____ |
| Cake table | _____ | _____ |
| Driveway | _____ | _____ |
| Entrance | _____ | _____ |
| Floating flowers | _____ | _____ |
| Free-standing displays | _____ | _____ |
| Garlands | _____ | _____ |
| Gift table | _____ | _____ |
| Guestbook table | _____ | _____ |
| Guest table displays (high set) | _____ | _____ |

|  | Qty | Type |
|---|---|---|
| Guest table displays (low set) | _____ | _____ |
| Hanging arrangements | _____ | _____ |
| Petals for scattering | _____ | _____ |
| Potted trees or plants | _____ | _____ |
| Restrooms | _____ | _____ |
| Serving platters | _____ | _____ |
| Sideboards | _____ | _____ |
| Stage | _____ | _____ |
| Staircase | _____ | _____ |
| Topiaries | _____ | _____ |
| Vase displays | _____ | _____ |
| Windowsills | _____ | _____ |

☐ Consider the size of the reception venue when selecting the number of flower arrangements

☐ Discuss the placement of your selected flower arrangements with your reception manager

☐ Hire or purchase vases for table displays

☐ Select vase fillers
- Acrylic gems
- Aquarium gravel
- Bath salts
- Berries
- Cinnamon sticks
- Citrus fruit
- Coloured crystals
- Dyed water
- Glass beads
- Pearls
- Polished rocks
- River rocks
- Shredded cellophane
- Themed ornaments
- Water gel beads
- Other …

☐ Arrange your own wedding flowers
- Most flowers will last 4–6 days so purchase before the wedding morning and store in a refrigerator
- Use buds which are just beginning to open
- Thoroughly clean, rinse and dry vases
- Purchase a quality flower food and follow the mixing directions carefully
- Cut stems at an angle with a clean, sharp pruner and put in water immediately
- Remove leaves below the waterline
- Pack flowers loosely in vases

Change water and trim stems every 24 hours
Keep in a cool environment (18–22°C) and away from direct sunlight

*Avoid stems which have drooping leaves, leaves with spots or yellowing patches. Look for firm upright petals.*

☐ Consider different ways to preserve the wedding flowers for the day
Have buttonholes and corsages wired to prevent wilting
Revive wilting flowers by trimming 3cm from the stem, plunging into boiling water and leaving to cool
Ask your florist what needs to be done to keep them looking fresh throughout the day

☐ Preserve your bridal bouquet or select a few flowers from your bouquet after the wedding as a keepsake

| | |
|---|---|
| Frame | Potpourri |
| Hang and dry | Press |

☐ Arrange for flowers to be sent to special people when you are on your honeymoon

| | |
|---|---|
| Attendants | Helpers |
| Parents | Special guests |
| Other … | |

## Flower Top Tips

- Avoid dyed flowers and flowers with pollen intact as they can stain your attire
- Take body figures into account when choosing the bridesmaid bouquets so they aren't too big or small for the person
- Tie fabric matching the bridesmaid dresses around flower stems
- A daisy ring makes a cute flower girl headpiece
- If you aren't permitted to toss flower petals have the flower girls hand single stems to guests sitting on the aisle
- Hold your bouquet with two hands in front of your navel
- Point the heads of your flowers toward the camera in wedding photographs
- Be careful of sudden exposure to cold air and direct sunlight
- A single flower in each napkin makes a stylish statement on your reception tables

# 20
# Transport

When selecting your transport, consider the size of your dress (is it very full or difficult to manoeuvre?), the number of passengers and your budget. Borrowing transport from friends, family or co-workers will not only save you money, but will open up options for a fully unique and personalised journey.

## Transport Ideas

☐ Select the type of transport to take you to the ceremony, to the reception and for leaving the reception

- Antique truck
- Army tank
- Bicycle
- Boat
- Bus
- Camelback
- Cinderella carriage
- Classic car, e.g. EH Holden, 1950s Cadillac
- Classic American car, e.g. Chevy, Dodge
- Classic luxury car, e.g. Rolls Royce, Jaguar, Aston Martin, Bentley
- Coach
- Convertible, e.g. VW beetle, Audi, Renault
- Fire engine
- Float
- Four-wheel drive, e.g. Hummer, Jeep, BMW
- Golf cart
- Gondola
- Helicopter
- Horse drawn carriage
- Horseback
- Hot-air balloon
- Hot rod
- Ice-cream truck
- Jet ski
- Kombi van
- Light plane
- Limousine
- Mini Cooper
- Mini van
- Motorcycle e.g. Harley Davidson, BMW, Yamaha cruiser
- Motorcycle side car
- On foot, e.g. walk
- Parachute, e.g. skydive, parasail
- Party bus
- Police car
- Quad bike
- River cat
- Scooter

| | |
|---|---|
| Sea plane | Taxi, e.g. British taxi |
| Sedan chair | Tram |
| Speed boat | Utility vehicle |
| Sports car, e.g. Corvette, | Vintage car |
| Ferrari, Mustang, Porsche, | Vintage school bus |
| Lamborghini | Water taxi |
| Stretch car, e.g. Rolls Royce, | Yacht |
| Ford, Hummer | Your own car |
| Tandem bicycle | Other ... |

## Who Rides With Whom

☐ Decide how the following people will arrive at the ceremony

| | |
|---|---|
| Bride | Ring bearer |
| Bridesmaids | Pageboys |
| Flower girls | Junior attendants |
| Bride's father | Ushers |
| Bride's mother | Groom's parents |
| Groom | Travelling guests |
| Groomsmen | |

☐ Ensure the bridesmaids travel to the ceremony ahead of the bride

☐ Decide how the following people will travel between the ceremony and reception

| | |
|---|---|
| Bride | Bride's parents |
| Groom | Groom's parents |
| Attendants | Travelling guests |

☐ Decide how the following people will leave the reception

| | |
|---|---|
| Bride | Bride's parents |
| Groom | Groom's parents |
| Attendants | Travelling guests |

☐ Purchase wedding transport decorations for inside and out

| | |
|---|---|
| Floral wreaths | Red carpet |
| Flower petals | Ribbons |
| Flowers | Stickers |
| Magnetic wedding signs | Tulle dressing |
| Party lighting | Tulle sashes |
| Other ... | |

*Ask your hire company if they can provide some of these.*

☐ Determine when and where the transport decorations need to be delivered

☐ Select items you require in your wedding transport

Bar

Drinks, e.g. chilled champagne, soft drink, bottled water

- Esky
- Fruit platter
- Glassware, e.g. champagne flutes
- Ice
- Snacks, e.g. canapés
- Stereo
- Sweets
- Tissues
- Umbrellas
- Other …

☐ Appoint parking attendants to direct traffic at the ceremony and reception
- Professional attendants
- Provided by your transport company
- Ushers
- Family members
- Friends

☐ Complete the following if you are using your own or borrowing vehicles
- Have a professional service
- Have a professional safety check, e.g. tyres, oil, water
- Wash the exterior
- Detail the interior
- Fill with petrol the day before

## Transport Particulars

☐ Determine how many hours you will require the transport

☐ Decide who will drive your wedding transport
- Professional chauffeur
- Family member
- Friend
- Helper

☐ Ensure your drivers are certified to drive the chosen vehicles

☐ Install child seats and/or booster seats for young passengers, if necessary

☐ Inform your driver of the following
- The address of each collection point
- The time of each collection
- Photo locations
- Surfaces you will be travelling over, e.g. roads, driveways, grass, gravel, sand

☐ Complete the wedding vendor checklist for your transport company and chauffeurs on pages 10 and 11

☐ Have your attendants decorate your going-away car toward the end of the reception

| | |
|---|---|
| ▪ Balloons | ▪ Pom poms |
| ▪ Banners | ▪ Shaving cream |
| ▪ Crêpe paper | ▪ Shoes |
| ▪ Decals | ▪ String |
| ▪ 'Just married' flags | ▪ Tin cans |
| ▪ 'Just married' licence plates | ▪ Window clings |
| ▪ Liquid chalk | ▪ Other ... |

☐ Ensure the going-away car decorations are safe and legal

## Transport Top Tips

- View and test drive each wedding vehicle to ensure it is comfortable and mechanically sound
- Conduct a practice run to determine how long it takes to travel between locations on a similar day and time
- Charter vans or a bus if many of your guests will not have transport
- Ensure travelling guests have transport to and from the ceremony, reception and back to their accommodation
- Place traffic cones at the front of the wedding venue to reserve parking spaces for the bridal party
- Assign designated drivers for guests who will be drinking alcohol

# 21

# Music, Musicians and Entertainment

Music is the perfect way to entertain guests, celebrate and honour special moments in your wedding. Add energy and fun to your big day with a playlist personalised to you and your fiancé's taste. Select your musicians and entertainers wisely – they have the ability to calm rowdy guests and pep them back up when the time is right.

## Musicians

☐ Research potential wedding musicians
   ○ View professional musicians in action
   ○ Obtain and review live recordings

☐ Select music providers for your ceremony, reception and in between each event

| | |
|---|---|
| A cappella group | Harpist |
| Accordionist | Jazz band |
| African chanting group | Jukebox |
| Band | Karaoke machine |
| Bag piper | Orchestra |
| Cellist | Organist |
| Children's choir | Pianist |
| Choir | Pop band |
| Classical band | Rockabilly band |
| Classical guitarist | Singers |
| Cover band | Soloist |
| DJ | String quartet |
| Drum group | Tribute band |
| Flautist | Trumpeter |
| Flute duo | Violinist |
| Gospel group | Woodwind quartet |
| Guitarist | Other ... |

☐ Complete the wedding vendor checklist for your musicians on pages 10 and 11

☐ Book your musicians as soon as possible

## Ceremony Music

☐ Discuss music types and selections with your ceremony officiant
    Enquire if you are permitted to play music at the ceremony venue. If so, do you need a permit? Are you allowed to use speakers?
    Enquire if you are permitted to play secular music if you are in a religious venue
    Find out what type of music is not available or allowed at the ceremony

☐ Select music to accompany key moments in your wedding ceremony
    Guest arrival
    Prelude
    Processional
    Bride's entrance
    Ritual or symbolic act
    Signing of the register, e.g. a quiet and reflective piece
    Recessional, e.g. an upbeat, lively and celebratory piece
    Postlude

*Write the type of music or name of the piece that you have selected next to each item.*

## Reception Music

☐ Discuss music types and selections with your reception manager
    Arrange blocks of music types, e.g. fast, slow, classical, jazz
    Organise five songs per block

☐ Consider your guests when planning your music choices
    Consider the type of people invited
    Have your music range to cover a large age group

☐ Select the music genres that you would like on your reception playlist

| | |
|---|---|
| Alternative | Jive |
| Big band | Latin |
| Blues | Modern |
| Celtic | Oldies |
| Classic rock | Pop |
| Classical | Punk |
| Contemporary | R&B |
| Country | Rap |
| Cultural | Reggae |
| Disco | Rock |
| Folk | Rock ballads |
| Gospel | Swing |
| Heavy metal | Techno |
| Hip hop | Top 100 |
| Jazz | Other … |

☐ Talk to your fiancé and together decide on your perfect wedding song
   ☐ Double check that your DJ or band knows the song you have chosen for your first dance

☐ Select music to accompany key moments at your wedding reception
   ☐ Pre-dinner drinks/cocktail hour
   ☐ As the bridal party enters the reception
   ☐ Background music throughout the meal
   ☐ Cutting the cake
   ☐ First dance
   ☐ Attendants' dance
   ☐ Father-daughter dance
   ☐ Mother-son dance
   ☐ Group dancing
   ☐ Garter toss
   ☐ Bouquet toss
   ☐ Last dance
   ☐ Bride and groom send-off
   ☐ Other …

*Write the type of music or name of the piece that you have selected next to each item.*

☐ Give music providers a list of specific songs and genres that you do *not* want played

☐ Determine if your music providers will play continuously or provide recorded music when on breaks

☐ Arrange for your DJ or MC to:
   ☐ Build a festive atmosphere
   ☐ Read the crowd when making music choices
   ☐ Encourage guests to get up and dance throughout the reception
   ☐ Take music requests

☐ Create your own personalised music playlist for the reception
   ☐ Play from a CD or MP3 player controlled by your DJ, MC or a helper

☐ Find out if there are any music restrictions at the reception venue
   ☐ When music volume must be turned down
   ☐ When music must cease

☐ Organise auditory enhancement equipment or find out if your performers or ceremony and reception venues can supply them
   ☐ Amplifiers
   ☐ Lapel microphones for the ceremony
   ☐ Lapel microphones for the reception
   ☐ Microphone and PA for the ceremony
   ☐ Microphone and PA for the reception

- Music stands
- Sound system, e.g. a powerful one if you are outside
- Turntables

☐ Test music at the actual ceremony and reception venues

☐ Ensure the music will be loud enough to hear and still suitable for guests to have conversations

☐ Organise music and entertainment for the wedding after-party

## Guest Entertainment

☐ Provide music as entertainment

☐ Hire professional entertainers
- Acrobat
- Cabaret artist
- Cartoonist
- Cocktail entertainer
- Comedian
- Dancers, e.g. ballroom, Latin
- Escapologist
- Fire performer
- Fortune teller
- Illusionist
- Impressionist
- Other …
- Instrumental group, e.g. jazz ensemble
- Live ice sculptor
- Magician
- Mime artist
- Poet
- Singer
- Singing duo
- Singing group
- Street theatre act
- Tribute act
- Tribute band

☐ Complete the wedding vendor checklist for your entertainers on pages 10 and 11

☐ Provide games and activities
- Boules
- Bride and groom trivia
- Casino games
- Croquet
- Dance lesson
- Dancing e.g. the Chicken Dance, Nutbush, Macarena
- Ice breaker games on guest tables
- Karaoke
- Limbo
- Photo booth with props
- Volleyball

☐ Organise a surprise for guests at the reception, e.g. fireworks, laser light show, recite a poem, read a love letter from your past together

## Entertaining Children

☐ Hire a professional children's entertainer
    Balloonist
    Children's band
    Children's singer
    Clown
    Face-painter
    Puppeteer
    Story teller
    Other …

☐ Arrange for some fun games and activities for young guests
    Activity books
    Baby animal farm
    Board games
    Colouring placemats
    Craft table
    Electronic games
    Jumping castle
    Paper for children to draw a picture for you to keep
    Piñata, e.g. heart shaped
    Puzzles
    Toys
    Treasure hunt

☐ Create amusement bags for young guests that include snacks, toys, colouring books, crayons, puzzles and stickers

☐ Provide a play area for babies using a large rug and age-appropriate toys

☐ Organise a separate children's entertainment room with supervisors and activities
    Beanbags
    Board games
    Books
    Computer games and console
    Movies
    Puzzles
    Tables and chairs
    TV and DVD player

☐ Provide sleeping facilities for children who will require a nap

☐ Organise for child minding at the venue or at a nearby location such as a house or hotel room

# 22

# The Cake

Have your wedding cake reflect a combination of your individual tastes with an element of personal significance. Your cake will be on display for most of the reception and it's often a focal point of the room, so make sure it shows your style. If you (or someone close to you) is making the cake, be sure to use fresh, top quality ingredients – they are essential for a delicious cake that will earn rave reviews.

## Selecting a Baker

☐ Decide who will create your wedding cake
   Professional cake maker
   Catering company
   Reception venue baker
   Friend or family member
   You

☐ Complete the wedding vendor checklist for your baker on pages 10 and 11

☐ Select another option for obtaining your cake
   Purchase a shop cake and have it professionally iced and decorated
   Have a friend or family member bake it and have it professionally iced and decorated
   Bake it yourself and have it professionally iced and decorated
   Purchase a bakery cake

☐ Provide your baker with all of your cake ideas and sketches
   Tell your baker what you *don't* want
   Inform your baker how long the cake will be on display on the day

☐ Taste test samples of cakes

☐ Order your wedding cake
   Order 2–3 months in advance
   Determine how long the cake will take to create

- [ ] Arrange for delivery of your wedding cake

- [ ] Record the following cake particulars in your wedding file:
  - Delivery date
  - Delivery time
  - Delivery destination
  - Where the cake will be assembled after transport
  - Where the cake will be stored
  - What happens to leftovers

## DIY Wedding Cake Top Tips

- Find a good recipe that is specifically designed for wedding cakes
- Purchase the highest quality ingredients you can afford
- Bake at least one trial cake very early on
- Practise not only baking but also assembling, freezing and thawing the cake
- Consider hiring cake tins and equipment
- Prepare extra batter, icing and filling
- Use a revolving stand for decorating
- Square cakes are more efficient as they have less wastage and provide more slices
- Determine if your reception venue will charge a cake cutting fee

## Style and Size

- [ ] Review cake pictures in books, magazines and online

- [ ] Sketch your dream wedding cake in your wedding file
  - Design and print your perfect wedding cake style using free software online

- [ ] Select a cake design that suits the theme and style of your wedding
  - Use your wedding gown as inspiration for the cake design
  - Use your ceremony building as inspiration for the cake design

- [ ] Calculate how large your wedding cake must be
  - Have your baker recommend an appropriate size
  - Consider the number of guests attending
  - Consider the size of each portion
  - Allow extra cake for guests to take home
  - Allow extra cake to send to absent guests

- ☐ Determine the portion size
  - Consider the cake type, e.g. sponge cakes require larger portion sizes than mud cakes
  - Serve large portions if the cake will be the only dessert
- ☐ Determine how your wedding cake will be divided:
  - The entire cake will be cut into even portions
  - The bottom tiers will be cut into portions and the top tier saved
  - The wedding cake will be kept intact and another rectangular 'sheet' cake of the same flavour will be cut for guests
  - Other …

## Shape and Display

- ☐ Select the shape of your wedding cake

| | |
|---|---|
| Diamond | Rectangle |
| Heart | Round |
| Hexagon | Square |
| Oval | Themed shape |
| Petal | Other … |

*Consider selecting a different shape for each tier.*

- ☐ Select how your wedding cake will be displayed
  - Boxed miniature cake display
  - Centrepiece cake – a small cake at the centre of every table
  - Croquembouche – a profiterole tower
  - Cupcake tower
  - Cupcake tower with a small cake as the top tier
  - Individual cakes tower
  - Single tier cake
  - Multiple tier cake
  - Other …

- ☐ Decide what the cake will be displayed on
  - Cake board
  - Pedestal stand
  - Plate, e.g. glass, ceramic, crystal
  - Platter
  - Stand

- ☐ Select the number of tiers for your wedding cake

| | |
|---|---|
| 1 | 4 |
| 2 | 5 |
| 3 | 6 |

- ☐ Decide how the tiers will be separated

| | |
|---|---|
| Cake boards | Columns |

- Covered cardboard discs
- Hidden columns
- Separator plates
- Spacer pegs
- Tiered cake stand
- Other ...

☐ Decide how each tier will differ
- Colour
- Design
- Embellishments
- Flavour
- Shape
- Size

## Flavour and Filling

☐ Select the type of wedding cake
- Black forest
- Cheesecake
- Dacquoise
- Fruit
- Fruit liqueur
- Fudge
- Génoise
- Ice-cream
- Marble
- Mud
- Pound
- Red velvet
- Sponge
- Tart
- Tiramisu
- Trifle
- Truffle
- Other ...

☐ Select one or more wedding cake flavours
- Almond
- Amaretto
- Apricot
- Banana
- Blackberry
- Butter
- Butterscotch
- Caramel
- Carrot
- Champagne
- Cherry
- Choc mint
- Chocolate
- Coconut
- Cookies & cream
- Cranberry
- Dark chocolate
- Double chocolate
- Fruit
- Hazelnut
- Honey
- Irish coffee
- Other ...
- Jaffa
- Lemon
- Lime
- Macadamia
- Mango
- Mint
- Mocha
- Orange
- Passionfruit
- Peach
- Peanut butter
- Pecan
- Pineapple
- Pistachio
- Pumpkin
- Raspberry
- Rum & raisin
- Spice
- Strawberry
- Toffee
- Vanilla
- White chocolate

☐ Select one or more wedding cake fillings
　　Buttercream (plain, mocha, pistachio, rum, bourbon, orange)
　　Chocolate (chocolate fudge, peanut butter chocolate)
　　Cream cheese (plain, lemon, orange scented)
　　Cream (vanilla, coconut, lemon, banana, hazelnut)
　　Curd (orange, lemon)
　　Custard (vanilla, apple, banana, chocolate, strawberry)
　　Fresh fruit (strawberries, raspberries, blackberries, blueberries)
　　Frosting
　　Fruit preserve (lemon, apricot, raspberry, strawberry, cherry, pineapple)
　　Ganache
　　Mousse (chocolate, white chocolate, raspberry, strawberry, passion fruit, mango, peach, Kahlua, mocha)
　　Nuts (macadamia, almond, pecan)
　　Pralines
　　Toasted coconut
　　Whipped cream

## Icing

☐ Select an icing type
　　Buttercream
　　Cream cheese
　　Fondant (rolled or poured)
　　Fudge
　　Ganache
　　Glaze
　　Other …

　　Marzipan
　　Meringue
　　Modelling chocolate
　　Mousse
　　Royal
　　Whipped cream

☐ Select an icing colour(s)

☐ Select an icing flavour

## Embellishments

☐ Select one or more details for your wedding cake
　　Basket weaving
　　Borders
　　Bows
　　Butterflies
　　Buttons
　　Cascading flowers
　　Champagne flutes
　　Combined monogram
　　Cupids
　　Doves

　　Flower buds
　　Flower clusters
　　Flower petals
　　Frills
　　Fruit
　　Garlands
　　Hearts
　　Henna style designs
　　Horseshoes
　　Intertwined hearts

Kissing doves
Lace
Leaves and berries
Lettering, e.g. your names,
combined monogram, wedding
date
Love birds
Pearls
Polka dots
Ribbons

Shells
Stars
Swags
Swans
Swirls
Themed details
Trellis
Wedding rings
Zigzags
Other ...

☐ Select edible ingredients to create the cake details

Berries
Cachous (metallic sugar balls)
Chocolate art
Chocolate powder
Chocolate ribbon
Chocolate shavings
Coloured gel
Edible diamonds
Edible glitter
Edible images
Edible ink pens
Edible marker
Edible metallic paint
Edible pearls
Edible sequins
Edible shimmer dust
Other ...

Fondant
Food colours
Gum paste
Gum paste decorations
Icing
Marzipan
Meringue
Modelling chocolate
Piping gel
Royal icing decorations
Sprinkles
Sugar art
Sugar confetti
Sugar crystals
Sugar pearls
Wafers

*Many of these items come in metallics, pearls, pastels and bright colours.*

☐ Select other items to create the cake details

Beads
Glass decorations
Non-toxic flowers
Non-toxic leaves
Ribbon
Wedding stationery paper
Other ...

☐ Select a wedding cake topper

3D lettering, e.g. 'Love', 'I Do', 'Mr & Mrs', your combined monogram
Antique jewellery, e.g. a family heirloom brooch
Bells
Birdcage
Bow

Bride and groom figurines
Bride, groom and their children figurines
Characters
Chocolate art
Crown
Crystal flowers
Fairytale castle
Flags
Flowers (fresh or artificial)
Intertwined hearts
Japanese love symbol, e.g. double happiness
Religious symbol
Scene
Themed ornament
Tilted champagne flutes
Wedding motif
Wedding rings
Wedding vehicle, e.g. horse and carriage, pumpkin coach, wedding car
Other …

## Serving and Saving the Cake

☐ Select where your wedding cake will be displayed
Reception entrance
On the head table
In the reception room on its own table

☐ Select items for your cake table
Bouquet
Candles
Scatters, e.g. beads, flowers, petals, glitter, sugared almonds
Table covering, e.g. silk, tulle, lace
Table swag, e.g. garlands, wreaths
Other …

☐ Ensure the cake table is kept clear of high traffic areas and children

☐ Purchase a cake knife and cake server set
Determine if your reception manager can provide them on the day

☐ Select items to serve with your cake
Brandy butter
Caramel sauce
Chocolate flakes
Clotted cream
Custard
Fresh fruit, e.g. seasonal berries

- Fruit coulis
- Glazed cherries
- Ice-cream
- Sorbet
- Sprinkling of cocoa or icing sugar
- Strawberries and cream
- Wafers
- Warm fudge sauce
- Whipped cream (plain or flavoured)
- Other …

☐ Decide how the cake will be served
- A generous slice as dessert
- A finger slice served with coffee after dessert

☐ Have cake slices placed in cake bags or boxes for each guest to take home

☐ Arrange for cake slices to be sent to absent guests

☐ Save the top layer of your wedding cake to freeze and share on a significant occasion
- Your first wedding anniversary
- The birth of your first child
- The baptism of your first child

☐ Have a baker create a small replica of your wedding cake to share on your first anniversary if a fresh cake is more appealing

# 23
# Gifts

Traditionally, wedding gifts were given to help the wedding couple establish their new home. However, if you already have a fully furnished house, request items or experiences that you have always dreamed of. When giving gifts to members of your bridal party, parents and other special people, select thoughtful, quality items that will last for decades.

## Gift Registry

- [ ] Decide what you both want for wedding gifts
    - Material gifts
    - Funds toward expensive items, e.g. honeymoon, mortgage, house renovation
    - An experience
    - Donations for a charity (or charities) close to your heart

- [ ] Select a gift registry type
    - Department store
    - Specialty store
    - Shopping centre (register with multiple stores within one shopping complex)
    - Gift card (nominate various stores for guests to purchase a gift card)
    - Online store
    - Wedding gift registry company
    - Wishing well

- [ ] Build your gift registry list
    - Be specific with each gift selected, e.g. indicate the make, model and colour

- [ ] Create your own gift registry list
    - Item description
    - Price
    - Store name
    - Store location

☐ Decide how you will distribute the gift registry information
    With your wedding invitation
    With your bridal shower invitation
    Attendants to distribute
    Close family member or friend to distribute
    Information sent only if asked for
    Displayed on your wedding website

☐ Nominate someone to be contacted with questions about the gift registry, e.g. your mother

## Gift Registry Top Tips

- Organise your registry a minimum of 3–6 months in advance
- Select stores that allow you to build and view the gift list online
- Choose stores with a good reputation and return policy
- Select a range of prices
- Allow guests to pool their contributions toward expensive items
- Add more gifts than you actually expect to receive to your list
- Request gift selections to be completed by a certain date
- Stores offering gift wrapping and delivery are ideal
- Ensure the store is convenient for all of your guests, e.g. online viewing and purchasing

## Wedding Gifts Theme

☐ Theme your wedding gifts

☐ Select one or more of the following wedding gift themes

| Theme | Examples |
| --- | --- |
| Antiques | antique furniture, artwork, vintage jewellery |
| Appliances | bread maker, carving knife, coffee grinder, coffee machine, electric toothbrushes, food processor, hand held vacuum, iron, toaster |
| Bar and cellar | barware, bar fridge, cocktail shakers, glassware, ice bucket, port, whisky, wine, wine cooler, wine racks |
| Bathroom | aromatherapy products, bath mats, bath sheets, bathroom cabinet, flannels, hand towels, robes, scales |
| Bed linen | bedspread, duvet covers, electric blanket, pillow covers, sheet sets, valance |
| Bedroom | cushions, rug, armchair, bed frame, side tables, bedroom suite, chest of drawers |

| Camping | barbecue, beds, binoculars, chairs, lanterns, picnic table, tent |
| Cooking | baking tins, blender, carving dish, cast iron cookware, microwave cookware, mixing bowls, saucepans, soufflé dishes |
| Crockery | casserole dishes, coffee pot, serving dishes, teacups and saucers, teapot |
| Crystal | candlesticks, clock, glassware, serving platters |
| Cutlery | carving set, knife rack, knife sharpener, salad servers, silver plated set, stainless steel set, steak knives |
| Dining | candelabra, candles, napkin rings, place mats, silk napkins, tablecloths, table linen |
| Electronics | camera, clock, GPS, mobile telephones, speakers, stereo, video camera |
| Entertainment | computer games, DVDs, DVD player, games console, media player, MP3 player, television |
| Experiences | cooking class, cruise, hot air ballooning, helicopter flight |
| Fitness | rowing machine, sports equipment, treadmill, weights bench, weights set |
| Furniture | bookcase, coffee table, dining suite, lounge suite, office chair, storage unit |
| Games room | bean bags, pinball machine, snooker table, table soccer, table tennis |
| Garage | cabinets, cordless drill, drawer sets, power tools, tool box, weatherproof stereo |
| Garden | garden shed, hedge trimmer, ladder, lawn mower, plants, wheelbarrow, whipper snipper |
| Glassware | beer mugs, brandy glasses, champagne flutes, jugs, red and white wine glasses, tumblers |
| Home accents | artwork, bowls, candles, indoor plants, ornaments, paintings, photo frames, throw rugs, vases |
| Home office | chair, computer, desk, fax machine, laser printer |
| Honeymoon | activities, beach towels, journal, luggage, travel guides |
| Kitchen | juicer, knife set, mixing set, pressure cooker, salad bowl, scales, spice rack, Tupperware, wok |
| Library | Bookends, book sets, cookbooks, travel books |
| Mortgage | donations for a house deposit, donations toward mortgage |
| Outdoor entertainment | barbecue, barbecue tools, daybed, dining table, hammock, outdoor heater |
| White goods | dishwasher, freezer, refrigerator, tumble dryer, washing machine |

- ☐ Select where your wedding gifts will be delivered
  - Your home
  - Wedding reception
  - Bride's parents' home
  - Groom's parents' home

- ☐ Record the date and time that your wedding gifts will be delivered in your wedding file

- ☐ Decide where you will display your gifts, e.g. arranged on the reception gift table or at home

- ☐ Move name tags out of sight to avoid guest awkwardness, e.g. attach under the gift
  - Do not reveal the amount of money people give

- ☐ Appoint someone to move gifts brought to the reception to a storage space if you are not placing them on display

- ☐ Place a wishing well, birdcage or 'card box' on the reception gift table

- ☐ Decide when your wedding gifts will be opened
  - The next day with key guests at a small gathering
  - As they arrive at your designated location, e.g. your home
  - After your honeymoon

## Gifts for Attendants and Helpers

It's traditional (and thoughtful) to give your attendants, helpers and close family members a thank you gift. And don't forget to give one to your fiancé!

- ☐ Select who you will give a gift of thanks

| | |
|---|---|
| Groom | Bride's parents |
| Maid of honour | Groom's parents |
| Bridesmaids | Helpers |
| Best man | Ceremony readers |
| Groomsmen | Speech makers |
| Flower girls | Officiant |
| Ring bearer | Financial contributors |
| Pageboys | Wedding coordinator |
| Junior attendants | Special family members |
| Ushers | Outstanding vendors |

- ☐ Inform your fiancé if you will be giving him a special gift so he can do the same for you

☐ Decide on the types of gifts you will give
    Items to wear on the day
    Keepsakes
    Practical items
    Humorous items
    Items relating to an interest or hobby
    Personalised items with your names and wedding date
    Personalised items with their name
    Thank you cards
    A letter or note expressing thanks
    Other ...

☐ Consider the following gift ideas
    Aftershave
    Book set
    Box of chocolates
    Charm bracelet
    Cigars
    Clock
    Cologne
    Cosmetic case
    Cuff links and studs
    Engraved compact
    Engraved keychain
    Engraved letter opener
    Engraved pen
    Experience, e.g. hot-air balloon ride, dinner cruise
    Framed photograph of them at your wedding
    Gift basket filled with fruit, wine, tea and gourmet snacks
    Gift certificate, e.g. day spa, manicure, pedicure, massage
    Handkerchief
    Jewellery
    Jewellery stand
    Jewellery box
    Lingerie
    Locket
    Luggage
    Manicure set
    Money clip
    Music box
    Passport wallet
    Pendant
    Perfume
    Photo album
    Photo frame (digital or standard)

- Piece of art
- Port
- Purse
- Restaurant voucher
- Scarf
- Scented bath oil
- Silk tie
- Silver pen set
- Spa treatment
- Stationery
- Swiss army knife
- Tickets to a sports event, concert, movie, musical, opera, orchestra
- Towels
- Vase
- Wallet
- Watch
- Wine
- Other …

*Find a more detailed list of gifts on page 231.*

## Bomboniere

Bomboniere, also called favours, are the gifts given to your guests as a symbol of your appreciation for their attendance. They are often kept as keepsakes to remember the day by.

☐ Choose meaningful bomboniere for your wedding guests

☐ Select the type of bomboniere you will give
- Edible
- Humorous
- Keepsakes
- Personalised items with the guest's name
- Personalised items with your names and wedding date
- Practical
- Themed
- Other …

☐ Decide where to place bomboniere at your reception
- Above each guest's table setting
- On each guest's bread plate
- In each guest's wine glass
- In the middle of each guest table as a centrepiece
- Arranged on a table for guests to take upon departure

☐ Select from the following bomboniere ideas
  Bottle openers
  Boutique/microbrewery beer
  Candles
  Champagne
  Charity donations in lieu of gifts
  Chocolate art (themed)
  Chocolate bouquets
  Chocolate covered coffee beans
  Chocolate truffles
  Coasters
  Corkscrews
  Cupcakes
  Etched wedding glassware (beer or wine glasses)
  Flowers
  Fortune cookies
  Fudge
  Homemade jam
  Homemade baked treats
  Homemade bath salts or fizzers
  Homemade soap stacks
  Macaroons
  Matchbooks or matchboxes
  Miniature potted flowers/plants
  Miniature bottles of wine, port or spirits
  Miniature tarts
  Packets of flower seeds
  Rock candy
  Stubby holders
  Sugared almonds
  Sweet bags
  Themed ornaments
  Wine (red, white, sparkling)
  Wine charms
  Wine stoppers
  Other …

☐ Personalise your bomboniere with:
  Your names                 Wedding motif
  Combined monogram          Themed graphic
  Wedding date               Guest name

*Print labels, etch, engrave, pipe with icing or have personalised by a professional.*

☐ Organise a candy buffet
  Display beautiful glass canisters and confectionery scoops
  Offer matching favour boxes in themed colours

*Top Ideas for Gifting*

- Distribute gifts to your attendants at the wedding rehearsal
- Creating your own original wedding favours can be an enjoyable activity
- Order extra bomboniere for yourselves
- Top ideas for the groom to give his bride are jewellery, a hand written letter or poem, pearls or lingerie for the wedding night
- Top ideas for the bride to give her groom are cufflinks and studs, an engraved watch, a wallet or tickets to an event

## Gift Presentation

☐ Present bomboniere and attendant gifts in an attractive way
   Wrap gifts in high-quality paper and ribbon

☐ Include a message of thanks
   Attach 'thank you' tags to bomboniere
   Write a thank you card or letter for attendants and helpers

*Ensure cards or tags are attached securely.*

☐ Select how you will package your gifts and bomboniere
   Box lined with tissue paper
   Cellophane bag
   Clear plastic box
   Corrugated box
   Embossed box
   Fabric bag
   Glass jars with a ribbon
   Heart-shaped box
   Miniature paper bag
   Noodle box
   Paper cone
   Themed gift box
   Tin container
   Tissue paper wrapping
   Tote bag
   Vellum sachets
   Other …

☐ Embellish packaging with ribbon, flowers, braid, beads or feathers

# 24
# Rehearsals, Itinerary and Emergency Kit

Wedding rehearsals can help to calm your nerves and ensure that your big day runs smoothly. You don't have to have an official rehearsal, but it's a good idea – especially if you have more than one attendant and/or children involved. If possible, have everyone involved in the organisation of your wedding attend.

## Wedding Rehearsal

☐ Select a day for the wedding rehearsal
- 1 week before your wedding
- 2–3 days before your wedding
- The evening before your wedding

☐ Send an invitation or inform participants of the rehearsal details
- Date
- Location
- Start and end time
- What to bring
- If food and drinks are provided

☐ Select who will be invited to the wedding rehearsal
- Bride
- Groom
- Bride's attendants
- Groom's attendants
- Junior attendants
- Officiant
- Officiant's spouse
- Parents of the bride
- Parents of the groom
- Ushers
- Ceremony readers
- Musicians
- Speech makers
- Wedding coordinator
- Banquet manager
- MC
- Spouses of attendants
- Children of attendants
- Other family members
- Other …

☐ Stage your rehearsal at a similar time of day as the ceremony and reception, particularly for outdoor weddings

☐ Ensure the ceremony and reception venues are available on your chosen day

☐ Simulate the venue if you can't rehearse at the actual location
    Draw and distribute diagrams/pictures

☐ Use props for your rehearsal to replicate bouquets, the ring pillow, lecterns etc

☐ Have a trusted person stand in for those who are not able to attend
    Inform the missing members of the procedures

☐ Organise a meal for after the wedding rehearsals

☐ Decide on the type of meal
    Backyard barbecue
    Cocktail party
    Dinner at a restaurant
    Other …

☐ Decide who will provide a toast at the rehearsal gathering
    Bride
    Groom
    Parent of the bride
    Parent of the groom
    Maid of honour
    Best man
    Other …

*Be sure to thank everyone for their participation and support.*

☐ Present gifts to your attendants and special helpers
*Find a detailed list of gift ideas on page 229.*

☐ Determine who will pay for the rehearsal gathering
    Groom's parents
    Bride's parents
    Bride and groom

☐ Arrange necessary documents to take to the wedding rehearsal, e.g. marriage licence, the witnesses' proof-of-age documents

## What to Rehearse for the Ceremony

☐ Have your officiant complete the following:
    Indicate the roles of each member of the bridal party
    Outline any rules and regulations
    Run through details of the service

- [ ] Complete an entire ceremony run through
    - Processional with music, e.g. where and how everyone will enter
    - Officiant delivers the welcome
    - The bride is presented
    - Officiant rehearses the introduction and charge to the bride and groom
    - Readers practise their lines
    - Musicians do a sound quality check
    - Bride and groom practise vows (unless they are to be kept secret)
    - Officiant completes the remainder of the ceremony
    - Rehearse places for the symbolic act, signing of the register and the presentation of the couple
    - Recessional, e.g. how everyone will vacate the ceremony

- [ ] Ensure you are aware of the following
    - Where you and your attendants will stand
    - When to sit
    - When to kneel
    - How you will kiss
    - How to link arms
    - Timing and prompts
    - Any other special requirements

- [ ] Ensure your attendants and helpers take the wedding rehearsal seriously

- [ ] Have a helper sit at the back of the ceremony venue during the rehearsal to ensure your vows, the music and people delivering readings can be heard loud and clear

## What to Rehearse for the Reception

- [ ] Have your reception manager specify the following
    - Details and timing of the reception
    - Rules and regulations

- [ ] Complete an entire reception run through
    - Grand entrance, e.g. order of entry
    - Toast makers practise their toasts
    - Speech makers practise their speeches
    - Cutting of the cake, e.g. how you will place your hands
    - Have a dance rehearsal on the actual dance floor you will be using
    - Bouquet toss, e.g. practise throwing elegantly
    - Garter toss, e.g. how and where you will sit
    - Send-off places and order, e.g. farewell arch

## Other Things to Rehearse

☐ Practise moving gracefully in your wedding gown and shoes
- Walking
- Sitting
- Kneeling
- Dancing
- Getting in and out of transport

☐ Practise good posture for standing and sitting
- Straight back
- Shoulders back
- Tuck in your bottom
- Pull in your stomach
- Take shorter steps rather than large strides
- Walk with your feet hip width apart for good balance

☐ Rehearse your wedding vows
- Read aloud
- Record and listen to yourself
- Pace yourself
- Have someone else listen to you read aloud

## Wedding Day Itinerary

☐ Create a wedding day itinerary
- Include detailed instructions of everything that will take place on the day
- Include a breakdown of the day in timeline format (include locations as necessary)

☐ Include the following in your wedding day itinerary:
- Pre-ceremony run sheet, e.g. hair, make-up, dressing time
- Ceremony run sheet (including set-up and clean-up)
- Processional and recessional order
- Ceremony seating plan
- Reception run sheet (including set-up and clean-up)
- Reception seating plan
- Venue addresses and maps
- Tasks to be completed on the day and names of those who will complete them
- Contact names and mobile numbers of attendants, key helpers, vendors and your wedding coordinator

☐ Make several copies of your wedding day itinerary and distribute to:

| | |
|---|---|
| Attendants | Reception manager |
| Ceremony manager | Ushers |
| Key helpers | Vendors |
| Parents | Wedding coordinator |

*Distribute a week before your wedding day and don't forget to keep a copy for yourself and your fiancé.*

☐ Ensure everyone reads the wedding day itinerary
   Ask if anyone has questions or needs further clarification of certain items

☐ Determine how you and your fiancé will keep from seeing each other on the day

☐ Decide who you want to be with you on the wedding morning

| | |
|---|---|
| Bridesmaids | Grandparents |
| Mother | Flower girls |
| Father | Close family |
| Children | Other ... |

☐ Decide how you will celebrate your wedding morning
   Enjoy a full breakfast with the foods you love
   Celebrate with champagne
   Take part in relaxing activities, e.g. swimming, golf, taking a bath, having a massage

☐ Tell your parents how important they are to you (parents are often just as anxious as you)

☐ Thank your attendants, friends and family for being with you on such an important day

☐ Confirm that all bridal party members are prepared

☐ Send the going-away car and honeymoon luggage to the reception venue or to your first-night accommodation

☐ Tie the rings to the ring pillow and give it to someone to keep safe until the ceremony

☐ Move your engagement ring from your left hand before the ceremony
   Move to your right hand
   Put it on a chain around your neck
   Give to a trusted friend or family member for safe keeping
   Leave at home
   Other ...

# Emergency Kit

☐ Prepare a wedding day emergency kit
  Consider your attendants and what they may need as well, e.g. bottled water
  Pack at least a week in advance

☐ Select items for your emergency kit
  Adhesive bandages
  Bottled water
  Cash
  Comb
  Comfortable shoes, e.g. ballet flats
  Copy of written vows
  Deodorant
  Double-sided tape
  Duct tape
  Glue
  Hairspray
  Hair pins
  Handkerchiefs
  High-energy snacks, e.g. protein bars
  Keys
  Medication
  Mints
  Mirror
  Mobile phone
  Paracetamol
  Safety pins
  Scissors
  Sewing kit (including white thread)
  Stockings/pantyhose
  Tissues
  Touch-up make-up
  Tweezers
  Wedding day itinerary
  Wet wipes
  White chalk or powder (for a dirty or stained gown)

☐ Give your emergency kit to a helper on the wedding morning

# 25
# Ceremony: Sequence of Events

Once the day has begun try not to get too concerned if the schedule isn't running perfectly. Some things are bound to go wrong, so take a deep breath and handle them as best you can (or get someone else to handle them for you!). The day will go quickly – enjoy every second.

## Typical Ceremony Sequence of Events

1. Prelude
2. Processional
3. Welcome
4. Congregation is seated
5. Presentation of the bride
6. Introduction
7. Charge to the bride and groom
8. Readings
9. Declaration of intent to marry
10. Vow exchange
11. Ring exchange
12. Ritual or symbolic act
13. Conclusion
14. Declaration of marriage
15. First kiss
16. Signing of the register
17. Presentation
18. Recessional

## Prelude

☐ Arrange for pre-processional music to begin 30 minutes before the ceremony

☐ Ask your guests to arrive 20–30 minutes before the ceremony

☐ Arrange for the groom and his attendants to arrive 20 minutes before the ceremony

☐ Enlist helpers to hand out programs at the ceremony entrance
- Children
- Close friends
- Family members
- Junior attendants
- Ushers
- Other …

☐ Appoint assistants to seat your guests
- Ceremony manager
- Groomsmen
- Other …
- Junior attendants
- Ushers

- [ ] Inform your seating assistants of who will sit where
  - Have the bride's guests sit on the left
  - Have the groom's guests sit on the right
  - Seat the bride's parents in the front row (or the second row if you have a large wedding party who will fill the front row)
  - Seat the groom's parents in the front row (or the second row if you have a large wedding party who will fill the front row)
  - Have immediate family members sit behind the parents of each family
  - Have all other guests sit behind the reserved rows from front to back as they arrive

- [ ] Reserve the front few rows with ribbons for close family and special guests

- [ ] Consider the following alternatives to traditional seating
  - Mix guests between the left and right sides
  - Seat all guests from front to back as they arrive
  - Have guests stand in a circle or semicircle
  - Seat guests in a U shape
  - Seat guests in semicircular rows
  - Seat half of your guests in a circle and have the other half stand behind them

- [ ] Have the mother of the groom seated five minutes before the ceremony is to begin

- [ ] Have your ushers or helpers light candles

- [ ] Have your officiant inform guests to turn phones and other devices to silent

- [ ] Have the mother of the bride seated immediately before the ceremony is to begin
  - Arrange for her to be escorted to her seat by an usher or male attendant

*The seating of the mother of the bride signals the beginning of the ceremony.*

- [ ] Have your ushers roll out the aisle runner as soon as the mother of the bride is seated (if not already done)

- [ ] Decide how the groom will enter the ceremony
  - Lead by the officiant with his attendants from a side room
  - Lead by the officiant with his attendants from the side of the venue (good for outdoor venues)
  - Walk down the aisle with his attendants immediately before the mothers are seated
  - Escort his mother to her seat and join his groomsmen at the top of the aisle
  - Participate in the processional, e.g. officiant is followed by the groom, his groomsmen, the bridesmaids, etc
  - Walk with the bride down the aisle

- ☐ Ensure the bride does not arrive early or before the groom
    - Have a family member confirm when the groom has arrived at the ceremony venue

- ☐ Have your maid of honour complete the following upon arrival
    - Arrange your skirt, train and veil
    - Check your make-up and hair
    - Hand the rings to the ring bearer (if not already done)

- ☐ Ensure your bridesmaids, flower girls and pageboys stand in order at the ceremony entrance

## Processional

- ☐ Select an escort for the bride

| | |
|---|---|
| Father | Son |
| Mother | Daughter |
| Both parents | Groom |
| Stepfather | Other family member |
| Brother | Close friend |
| Sister | Other … |

- ☐ Have the bride take the escort's right arm

- ☐ Appoint a helper to signal the processional music to begin

- ☐ Have the groom, best man and groomsmen stand and face guests when the processional music begins

- ☐ Have your officiant signal the congregation to rise

- ☐ Determine your processional order
    - __ Bridesmaids, e.g. in reverse order with your maid of honour being last
    - __ Flower girls
    - __ Ring bearer
    - __ Bride and her escort
    - __ Pageboys

- ☐ Consider the following alternatives to a traditional processional
    - Bridesmaids walk in pairs
    - Bridesmaids and child attendants walk in pairs
    - Bridesmaids and groomsmen walk in pairs
    - Include parents
    - Include grandparents

- ☐ If your ceremony venue has two aisles, decide how you will use each
    - Processional to use one aisle and recessional to use the other
    - Bridesmaids to use one aisle and groomsmen to use the other

- [ ] Walk down the aisle with your escort
  - Walk at a slow pace
  - Smile
  - Walk with good posture
  - Try to relax
- [ ] Ensure the groom looks at his bride as she makes her way down the aisle
- [ ] Have the bride stand to the left of the groom
- [ ] Face the officiant
- [ ] Have your maid of honour arrange your skirt, train and veil
- [ ] Have your ring bearer present the rings (if not presenting at the ring exchange)
  - Have the ring bearer place the rings on the altar
  - Have your best man present the wedding band and take a step to the side and slightly behind the groom
- [ ] Try your best not to fidget or appear nervous once the proceedings begin

## Welcome

- [ ] Have your officiant perform the following
  - Welcome guests on behalf of the couple
  - Introduce him or herself
  - Highlight the significance of marriage
  - Ask if anyone present objects to the marriage
  - State opening remarks, e.g. the call to worship
  - Deliver an opening prayer if you are including religious or spiritual aspects

## Congregation is Seated

- [ ] Have your officiant instruct guests to be seated

## Presentation of the Bride

- [ ] Have your officiant ask the bride's escort to present the bride with one of the following questions
  - Who blesses this union?
  - Who brings this woman to be married?
  - Who gives this woman to be married to this man?
  - Who gives this woman to this man?
  - Who presents this bride for marriage?
- [ ] Have the bride's escort reply 'I do' or a variation, e.g. 'Her mother and I do'

- ☐ Have the bride's escort lift the bride's veil (alternatively, the groom can do this just before the first kiss)
- ☐ Have the bride's escort kiss and hug the bride and shake the groom's hand
- ☐ Have the bride's escort take a seat next to the bride's mother

## Introduction

- ☐ Have your officiant narrate the following
  - How you first met
  - How you fell in love
  - The proposal details
  - Why you are getting married
  - How you will strive to make your marriage work
  - Other …
- ☐ Arrange for a hymn or worship song, if desired
- ☐ Have your junior attendants move to their allocated seating or with their parents

## Charge to the Bride and Groom

- ☐ Have your officiant direct a charge to you both
  - Remind you that the wedding commitment is of a serious nature
  - Remind you of your duties and roles in the marriage
  - Outline the significance and magnitude of your vows
  - Declare that you recognise the importance of your commitment
  - Announce that you are devoted to honouring the commitment for the rest of your lives
  - Other …

## Readings

- ☐ Arrange for 2–3 readings
- ☐ Select people to deliver readings that are special to you as a couple
- ☐ Select the type of readings that you will include
  - Passages
  - Scriptures
  - Poems
  - Verses
  - Excerpts from literature
  - A reading written by yourself
  - A reading written by a close friend or family member

- [ ] Ensure the readings are both meaningful and appropriate for the ceremony venue

- [ ] Have your readings focus on marriage and togetherness

- [ ] Refer to your officiant for suggestions and where to look for readings

- [ ] Have your officiant provide a homily (a short sermon)

## Declaration of Intent to Marry

- [ ] Have your officiant provide a statement expressing the declaration of intent to marry as outlined by the Marriage Act

- [ ] Have your officiant ask if each of you has come of your own free will to marry, e.g. 'Will you have this woman to be your wife?' and 'Will you have this man to be your husband?'

- [ ] Both reply to the question with 'I do' or 'I will'

## Vow Exchange

- [ ] Select the type of vows you will read
    - Traditional
    - Traditional with some personal additions
    - Tailored to you both
    - Written by each of you

- [ ] Determine if you and your fiancé will read the same or different vows

- [ ] If you and your fiancé are writing your own vows, begin writing them eight weeks in advance
    - Read over sample wedding vows online, in books or from your officiant

*View the extensive list of 'Words for Ceremonial Vows' found at www.TheWeddingChecklist.com.au*

- [ ] Select items to include in your vows
    - Passage
    - Poem
    - Verse
    - Excerpt from literature
    - Cultural traditions
    - Religious customs
    - Your personal beliefs about marriage
    - Mention special people, e.g. children, close family members

- [ ] Have someone read over your written vows
    - Ask them to make corrections and suggestions
    - Select a second person to read over your final version

- ☐ Have your officiant approve your vows

- ☐ Decide how you will deliver your vows on the day
    - Repeat your officiant
    - Read from handheld notes
    - Recite from memory
    - Deliver in more than one language
    - Other …

- ☐ Ensure you and your fiancé both take a copy of your vows to the ceremony
    - Place a spare copy of each in the wedding emergency kit

- ☐ Have your officiant ask you to face each other and join hands for your ceremony vows

- ☐ Have your maid of honour hold the bridal bouquet

## *Wedding Vow Top Tips*
- Be passionate and sincere
- Write from your heart
- Keep it short (it's about quality not quantity)
- Be creative, e.g. use your favourite musician as inspiration
- Ensure they are positive

## Ring Exchange

- ☐ Have the ring bearer present the wedding bands to your officiant at a prearranged moment

- ☐ Have your officiant explain the significance of your wedding rings

- ☐ Have your officiant bless/honour your wedding bands
    - Have your officiant pass the rings around for your guests to bless or make a wish for you

- ☐ Have your officiant pass the bride's wedding ring to the groom
    - The groom places the wedding ring halfway along the fourth finger of the bride's left hand
    - The groom makes his promise to the bride
    - The groom pushes the ring all the way on

- ☐ Have your officiant pass the groom's wedding ring to the bride
    - The bride places the wedding ring halfway along the fourth finger of the groom's left hand
    - The bride responds with the same promise to the groom
    - The bride pushes the ring all the way on

☐ Consider the following alternatives to exchanging rings
  - Covenant of salt or sand
  - Hand fasting
  - Planting seeds
  - Sand pouring
  - Sharing a glass of wine
  - Unity candle

*These unity rituals can be included as well as exchanging rings.*

## Ritual or Symbolic Act

☐ Select a ritual or symbolic ceremony to include in your wedding ceremony
  - Breaking of the glass
  - Candle lighting e.g. unity candle, family unity candle
  - Communion
  - Family medallion ceremony
  - Hand ceremony
  - Hand fasting ceremony
  - Irish wedding bell
  - Jumping the broom
  - Mass
  - Rose ceremony
  - Sand ceremony
  - Sharing of wine
  - Unity bowl
  - Wishing stone ceremony
  - Other …

*Find definitions and explanations of each ritual or symbolic act at www.TheWeddingChecklist.com.au*

## Conclusion

☐ Have your officiant give a short address
  - A piece of literature or a poem
  - Closing words and/or prayers
  - Benediction (blessing)

## Declaration of Marriage

☐ Have your officiant pronounce you as husband and wife
  - Proclaim that you are married
  - Signal you to share your first kiss

# First Kiss

☐ The groom lifts the bride's veil (if not already done)

☐ Share your first kiss as a married couple
　　Step toward each other
　　Decide where you will put your hands
　　Move your heads toward each other slowly
　　Take your time, e.g. a few seconds

☐ Share a short second kiss

# Signing of the Register

☐ Have your selected reading or music piece begin for the signing of the register

☐ Move to the place where you will be signing the marriage documents

☐ Have your officiant, two witnesses, photographer and videographer join you

☐ Sign your marriage documents

☐ Pose for photographs with your marriage certificate
　　Hold the marriage certificate together

☐ Have your maid of honour return your bouquet after the signing of the register

# Presentation

☐ Have your officiant provide words before your presentation
　　Pray for you
　　Offer good wishes to you as a newly married couple
　　Congratulate you as newlyweds

☐ Have your officiant present you to your guests with your new names and titles
　　Ensure your officiant knows what you would both like to be called once married
　　Ensure your officiant knows the correct pronunciation

☐ Arrange for items to be released
　　Butterflies
　　Doves
　　Fireworks
　　Helium balloons
　　Sky lanterns

*Consider council restrictions before planning this aspect.*

# Recessional

- ☐ Have your recessional music begin

- ☐ Ensure you link arms with your husband
    - Take your husband's left arm

- ☐ Have your officiant ask guests to rise and applaud

- ☐ Determine your recessional order
    - __ Bride and groom
    - __ Pageboys
    - __ Flower girls
    - __ Ring bearer
    - __ Maid of honour and best man
    - __ Bridesmaids and groomsmen in pairs
    - __ Bride's parents
    - __ Groom's parents
    - __ Honoured guests
    - __ Guests (guided by ushers one row at a time)

- ☐ Decide how you will exit the wedding ceremony
    - Walk slowly and savour your first few moments of marriage
    - Hug, kiss and thank each guest as you vacate
    - Dance down the aisle
    - Have a salute or military exit
    - Other …

- ☐ Arrange for guests to congratulate you using one of the following:

| | |
|---|---|
| Bells | Poppers |
| Bird seed | Rice (uncooked) |
| Bubbles | Sparklers |
| Confetti | Streamers |
| Flower petals | Whistles |
| Other … | |

*Check if there are council restrictions for using these items.*

# Shortly after the Ceremony

- ☐ Have a group photo taken at or outside the ceremony venue before guests disperse

- ☐ Ensure the bride and groom leave the ceremony location first

- ☐ Have your driver provide snacks and drinks for the bridal party

- ☐ Have your ushers ensure that no one has left anything at the ceremony venue

☐ Have your ushers take flower arrangements from the ceremony venue to be placed at the reception venue

☐ Provide entertainment for your guests if there will be a long wait between your ceremony and reception
    Provide music and/or entertainment
    Serve drinks
    Serve nibbles
    Suggest nearby amusements, e.g. park, beach, zoo, botanical gardens

*Find a detailed list of entertainment ideas on page 215.*

## Personalising your Ceremony

☐ Include your children in the ceremony

☐ Remember loved ones with a memorial tribute
    Add their favourite flower or herb to your bouquet
    Include a floral wreath
    Light a candle
    Place their photograph on the altar
    Play their favourite song or piece of music
    Refer to them in a reading
    Wear a memento
    Write a tribute in your wedding programs
    Other …

☐ Honour special people who couldn't attend with:
    A piece of music    Scripture
    Poem    Song
    Reading    Other …

☐ Include family heirlooms in the ceremony
    Brooch    Piece of clothing
    Coat of arms    Piece of linen
    Cufflinks    Small piece of furniture
    Family clock    Watch
    Jewellery, e.g. a ring, necklace, earrings    Other …

☐ Include elements from each of your cultures in the ceremony

☐ Surprise your fiancé at the ceremony with a:
    Love letter    Reading
    Piece of music    Short passage
    Poem    Song
    Quote    Other …

*Ensure your officiant knows of your plans.*

# 26

# Reception: Sequence of Events

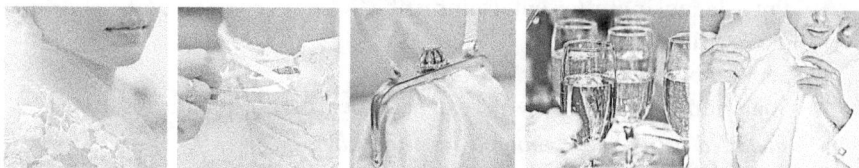

The hard work is finally over and now it's time to party. Right? Well, if you are organised this will be the case. Researching, organising, delegating and planning your reception to the minute will free up the night for you to celebrate and enjoy yourself.

## Typical Reception Sequence of Events

1. Pre-reception drinks and appetisers
2. Guests enter and are seated in reception room
3. Bridal party grand entrance
4. Blessing by your officiant
5. Toast to the bride and groom
6. Toast to the parents
7. Entrees served
8. Main meal served
9. Tables cleared and champagne served
10. Speeches delivered
11. Cake cutting
12. Cake served
13. First dance
14. Father–daughter dance
15. Mother–son dance
16. Bridal party dance
17. Open dancing
18. Dessert and coffee served
19. Dancing continues
20. Bouquet toss
21. Garter toss
22. Bride and groom send-off

☐ Select the events you want to take place and estimate the beginning and end time

  Give a copy of your reception sequence of events to your MC and reception manager

☐ At the reception, have your MC and reception manager monitor the time and ensure the reception stays on schedule

## Grand Entrance

☐ Ensure the hosts of the reception arrive first

☐ Have your guests wait in the bar/foyer until they are advised to enter the reception area

☐ Change your gown and hairstyle before the reception

☐ Assemble your receiving line (a line to welcome guests)
    Bride and groom
    Bride, groom and attendants
    Bride, groom and both sets of parents

☐ Ensure your photographer and videographer are ready for your entrance

☐ Select how you will enter the reception room
    Dancing
    Elaborate double door entrance
    Motorcycle
    Red carpet entrance
    Themed entrance
    Through a decorated archway
    To live music, e.g. bagpipes
    Via a grand staircase
    Other …

☐ Select who your MC (Master of Ceremonies) will announce
    Bride and groom only
    The attendants and the bride and groom
    Both sets of parents, the attendants and the bride and groom
    Children of the bride and groom, the attendants and the bride and groom
    Other …

☐ Ensure your MC is comfortable with the pronunciation of all names
    Inform your MC of your new (married) names

☐ Have your attendants stand behind their seats until you are announced

☐ Give your MC written instructions of your order of entry as well as the sequence of events

## Speakers, Speeches and Toasts

An MC or toastmaster can make a huge impact on your wedding reception. Select an MC with a strong, clear voice with plenty of confidence and good humour. Their fresh and energised temperament should set the mood and help everyone have a good time while not detracting focus from the newlyweds.

☐ Appoint an MC
    Attendant                Hired professional
    Friend or family member    Trained public speaker
    Parent of the bride        Venue manager
    Parent of the groom       DJ

*You can appoint more than one person to share the tasks of the MC.*

- ☐ Ensure your MC is:
    - A creative thinker (and can think on their feet)
    - Adaptable
    - Entertaining
    - Enthusiastic
    - Flexible to your needs
    - Trustworthy
    - Willing to follow your instructions and satisfy your requests

- ☐ Have your MC confirm their main responsibilities
    - Make sure the reception runs on time
    - Liaise with speech makers throughout the night, e.g. remind them to use the bathroom 10 minutes before they are to begin
    - Other …

- ☐ Complete the wedding vendor checklist for your wedding MC on pages 10 and 11

- ☐ Select what your MC will announce
    - Inform guests when to be seated
    - Announce the entrance of the bridal party
    - Announce the bridal couple's entrance
    - Provide a welcome speech
    - Introduce toast makers
    - Grace (if your officiant is not in attendance)
    - Introduce speech makers
    - Thank each speech maker and introduce the next
    - Announce the cake cutting
    - Toast the bride and groom
    - Invite guests to gather around the dance floor for the first dance
    - Announce each attendant as they enter the dance floor
    - Invite all guests to share the dance floor
    - Pass to the DJ for requests
    - Announce last songs and drinks
    - Provide a goodnight announcement

- ☐ Select what you would like the MC to include in their opening speech
    - Welcome guests
    - Introduce themselves
    - Introduce the bride and groom
    - Introduce the photographer and videographer
    - Set the scene
    - Outline the order of events
    - Explain how the food will be served and when the meal will begin
    - Housekeeping, e.g. toilet locations, designated smoking areas
    - When the bride and groom will depart
    - Other …

- ☐ Inform your MC of any other particulars that you would like announced, e.g. gifts to be placed on the gift table

- ☐ Select what you would like included when the MC introduces speech time
  - Guests to face the bridal table
  - Guests to turn phones and other devices to silent
  - Compliments to the chef
  - Other …

- ☐ Select what you would like included in the goodnight announcement
  - Refer to driving safely home
  - Thanks to everyone for making the reception a success
  - Where partygoers can go to continue their night
  - Other …

- ☐ Ensure your MC will be wearing appropriate attire and shoes

- ☐ Decide when the main speeches will be
  - Before the meal
  - During the meal
  - Between the main meal and cake
  - After dessert
  - Spread throughout the reception, e.g. between courses
  - Other …

- ☐ Select your speech makers
  - Bride
  - Groom
  - Best man
  - Groomsmen
  - Maid of honour
  - Bridesmaids
  - Father of the bride
  - Father of the groom
  - Mother of the bride
  - Mother of the groom
  - Close family members
  - Your children
  - Officiant
  - Other …

*Aim for no more than eight speeches.*

- ☐ Inform each speaker that you would like their participation
  - Ensure they are comfortable with public speaking and actually willing to make a speech

- ☐ Advise each speaker what you expect of them
  - A brief speech, e.g. a maximum of five minutes
  - Humorous but not offensive
  - Other …

- ☐ Inform speech makers of any points which are off-limits, e.g. family divorce, feuds, topics which may offend certain guests

☐ Decide what you will include in your speech
　　Compliment the groom
　　Acknowledge the help given to you by your attendants
　　Toast the flower girls, pageboys and ring bearer
　　Pay tribute to your parents and family
　　Thank the groom's family for their support
　　Thank everybody for their kind wishes, gifts and cards
　　Thank florist, caterers, baker, etc
　　Thank anyone else who has contributed to the wedding
　　Other …

☐ Decide what the groom will include in his speech
　　Thank the mother and father of the bride for supporting the marriage
　　Pay tribute to his own parents and family
　　Thank guests for attending
　　Compliment the bride
　　Acknowledge the help given to him by his attendants
　　Toast the bridesmaids
　　Present gifts to the attendants
　　Other …

☐ Talk with the father of the bride and decide what he will include in his speech
　　How proud he and his wife are of their daughter
　　Relate to the bride's family life and growing up
　　Welcome his new son-in-law
　　Welcome the parents of the groom
　　Provide words of wisdom and well wishes to the bride and groom
　　Emphasise his confidence in their future
　　Toast the bride and groom
　　Other …

☐ Talk with the best man and decide what he will include in his speech
　　Thank the groom for appointing him as the best man
　　Compliment the bride and groom
　　Compliment and toast the bridesmaids
　　Respond on behalf of bridesmaids
　　Provide an informal story about the groom
　　Discuss highlights of the bridal couple's relationship
　　Read emails and letters from guests who were unable to attend
　　Grant the bride and groom good wishes for their future together
　　Toast the bride and groom's families
　　Other …

☐ Have speakers liaise with each other so they don't double up

☐ Organise microphones and speakers for speech makers

☐ Provide an 'open microphone' after your prearranged speeches
    Have your MC monitor the open mic session

☐ Inform your waitstaff or ushers to:
    Fill and distribute toasting glasses just before the speeches and toasts begin
    Deliver water to speech makers

## Top Tips for Speech Makers

- Be sincere
- Don't offend or embarrass anyone
- Draft and memorise your speech well in advance
- Rehearse, rehearse, rehearse
- Use cue cards if needed
- Speak slowly and clearly
- Look at the audience when speaking
- Do not drink too much alcohol prior to your speech if it may hinder your performance

## Meal and Mingling

☐ Have your officiant say grace before the meal, if desired
    Have your MC or father of the bride say grace if your officiant is not attending the reception

☐ Ensure you, the bridal couple, begin your meal first

☐ Spend some time with your guests at the reception
    Visit each guest table throughout the night and thank everyone for attending
    Stay put and let guests come to you (great for stand up receptions)

☐ Encourage your friends and family to mingle
    Inform your ushers or attendants that you would like their help with this

☐ Throughout the reception have attendants and guests tap a toasting glass with a spoon to signal you to kiss

☐ Take a few minutes to watch your guests partying

☐ Take a few minutes during the night to be alone with your new husband

## Cutting the Cake

☐ Decide when the cake cutting will be
    After the last speech
    After your grand entrance, if your photographer is only attending the beginning of the reception
    Other …

☐ Have your MC announce the cake cutting
    Gather guests in a circle around the cake table
    Invite guests to make a wish for the bride and groom
    Invite guests to take photos after the professional photographer

☐ Cut your wedding cake
    The bride and groom stand behind the cake table
    The bride picks up the knife
    The bride holds the cake knife with her right hand, the groom's right hand is placed on top and the bride's left on top of that and the groom's left hand underneath
    Ensure your rings are in view
    Pose for photographs
    Cut the first slice of cake together

☐ Share the first slice by feeding each other a small piece

☐ Have your caterers take the cake away for portioning and distribution

## Dancing

☐ Attend dancing lessons with a:
    Choreographer
    Dance instructor
    Dance school
    Family member
    Friend

☐ Decide how many lessons you will need, e.g. four × one-hour sessions

☐ Purchase learn-to-dance aids
    Books
    Dance software
    Instructional DVDs
    Internet videos, e.g. YouTube

☐ Select when you will have your first dance
    After the cake is cut
    After your grand entrance, if you wish for guests to dance before the main meal or if your photographer is only staying for the beginning of the reception

- ☐ If you want guests to dance throughout the reception have your DJ invite them to dance at the beginning as they may be waiting for your first dance before they will use the dancefloor

- ☐ Allocate helpers to clear space for the dance floor

- ☐ Have your MC introduce the wedding dances
  - Invite guests to stand around the dance floor
  - Announce each pair of dancers as they enter the dance floor
  - Invite all guests to share the dance floor

- ☐ Decide which dances will be performed and the order
  - Bride and groom (first dance)
  - Bride's parents and groom's parents enter the dance floor and they dance
  - Bride dances with her father (father–daughter dance)
  - Groom dances with his mother-in-law
  - Groom's parents continue dancing together
  - Bride dances with her father-in-law
  - Groom dances with his mother (mother–son dance)
  - Bride's parents rejoin and dance together
  - Wedding attendants join in
  - Guests join the dancing (open dancing)

*Allow your attendants to dance with a partner of their choice rather than having them dance together, particularly if you only have one of each.*

- ☐ Choose a first dance style
  - Bollywood
  - Cha-cha
  - Disco
  - Foxtrot
  - Freestyle
  - Mambo
  - Quickstep
  - Rumba
  - Other …
  - Salsa
  - Samba
  - Slow rhythm dance
  - Swing
  - Tango
  - Two-step
  - Viennese waltz
  - Waltz

- ☐ Select an alternative to a traditional first dance
  - Have your attendants and guests dance with you from the beginning
  - Perform a choreographed dance with your attendants
  - Perform a duet
  - Play a piece of music together (if you play instruments)
  - Play a photo slideshow of your lives with your wedding song playing in the background
  - Provide a dance lesson for your guests

☐ Select other cultural or special dances
- Anniversary dance
- Children's dance
- Farewell dance
- Gladdening of the bride
- Horah
- Kalamatiano
- Krenzl
- Mizinke
- Money dance (dollar dance)
- Pani Mloda
- Snowball dance
- Tsamiko
- Tsifteteli
- Veil dance
- Wish dance
- Zembekiko

## Bouquet Toss

☐ Prepare for the bouquet toss
- Gather your throwing posy
- Have your MC gather unmarried women
- Gain some height, e.g. from a step or a stage
- Turn around so your back is facing the crowd
- Throw your bouquet over your shoulder

## Garter Toss

☐ Prepare for the garter toss
- Have a helper to bring a chair to the dance floor after the bouquet toss
- Have your MC gather unmarried men and invite the bride to sit on the chair
- The groom removes the bride's garter
- The groom flings the garter to the single men

## Send-off

☐ Change into your going-away outfit
- Have your maid of honour help you to do this

☐ Decide how you will depart the wedding reception
- Farewell arch
- Farewell circle
- Farewell dance
- Guard of honour
- Move to each table and say goodbye to your guests
- Sky lantern send-off
- Sparklers send-off
- Other …

- ☐ Enlist a friend or family member to drive you to your first night accommodation
    - Remind your new husband to carry you over the threshold
    - Organise for someone to collect your wedding attire from first night accommodation if you are going straight to your honeymoon

- ☐ Have your DJ or MC inform guests what to do once you have left

- ☐ Decide not to have a send-off
    - Provide a welcome circle at the beginning of the reception instead of a farewell circle
    - Stay at the reception and party until the very end

*Inform guests who might like to leave early that you will be staying until the end.*

## After the Reception

- ☐ Organise for your wedding centrepieces and main decorations to be given to special guests
    - Attendants
    - Helpers
    - Close family
    - Close friends
    - Other ...

- ☐ Give a trusted family member or friend a list of items to take home after the reception
    - Bridal bouquet
    - Cake topper
    - Decorations, e.g. flowers, centrepieces
    - Gifts
    - Guestbook
    - Horseshoes
    - Seating chart, place cards, table names
    - Sheet music
    - Speech notes
    - Wedding emergency kit
    - Other ...

- ☐ Have your parents or head attendants ensure your guests haven't left anything behind

- ☐ Have your wedding hosts settle outstanding accounts at the end of the reception
    - Organise for tips to be distributed last

- ☐ Ensure your wedding hosts leave the reception last

- ☐ Organise an after-party
  - Change your outfits
  - Have your bridal party change their outfits

- ☐ Decide where you will have the after-party
  - At the beach with a bonfire
  - Club or bar
  - Family member or friend's hotel room
  - Family member or friend's home
  - First night accommodation
  - First night hotel, e.g. pool area, barbecue area, games room
  - Other …

*You will be tired from the long day so don't feel compelled to party on.*

- ☐ Plan for a catch up with attendants, close family, helpers and travelling guests the next day, e.g. brunch, lunch, group activity

- ☐ Arrange for a gift opening party
  - Plan this for after your honeymoon
  - Invite attendants, close family and friends

- ☐ Remove stains from your wedding attire as soon as possible
  - Arrange for a friend or family member to do this if you are going straight to your honeymoon

- ☐ Preserve your wedding attire
  - Have your gown professionally cleaned
  - Have your gown restored
  - Purchase a storage and preservation box
  - Place acid-free tissue paper in-between the folds of your gown
  - Have your veil, shoes, hat and bag professionally cleaned

- ☐ If hired, arrange for your wedding gown to be returned

- ☐ Preserve your bouquet and mount in a bouquet shadow box

- ☐ Create a portfolio or decorate a storage box to store keepsakes and objects with sentimental value
  - Bridal bouquet ribbon
  - Bow tie
  - Cake topper
  - Cufflinks
  - Decorations
  - Emails from absent guests
  - Garter
  - Guestbook
  - Horseshoes
  - Invitation
  - Menu

Napkins
Personalised clothing
Photographs
Place cards
Printed copy of your wedding website
Sheet music
Shoes
Speech notes
This book
Vows
Wedding DVD
Wedding file
Other …

## Top Tips for After the Wedding

- Contact friends and family who didn't attend to share your details and memories of the day
- Write a note to both sets of parents and your attendants thanking them for all of their support
- Write a letter of thanks to vendors who were exceptional
- Allow your engaged friends and family to look through this book
- Create a scrapbook of the day
- If you choose not to preserve your wedding gown, dye or alter it so you can wear it again
- Frame your favourite photographs and display around your home

# 27
# Honeymoon

Your honeymoon is about spending uninterrupted time together to relax and unwind after the stress of your wedding. Whether you are planning to travel around the world or stay local, the best advice is to make bookings early for the best choices and discounts.

## Finding the Perfect Honeymoon Spot

☐ Discuss your dream honeymoon destination with your fiancé

☐ Decide what type of holiday appeals to both of you

| | |
|---|---|
| Adventurous | Luxurious |
| All-inclusive | Pampering |
| Camping | Quiet and relaxing |
| Cultural | Romantic |
| Eco friendly | Sporty |
| Exotic | Tropical |
| Fairytale | Touring |
| Family | Volunteering |
| Other ... | |

☐ Select an accommodation type

| | |
|---|---|
| Beach house | Houseboat |
| Bush cottage | Island resort |
| City apartment | Motorhome |
| Countryside inn | Mountain chalet |
| Cruise ship | Rainforest bungalow |
| Eco lodge | Riverside hotel |
| Farm stay | Rustic cabin |
| Forest retreat | Ski lodge |
| Health retreat | Spa resort |
| Other ... | |

☐ Select from the following honeymoon activities

| | |
|---|---|
| Bush walking | City tour |
| Caravanning | Cruising |

| Cycling/bike tour | River rafting |
| Four-wheel driving | Safari |
| Golf | Sailing |
| Health and beauty treatments | Scuba diving |
| Horse riding | Shopping |
| Island tours | Sight-seeing |
| Kayaking | Skiing |
| Motorbiking | Snowboarding |
| Mountain biking | Sports |
| Mountain climbing | Swimming |
| Music festival | Tasting, e.g. food, wine |
| Other … | |

## Top 10 Honeymoon Hotspots

- British Isles
- Canadian Rockies
- Caribbean
- Fiji
- French Riviera

- Great Barrier Reef
- Hawaii
- Maldives
- Mexico
- Rome

## Research and Decisions

☐ Determine when you will leave for your honeymoon
  - Immediately after the wedding reception
  - The day after the wedding
  - Several days after the wedding
  - Postponed to a later date

☐ Decide how long you will spend on your honeymoon

☐ Decide how far you would like to travel
  - Local
  - Regional
  - Interstate
  - International

☐ Consult a travel agent to assist you with your honeymoon plans
  - Accommodation
  - Activities
  - Car hire
  - Creating your itinerary
  - Flights
  - Industry discounts
  - Knowledge of the location/insider information
  - Support while on your honeymoon

- ☐ Tour packages
- ☐ Transfers
- ☐ Travel insurance

☐ Complete the wedding vendor checklist for your travel agent on pages 10 and 11

☐ Research the possibility of inclement weather
- ☐ Cyclones/hurricanes
- ☐ Freezing temperatures and extreme cold
- ☐ Gloomy weather
- ☐ High humidity
- ☐ Intense heat
- ☐ Rainy seasons
- ☐ Storms
- ☐ Other …

☐ Research your chosen honeymoon destination
- ☐ Browse travel brochures and magazines
- ☐ Discuss your plans with family, friends, work colleagues or neighbours who have been to your destination
- ☐ Obtain advice from your travel agent
- ☐ Purchase a guidebook
- ☐ Search online

☐ Search online for up-to-date reviews and blogs on the following
- ☐ Car hire
- ☐ Destinations
- ☐ Flights
- ☐ Holiday packages
- ☐ Hotels
- ☐ Resorts
- ☐ Restaurants
- ☐ Shopping
- ☐ Things to do
- ☐ Transport
- ☐ Weather
- ☐ Other …

☐ If you are visiting another country, check with the embassy for advice on travelling to your chosen location
- ☐ Contact the consulate of the destination country
- ☐ Contact the tourist board of the destination country

☐ Obtain health and hygiene advice on the destination from your doctor or the Department of Health
- ☐ Food and drinking water standards
- ☐ General hygiene
- ☐ Preventative measures
- ☐ Vaccinations
- ☐ Other …

☐ Investigate customs and etiquette of your honeymoon location

| | |
|---|---|
| Body language | Laws |
| Dress | Meeting and greeting |
| Drinking | Personal space |
| Eating and dining | Public behaviour |
| Language | Tipping |

## Itinerary

☐ Plan and book tours and activities
    Conduct online research
    Obtain a list from your travel agent
    Obtain a list from your accommodation manager

☐ Create an itinerary – be sure to leave plenty of time to relax together!

☐ Include a list of honeymoon locations and emergency phone numbers

☐ Make copies of your itinerary, locations and emergency phone numbers
    Pack a copy in your hand luggage
    Pack a copy in your checked luggage
    Give a copy to two sets of people

## Passport and Legal Documents

☐ Make all travel arrangements in your maiden or passport name and officially change your name once you arrive home

☐ Apply for a passport
    Allow at least three months for the application process

☐ Update passports
    Allow at least three months for the updating process

*Some countries require that you have more than six months validity on your passport by the end of your visit.*

☐ Apply for the necessary travel visas

☐ Arrange travel insurance
    Obtain professional advice in regards to the type and level of cover you will need
    Ensure that medical insurance is included in your travel insurance policy

☐ Give photocopies of your passports to a trusted friend or family member

## Money

☐ Begin saving for your honeymoon
*Refer to page 25 for a detailed honeymoon budget.*

- ☐ Set aside a portion of your honeymoon funds for spending money
- ☐ Budget for extra travel costs, e.g. taxi fares, airport transfers
- ☐ Ensure your credit cards and debit cards will work in the honeymoon region
  - ☐ Pay off your credit cards in advance for honeymoon spending
- ☐ Obtain foreign currency
- ☐ Pre-pay personal and household bills that may arrive during your honeymoon

## Items to Organise

- ☐ Apply for recreational leave from your workplace
  - ☐ Before the wedding
  - ☐ The wedding day
  - ☐ The honeymoon
  - ☐ Time after to recover
- ☐ Organise childminding for when you are on your honeymoon
- ☐ Organise pet boarding for when you are on your honeymoon
  - ☐ Kennel
  - ☐ Cattery
  - ☐ Neighbours
  - ☐ Friends
  - ☐ Family
  - ☐ House-sitter
- ☐ Organise a house-sitter for when you are on your honeymoon
- ☐ Organise a mail hold with your local post office
  - ☐ Start the mail hold on the day of your wedding
  - ☐ Start the mail hold on the first day of your honeymoon
  - ☐ Ensure your mail is held in both your maiden and married names
- ☐ Organise for a neighbour to put out and bring in your garbage bins
- ☐ Prepare and freeze meals to have when you arrive home
- ☐ Turn on your home phone answering machine
- ☐ Have your mobile phone set to global roaming
  - ☐ Check with your service provider about cost
- ☐ Organise for airport transfers to and from home

## Packing

- ☐ Determine the amount of luggage you can each take on your honeymoon
  - ☐ Hand luggage
  - ☐ Checked luggage
- ☐ Review hand luggage and checked luggage guidelines, e.g. weight limits
- ☐ Purchase bags and suitcases

- [ ] Purchase luggage accessories
  - Anti-tamper tags
  - Elastic luggage straps
  - Name and address tags
  - Padlock sets
  - Portable luggage scale
  - Other …

- [ ] Purchase a secure travel wallet for storing travel documents

- [ ] Go shopping with your fiancé for honeymoon outfits and accessories

- [ ] Pack your suitcases well in advance so you can focus on the wedding day
  - Pack non-essential items up to a month before

- [ ] Consider the following items when packing for your honeymoon:
  - Clothing, e.g. formalwear, casual clothing, pyjamas, swimwear
  - Underwear
  - Footwear (consider weather and activities)
  - Warm items, e.g. scarves, earmuffs, gloves, boots
  - Sun protection, e.g. hats, sunscreen, sunglasses
  - Beach towels
  - Toiletries
  - Medication (order in advance and obtain a doctor's note explaining large amounts of medication for Customs officials)
  - Insect repellent
  - Activity-related items, e.g. surfing, snorkelling, hiking, swimming gear
  - Camera, batteries and memory cards
  - Video camera and equipment
  - Battery rechargers
  - Universal travel power adapter
  - Stationery, e.g. pens, paper, envelopes
  - Reading material
  - Travel pillows
  - Other …

- [ ] Send honeymoon luggage to your first night accommodation

## Honeymoon Top Tips

- Research low season discounts
- Travel on a weekday if it is more economical
- If your flight is early in the morning, reserve accommodation near the airport for the night before
- Confirm flight information the night before to check for delays
- Have the groom or hotel manager decorate the honeymoon suite with rose petals, candles and chocolates
- Advise your accommodation that you are honeymooners; often you will receive complementary champagne and fruit
- Take time after your honeymoon to recover

# 28

# When Things don't go to Plan

No matter how much you try, your wedding might not be perfect – things may go wrong. The key is to be prepared and plan for the unexpected.

☐ Consult with your officiant or wedding coordinator if you have any concerns or problems with the ceremony

☐ Consult with your reception manager or wedding coordinator if you have any concerns or problems with the reception

☐ Contact your vendors if you are dissatisfied with their service
    Explain your concerns or problems
    Ask for a reduction in the bill
    Place a complaint
    Follow up with a letter or phone call to the company manager

## What Can Go Wrong on the Day

☐ Accept that mishaps will happen

☐ Be prepared for wedding day mishaps
    Write lists
    Rehearse
    Have back-up plans
    Carry an emergency kit

☐ Nominate a close friend or family member who is not an attendant to handle problems on the day
    Have them answer your phone
    Have them determine if there is something that can be done
    Have them solve the problem if they can, or come up with a way around the problem

☐ Review each of the following common wedding day mishaps
    Decide how you would deal with each one if it happened on your wedding day

# Top 50 Wedding Day Mishaps

1. You look tired from not sleeping the night before
2. You don't like the look of your make-up or hairstyle
3. You or your attendants have make-up issues, e.g. it is melting in the heat
4. Your hairstyle drops
5. There are problems with your own or your attendants' attire, e.g. tears
6. The bride or bridesmaid gowns become dirty or stained
7. The attire doesn't fit the bride, groom, attendants or junior attendants
8. You have shoe issues, e.g. your shoes become increasingly uncomfortable
9. An attendant or key helper does not turn up
10. A young attendant decides not to cooperate
11. The ring bearer forgets the rings or the rings go missing
12. Your attendants argue with each other
13. Your ushers or helpers are not doing their assigned tasks
14. Your florist does not deliver your exact order
15. Your flowers wilt and droop
16. The wedding transport breaks down
17. A large number of guests do not turn up
18. Too many guests turn up
19. The bride, groom or an attendant is feeling unwell
20. The bride, groom or an attendant drinks too much before the ceremony
21. The bride, groom or an attendant falls or trips at a critical moment
22. You, or your fiancé, get the giggles at the ceremony
23. Someone objects to or interrupts the ceremony
24. You can't get the rings to fit when exchanging rings
25. One of your readers or speech makers gets stage fright
26. There is an accident with a candle at the ceremony or reception
27. An unexpected weather change stops you from carrying out your perfect day
28. You are running late and the schedule falls very behind
29. One of your vendors does not show up
30. You don't have enough cash to pay a vendor on the day
31. Your photographer puts you in positions that you don't like
32. There is confusion with the ceremony or reception venue booking
33. Uninvited guests turn up to the reception
34. The food is not up to standard, e.g. main meals are cold
35. Guests complain that there is not enough food or drink
36. A guest or many guests have a reaction to the food
37. A speech maker says something inappropriate or talks for too long
38. An attendant or a guest becomes intoxicated and causes a scene
39. Someone gets injured while dancing
40. The reception room is not arranged as you requested
41. The air conditioner or heater breaks down
42. There is a power outage
43. The reception room is too small for the number of guests

44. The DJ doesn't play the requested music
45. Your entertainer proves to be non-entertaining
46. Your musicians or singers sound off-key
47. Music, audio, photography, kitchen or other equipment malfunctions
48. Gifts go missing
49. There are issues with the look of the cake, e.g. it is slanting
50. The cake doesn't provide enough portions for every guest

## Rescheduling your Wedding

☐ Inform your guests as soon as possible that you are rescheduling
your wedding

☐ Send each invited guest a printed card with the new wedding date

☐ Explain why you are rescheduling your wedding
    Include a separate hand-written note with a short explanation

☐ Communicate by word of mouth if you haven't yet sent invitations
    Personally inform your closest family and friends
    Have your family and friends spread the word to others

☐ Have a close family member or friend personally contact each invited guest
if the original wedding date is very close, e.g. 1–2 weeks away

☐ Review your wedding insurance policy
    Locate the 'rescheduling' clause

☐ Contact your wedding insurance company
    Apply for compensation
    Update your policy with the new wedding date

☐ Notify all vendors, venues, caterers and musicians of the postponement
details
    Notify in writing
    Apply for a full or partial refund
    Inform them of the new wedding date

☐ Notify your travel agent, accommodation and airline of the postponement
details
    Apply for a full or partial refund
    Inform them of the new honeymoon dates

## Cancelling your Wedding

☐ Inform your guests as soon as possible that you are cancelling your wedding

☐ Notify all invited guests that the wedding has been cancelled
  Send a printed card or hand-written note
  Have close family and friends spread the word

*You don't need to give a reason why the wedding has been cancelled.*

☐ Communicate by word of mouth if you haven't yet sent invitations
  Personally inform your closest family and friends
  Have your family and friends spread the word to others

☐ Have a close family member or friend personally contact each invited guest if the wedding date is very close, e.g. 1–2 weeks away

☐ Review your wedding insurance policy
  Locate the 'wedding cancellation' clause

☐ Contact your wedding insurance company
  Apply for compensation

☐ Notify all vendors, venues, caterers and musicians of the cancellation
  Notify in writing
  Apply for a full or partial refund

☐ Notify your travel agent, accommodation and airline of the cancellation
  Apply for a full or partial refund

☐ Decide who will cover the outstanding wedding costs

☐ Decide what will happen with the wedding and engagement rings
  Return the rings to whoever paid for them
  Return family heirloom rings to the family of origin
  Sell and split the profits
  Keep the rings

☐ Reimburse your attendants for anything they have personally spent on your wedding

☐ Return bridal shower gifts

☐ Return engagement gifts

☐ Return wedding gifts
  Keep gifts that you have already started using
  Buy identical replacements and send back if you have already begun using them

# Conclusion

Congratulations! You are now well on your way to a meaningful and unforgettable wedding day.

There is no 'right' way to plan a wedding. As long as it is what you want it to be and it is meaningful to both you and your fiancé you are on the right track. The key is to stay organised and allow plenty of time to achieve your plans and goals.

There will be times when you get stressed; remember how much you love your fiancé and how great it will feel to finally be married. Stress is a very natural part of wedding planning, try to enjoy even the stressful moments. If you become overwhelmed; look to your wedding file and this book for relief, it should help eliminate a lot of your anxiety.

Try not to get caught up in details that will not matter in the long term. And to have fun and enjoy the planning process. Ultimately, your wedding is only one day; maintaining a healthy marriage is the most important thing. Remember that you love each other and nothing else matters.

Wishing you a wonderful wedding day and beautiful life together.

**Please visit
www.TheWeddingChecklist.com.au
for more information**

- Attendant to-do lists
- Photography suggestions
- Flower types and availability
- Words for vows
- Wedding rituals defined
- Printable guest cards

and much more....

**www.TheWeddingChecklist.com.au**

# Invitation

If **you** have a great suggestion that other engaged couples would benefit from please submit it to:

info@theweddingchecklist.com.au

or

PO Box 381
Quinns Rocks, WA 6030
Australia.

Please be sure to include your name and suburb or town; if your ideas are selected you may be acknowledged in later book editions!

*Thank You*

Wishing you a wonderful wedding and a beautiful life together...

## Tenille Gregory

www.TheWeddingChecklist.com.au

# Share these ideas!

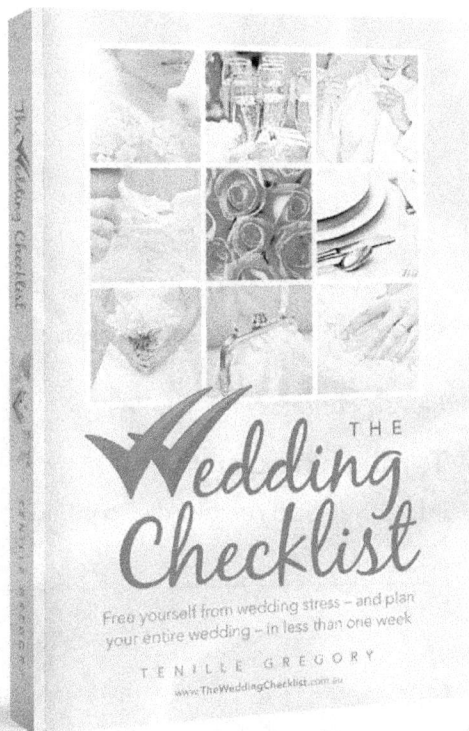

Pick up a copy for your engaged friends and family.
www.TheWeddingChecklist.com.au

# Bulk Orders

Bulk discounts start at 12 copies.

*Please contact*

**Tenille Gregory**
info@theweddingchecklist.com.au

www.ingramcontent.com/pod-product-compliance
Lightning Source LLC
LaVergne TN
LVHW021132080426
835509LV00010B/1332